Flavours
of
Arctic
Warmth

Molly Fletcher

ISBN 978-1-915292-07-0

Printed by Biddles Books Limited,
King's Lynn, Norfolk

Foreword

I began my life-long love affair with Norway in 1953. My aunt took each of her two nephews and nieces in turn away on holiday when we reached the age of 11. A decade later I was fortunate enough to work there for two years – and ever since, I've been privileged to enjoy a longstanding relationship with many Norwegian friends as well as two Norwegian god-daughters and their children.

I have wanted to write this book for more than 20 years. It appears now largely thanks to Covid lockdown, but also motivated by my personal knowledge of the increasing numbers of Brits who want to go on holiday to Norway. Advertised cruises on TV, with their glorious film sequences of the Lofoten Islands for example, are breath-taking inducements to visit such a beautiful country via the *Hurtigruten*. It seemed timely to tell some of my experiences from living in both the South and then the extreme North of the country nearly 60 years ago in the hope that they might take root in the fertile ground of some readers.

In my second year, I worked in a town called Vadsø, some 900 miles from Oslo, and deep inside the Arctic Circle. At the time it had a population of 2,500. Vadsø is situated in the county of Finnmark that has a population of 75,000 scattered across an area the size as Denmark. In the 1960s, life was basic and uncomplicated in a harsh and unforgiving climate. But the people who lived there were simply extraordinary.

What I tell about my time there is fundamentally true, although memory can play tricks with details. Judgments, perceptions and interpretations may also have changed into different understandings over the years. I was astonished to find many, many documents – letters, programmes, articles – I did not realise I had kept, but which emerged from a lockdown attic clearance. Such riches have further prompted my memory and although my interpretation of events may not be factually accurate in every detail, the story I tell is nevertheless essentially true. For example, I remember running an English Evening and what it consisted of, but according to some newspapers I have found, I apparently ran three.

I have not been able to find any of the people who I tell about here in detail. So, their names have been changed: their faces, however, appear before me whenever I write.

As I began to write, my story woke up slumbering recollections and emotions stored at the back of my mind. In turn, they have woven themselves into a wider tale that is underpinned by my love of Norway, its rugged, dramatic beauty and its strong, large-hearted and well-grounded people.

I hope I have written about connection: originally, mainly to those who lived in two spectacular geographical areas. The first in a group of small towns in Southern Norway; the second in the remote and freezing North. Both have their own unique landing places, which makes them special in their own right. But together, over time they have welded together to create a fulfilling adventure of a life-time. I am the person I am today partly because of the experiences I tell about in this book. How I have responded to them, the people I met and the lifelong friends I made, have all helped point the path of my personal growth over the years.

The stories I write about help to describe how important it is to understand what we work at and who we spend time with, because they create experiences that inevitably change us. If we pay attention, we may actually realise that and deliberately work at allowing our development to be shaped. However, if what we experience feels more like an endless series of warm baths, we may not realise until much later how deeply we have been impacted, or in what ways we are being changed, sometimes profoundly. Indeed, we may not even realise until later how we have become who we are as a result of what we have experienced, even many years ago. This is what writing this book has taught me.

This book is not a travelogue or an edited diary. It is a work of poetic non-fiction that tries to communicate what to me were exquisitely important experiences that touched me, that I was privileged to have lived through and that still bring me joy and inspiration to recall. I hope they also inspire the reader.

I owe debts of gratitude to many who have encouraged and advised me in this enterprise. Most particularly, I appreciate the time invested in wise counsel after reading excerpts here and there from family members. My daughter-in-law, Mary, and my granddaughter, Emily, in particular have been excellent critics. I also appreciate the timely and helpful advice I have had from my sons and my grandson. Dickon Fletcher has read most of the manuscript, always with a forensic, editorial eye and made many constructive comments. One of my Norwegian god-daughters reviewed one whole chapter in helpful, minute detail. My gratitude to the nine members of the entire Norwegian Busk family, whom I regard as my family too, is also considerable. Many other friends, including Lorraine Long, have read chapters and encouraged me consistently and unreservedly, not least my two Elderly Arctic Musketeer friends, Ann Jones and Margaret Wood, who took a memorable trip with me back to Finnmark a couple of years ago. One or two of Ann's photographs are also reproduced here.

However, my greatest thanks, my on-going and considerable debt, must go to my editor Jo Flack. It is not possible to overstate what I owe her. She has not only taught me an enormous amount about writing, but also, and more importantly, about how to reach for the honest detail. It is she who has encouraged me to write from my heart rather than my head. I have been particularly blessed to have benefitted from her meticulous attention to detail and style, using her knowledge and skills acquired from years as a journalist. Her forensic approach, her wisdom and dedication to the project have all been awesome. We have also always had tremendous fun in our editorial sessions together, sometimes aching with laughter! Most important of all, we have become great friends.

The process of an undertaking is usually as important as the product. That the Creator has challenged me to write every day for these last 18 months of 'in and out' lockdown has been an extraordinary experience in itself. But few will have been as privileged as I have been to engage with such an enthralling project, allowing me to escape into amazing and wonderful memories. Writing this book has allowed me to dig deep into them: apart from reinforcing my understanding of how important it is to connect with other people, they have also helped me to see how essential it is to recognise what we truly feel and experience.

We wake up fully when we see with our heart. It is the key to personal change, growth and love. It facilitates being truly alive. I feel blessed to have been shown that beginning to move closer to understand the importance of becoming who we are truly meant to be as we learn how to evaluate life's journey, is indeed to grasp our Maker's pearl of great price.

Chapter 1

A New Adventure for an Old

'Here you are then, ladies!' the driver announced, heaving our suitcases from his taxi. He set them down on the walkway in front of the hotel, hesitated, and then as he shut his boot said, 'Whatever are you all doing here, by the way - if you don't mind me asking?'

This was not the first time we had been asked that question, nor would it be the last. Our presence in such a remote part of the Norwegian Arctic Circle was a constant source of curiosity. We soon became aware just how much we stood out wherever we went. Sometimes we could be overheard speaking English to each other. Even so, clearly none of us was anyone's long lost, foreign relative who had made a pilgrimage to visit family from foreign parts. We would have been recognised at once if we had been, because everyone would have known we were coming and would have been looking out for us. We remained a curiosity.

My reply was the same every time we were asked. 'I used to live here.'

Such an unexpected reply produced even more astonished consternation. Inevitably the questioner always wanted to know more.

'Really? You LIVED here? When?' The taxi driver seemed utterly amazed, both by the sudden switch to Norwegian which he had not expected, as well as the actual answer to his question.

'In the 1960s.'

'That's an awfully long time ago: what on earth were you doing here then?

'I was teaching.'

'Teaching? Goodness me! But why on earth are you here now?'

'Because I loved it here. Everyone was so amazing and the pupils I taught were absolutely wonderful. I wanted to see for myself what, if anything, has changed. I mean now there are many more people living here, and many facilities have definitely improved, like this actual hotel,' I said waving my arm towards its entrance. 'There's much better access too.' I hesitated before adding.

'Also, I know that climate change is happening faster in the Arctic Circle than everywhere else. So, I wanted to try to see for myself what that means.'

The taxi driver still seemed astonished, and I thought he wanted to chat further by the look on his face. But he had another call and had to answer it. It was too cold to stand and chat anyway. So, I just offered my hand which he shook heartily.

As he drove off, I wondered how long it would be before lots of other people would know of our arrival. I suspected he would probably share the news of his surprising encounter with everyone at his family dinner table later on, and probably straight away with any work mates. If things now were as they were in the 1960s, the news of our presence would spread like wildfire.

After so many years, I had only recently begun to grasp just how much the experience of spending a year in Vadsø had changed me, even more than my previous year in the South of Norway had done. My two years in Norway had taught me an enormous amount about life and relationships, about work and having fun: some of which I grasped and absorbed at once. But there was also much that penetrated so deeply that it has taken years to appreciate properly.

I had gone to teach in a town 100 miles South of Oslo in 1965, straight after I finished my degree in History at the University of London. It was only 20 years after the war and the strong bond forged between the English and the Norwegians - as many subsequent Hollywood and Norwegian films bear witness – was still evident. At a time when Norway wanted its population to be more confident and fluent in speaking English, I was part of a scheme that sent young graduates to work in schools, organisations, clubs and businesses for a maximum of two years to work at all levels of communicating, developing confidence in using English with up-to-date idioms and fluency. It was a wonderful experience and planted a deep love of the country in my heart.

I was taken completely by surprise at the joy I felt this time as I first caught sight of Vadsø's surrounding landscape from the plane. As we flew from Tromsø, the view had slowly changed from one of lush green terrain in between mountains and lakes, with the occasional sight of a boat and a huddled few or even isolated homesteads to a terrain that seemed barren, deserted and often shrouded in wispy, grey mist. Even the sea had turned grey, a deep, dark gloomy grey that looked forbidding to swim in, fish from, or sail on. Indeed, the land below us seemed almost unendingly nondescript: dull and totally uninviting. I wondered if catching sight of it for the first time might sink many a heart which would not have expected such a dramatic change of scenery. But far from feeling daunted, I felt elated – thrilled even. I was overwhelmed by a whole range of emotions even as it began to bring old memories to the surface. My sense of joy only deepened and strengthened as we finally flew low over the fjord in our approach to landing at Vadsø's tiny, remote airport.

There had been no airport in Vadsø 50 years ago. The nearest one then was some 100 miles or so away by road or across the fjord by *Hurtigruten*: the latter, always unpredictable. It could not be relied on to appear at any port at its scheduled time and it only sailed in the direction of the town with the nearest airport every other day anyway. The road was also unreliable. Sometimes it had been impossible to keep open through the winter, especially if there had been a heavy fall of snow. So, I had never seen Vadsø from the air before. As it gradually came into view below the grey and misty cloud, the airport looked like a small coach or car park for visitors who might have come for the day, had been placed just outside the town. As we flew low passing the town itself, I could actually feel my heart leap. There it was to my left below me, its long row of different coloured houses clearly visible, with the church standing proud above the town's main and central road leading down to the harbour. To be sure, there seemed to be a few more buildings on the outskirts of the town than had been there before. But otherwise, it looked exactly the same as I remembered.

Our tiny, turboprop plane hit the ground and taxied along the shortest of runways to come to a halt close to the Arrivals entry – it was far too small to be called a Hall. It felt almost as if we were getting out of a limousine that was getting as close as possible to depositing its passengers into a building. Five minutes later at the most, the luggage had been taken from the plane and processed down the short luggage slide which could not have been more than six feet long. There was no need for any sort of carousel. Everyone grabbed their luggage as it was actually still in descent down the shute. They could as well have stood around the plane and received it straight away after disembarking from the hands of those who were processing it all.

We had been eyed somewhat curiously on our flight. Everyone else seemed to know each other and within a few minutes, the Arrivals area was deserted apart from the three of us and one airport official who probably had to see to bits of admin that needed to be processed before the plane took off to fly south later that day. Even the crew had disappeared: both of them! Since there was nowhere even to sit down or get a cup of coffee - not a chair or bench in sight - I thought they had probably driven into Vadsø where they could relax and pass the time before they needed to fly off again. There was no airport bus and no sign of a taxi. Everyone else, all 20 or so people - and all of them, male - had obviously made arrangements in advance to be collected. So, I approached the only man who was left on site and asked how we might get into the town. 'Would there be a taxi by any chance?'

There had only been one, little-used and so-called 'taxi' 50 years ago. The driver, like so many other people in the town then, had a full-time job, but like many other people who lived there, was willing to contribute to life's practical needs what help he could. I recall that he had agreed to be called on when anyone urgently needed to get out of Vadsø to go to a village along the coast or to the nearest town on some urgent errand at times when travel was especially challenging. The roads in Vadsø in those days were virtually impassable in winter. If they were not completely covered in deep snow, they were partially churned up with ice and mud. In any case, the town was so small that it was easiest to ski or spark along on an ice scooter to get where one needed to. Everywhere was within skiing distance anyway. I thought it was likely there would be taxis nowadays but could not be absolutely sure. On the other hand, here I was in an airport where there had not been one 50 years ago, so maybe times had changed about the availability of taxis too.

'Of course,' he said. 'I'll get you one straight away.'

As yet, he had not heard us speak amongst ourselves, so would have had no idea that we were not Norwegian, apart from how bewildered and out of place we must have looked. But then we were women after all! That alone made us stand out in our current situation. While we were waiting, however, he had a chance to hear us speak. He did not say anything. But the look on his face told us that he, like everyone else, was astonished by our presence and presumably was struggling to work out what on earth had brought us there. He too must have been wondering who we were and what three unaccompanied, elderly women were doing at this particular airport, miles from anywhere and well before the start of the tourist season.

In the short time we had to wait, I thought about our travel to date. It was two days since we had left England and the day before, the three of us had flown from Oslo to Tromsø in a standard, six-seater-across, jet. But this morning we had set off from a different part of Tromsø's airport, an area obviously set aside for local traffic, to board the much smaller plane only used for local flights – transport, post, deliveries and so forth as well as passengers. There had been no facilities in the area where we waited – no chance to get a cup of coffee or even a glass of water. There was one loo, fortunately, because we found ourselves having to wait a couple of hours or so before we were told our transport would be landing in the next few minutes. With such basic facilities, I could not help wondering how this could possibly be called Tromsø 'International' airport?

The plane taking us from Tromsø to Vadsø had been two and a half hours late. No one explained why it was late or apologised for it being so. I just assumed that local conditions beyond control explained the delay and everyone was used to that. I remembered just how bothered I always was throughout my two years in Norway about not being late! I smiled as I remembered how I endlessly asked myself whether or not it mattered, and how I never came to a proper conclusion.

At Tromsø, our luggage had been taken to our plane on a trolley pulled by a man pedalling a bicycle which towed the luggage behind. Our luggage was then 'put' into the plane by hand: there was no luggage shute from the ground into an aircraft hold. There was just a storage space where everything was stowed away by hand. It only took a couple of minutes for the 20 or so of us to board, and almost immediately, we took off, just two and a half hours later than scheduled.

Back in Vadsø, our taxi had arrived.

Ann and Margaret chatted away to each other in the back while I sat in the front trying to get a grip on the surprising strength of my emotions. I had no time to come up with any kind of answer because in no time at all we were at our destination. We could not have been more than a couple of miles at the most from the airport. It was only at that point we discovered that our driver knew enough English to speak to us as he helped us to unload.

We pulled our suitcases up the short access slope to the hotel entrance and were glad of the warmth that immediately enveloped us once we were through the swing doors. The one thing I noticed that had definitely NOT changed in Vadsø was the quality of the cold. So far in our travels it had always been at least a few degrees above zero: in single figures maybe, but never chillingly uncomfortable. Now, however, I remembered what the special Vadsø chill was like. It had always felt much colder here than anywhere else I had ever been in the Arctic Circle. Vadsø is totally exposed to the elements. It is not protected by tall buildings, trees, or anything else that might soften, or slow the harsh winds with the freezing cold gusts, blowing almost uninterrupted across from the Russian Steppes. The icy chill always sweeps unchallenged right through the whole of Vadsø.

The young, male hotel receptionist registered us and assigned us our keys. I could see he was fascinated by the three of us, but probably lacked the confidence to ask who we were and what on earth we were doing there. We settled into our rooms and agreed to take a breather for an hour or so to gather ourselves after travelling such a long way: more than 1,000 miles in the last 24 hours.

I was stunned to see the view – the same from all our rooms. It was of the wide, main street which led from the harbour through the hub of the town up to the town's residential area. I remembered it as the very heart of Vadsø which could be seen from practically every direction. It had been the fulcrum of all access and activity. In many ways, it looked exactly the same, just as I recalled it. My very first drive up this same street from the harbour in the early morning of the day I first arrived in 1964 came back to me as some of the emotions I experienced then also began to resurface. My shock was not that it had not changed – indeed it had. Now it was a tarmacked host to both moving and parked cars with proper pavements either side of it and a cycle track too. Fifty odd years ago, hardly anyone had a car apart from those who came from the South, and even they found they could rarely drive them because the roads were often barely passable. I was surprised, however, that this street was still the central hub of the town. Years ago, housewives, men going home from work and students lingered at the top of it to chat briefly en route home after school, and everything delivered to the town from the *Hurtigruten* made its way eventually up that main street, people as well as goods. However, now in addition at right angles to it, there were three or four restaurants and coffee shops – such were unheard of in my day. It felt powerfully comforting that the view could be both so different and yet exactly the same.

I could not remember what had been knocked down to make space for our hotel. I wanted to start exploring at once to try to find out. I longed to be out there wandering around, sleuthing, but knew I needed to rest a bit and gather myself or I would pay for it later. In any case, I needed to try to come to terms with my emotions. I had to try to identify and understand them before I engaged with any of the 'research' I had come to do. I wondered at first if it was just that I wanted to be young again – or maybe I was really longing to go back in time? In any event, I had not expected to feel so overwhelmed by feelings of wistful homesickness for the past. I had not realised so many past experiences and feelings would surface just because I was back in this remote place, so isolated and distant and cold. I understood that I needed to prepare myself to be surprised by further discoveries as I could feel strong responses of joy and nostalgia stirring in my spirit.

Chapter Two

Arrival

The coastal steamer sighed with each wave as it worked its way silently round the peninsula. It was raining hard, and sharp, wet arrows stung my face as I stood on deck. There was a heavy mist – the sort of quiet, damp sea mist to which I was to grow accustomed throughout the next 11 months, uncanny in its shrouding weight and always bitterly cold. The period of the midnight sun was over, but the whole day was still light, and it had been a fine day so far. The sun was well up in the sky although it was only 5 30am – the second week of August in 1965.

I thought it would be about half an hour before the boat would reach the harbour. Then, finally, my nine days at sea would end. The last few had been grim. I had company at the beginning of my trip - people travelling from Bergen like myself, to the far North: although most of them, only as far as Bodø. Thereafter, I had been on my own because my destination was by far the furthest - to a small town, further away from Oslo and closer to the Russian border even than the North Cape. At the same time, the coastline had become increasingly stark and rugged on the starboard side as we sailed further and further, into the Arctic Circle. We left behind the sight of farms and hamlets surrounded by mile after mile of rich, green pastures. Incessantly dotted along the shore, running down right to the sea, they had been an unfolding delight just to catch sight of during many previous days. I envied those who lived there surrounded by lush, fertile land running down, and almost into, the clear blue sea. To me, it seemed the epitome of the best possible lifestyle: dwellings close to nature, brightly painted houses whose gardens touched the water's edge with tiny jetties where small boats were moored.

So far, the weather had been good, but with few passengers to talk to, the last three days had been long and monotonous. In addition, there had been the frustration of having to change boats at Harstad. The so-called daily *Hurtigruten*, or coastal steamer, I had boarded and sailed in all the way north along the Norwegian coast from Bergen, had broken its propeller. We had been towed by a valiant tugboat, so, so slowly, for more than 24 hours into a dry dock where a new propeller could be fixed. It was early evening by the time we got there. Then, we had had to wait almost the whole day for a replacement vessel to come and take us further north to complete our various journeys.

At all the ports of call so far, the sailors would shout out the name in both English and Norwegian as well as the length of stay before the ship sailed on. Invariably, we could not avoid being woken up wherever we docked, but there was no need for such a call when it got to my destination. The estimated arrival time had been 4am, and even though we were now a couple of hours late, it was still early. It was unlikely that the *Hurtigruten* would be discharging or taking on many new voyagers simply for the fun of an excursion this far north. A few people perhaps might board because they wanted to go on to the next stop, for the airport, for example.

In due course, I was to discover that travelling within the Arctic Circle could be anything up to 48 hours behind schedule. To be only a couple of hours late was really remarkably punctual. I had long since shed any of my southern, city dweller's expectations that punctuality was essential or even at all important. None of the passengers I had travelled with so far seemed to be anxious because of a delay which would make them 'late'. I soon found out that where I was to spend the next 12 months, the word itself had little meaning. People arrived at their destination when it was possible to get there safely, and everyone accepted that alone as a triumph. Meanwhile, since I suspected there would be no announcement, I approached the nearest sailor, and in my slow Norwegian asked, 'is the next stop Vadsø?'

'Yes, it is!' was the reply, in that charming, attractive lilt that was the predominant feature of North Norwegian pronunciation.

'How long will it be until we get there?'

'Depends, Miss, on the mist. We might have difficulty getting into the harbour. Visibility is patchy, you see, and unpredictable. And we don't want to be grounded: not again!' He grinned.

I looked beyond him to where I imagined the coastline would be, and where it had been visible for most of the voyage. But now there was nothing to see: the mist was more like thick fog. The sun had gradually become invisible - although it still gave light, even through the thickened sea mist.

'Might be half an hour,' he ventured. 'Might be three quarters. We shall see.'

I knew I was already a day late for school since the whole procedure of changing boats had taken 27 hours. It made me feel tense because it meant I could not be properly prepared for my new venture. Up to this point in my life, being as late as I was would have made me feel very anxious because everything in my education and background had taught me that being punctual was a mark of one's character. Being late was seen as rude and inconsiderate. Even though the headmaster's response to my telegram from Harstad, where the ship broke down, had been both resigned and sympathetic. All passengers had been offered to send a free telegram if necessary, which was unusual in Norway in those days when money was so scarce.

People sensibly and inevitably took things as they came in this part of the world. There was no choice. Part of the transformational magic of Norwegian life was the calm serenity that always prevailed over all things practical.

I was beginning to feel uncomfortable, with a slightly sick feeling of anticipation which seemed to have come from nowhere. Sometimes I felt uneasy when I faced something new - not dread exactly - about what would be expected of me, and would I be up to it? There had been plenty of time since Bodø to have second, third and even fourth thoughts about teaching in so remote a place. But I kept telling myself, although Vadsø is remotely sited further to the East than Norway's famous West Coast crowned by the North Cape and had a population of only 2,500, it was and remains a key strategic and administrative town. Just under 50 miles from the Russian border, I knew the government in Oslo regarded it as a vital conduit of information and security in keeping peace with Russia. It had been chosen deliberately by the Norwegian government to be the most northerly county of Finnmark's administrative capital, and a NATO station had been built there soon after the organisation itself was founded. Vadsø was ideally placed to keep an eye on any Russian skulduggery from their submarines in the Barents Sea. Surely that would mean it was an important enough place to be in regular contact with the rest of the world at large, wouldn't it? I was bound to be fine working there, wasn't I?

On the voyage northwards, sailing always so close to the coast, I had been amazed to see some places, purporting to be towns where the steamer had stopped to unload and take on board supplies, post and people. It seemed from the *Hurtigruten* as if there was just a line of houses parallel to the harbour with a few other buildings scattered about and further away. Signs of moving traffic, or of any kind of vehicle, dwindled the further North we went. I was even more flabbergasted once the steamer had turned east after the North Cape. Thereafter, it seemed we stopped continually at what looked like just small clusters of a few different coloured homes, standing stoically and defiantly together near the coastline. They seemed miles from anywhere, enveloped by never ending, bleak-looking tundra as far as the eye could see. I could not help wondering what kind of life the people were able to enjoy - since they were likely to have been fairly isolated for probably close to 10 months of the year. How did they cope if they were ill and needed a doctor, or had severe toothache? Where did they actually go to school? I could not see any school buildings or hospitals in these small settlements where the *Hurtigruten* docked. I began to see what some Southern Norwegians who I had worked with actually meant when they said how different life was in the North. Many had been shocked when I told them I was going north for a year. Now, as we were within minutes of Vadsø, I began to see what they might have meant.

'You won't be able to stand it,' they had all said. 'Have you any idea what it's like? It's so different from what you've experienced here this last year - in ways it's not possible to tell you about. You're far too English: we give you three weeks at the most up there. And it will be a triumph if you survive that long!'

I had got used to hearing these sorts of comments. At the time they only served to make me more determined. But now, I was beginning to wonder if they did not have a point? Had my decision to come here been headstrong and foolhardy after all?

I had never really quite known what the Norwegians meant when they said that I was 'very English'. I had always supposed that it must have had something to do with living in London, or with being musical in a classical sort of a way, or because of the way I spoke and pronounced my words. I often found myself quite irritated when my personality, beliefs or personal values were attributed to, or confused with, my nationality. People had often said things like, 'I suppose you think that, because you're English?' Even so, I knew that all the misgivings about my spending a year in the Far North had been kindly meant. I was not entirely sure I knew what I had agreed to take on or why. I had just known that when such an enterprise had been suggested to me, I had jumped at the chance. My southern Norwegian friends thought being only 23, I was too young and inexperienced to undertake such an adventure.

But then all of a sudden, I realised the mist was clearing, or at least seemed to be thinning out. We were now sailing closer to the coast, and I sensed the ship turning sharply into what I presumed, but could not see, must be a harbour. I went below to collect my luggage.

When I returned to the departure deck some few minutes later, the ship was at the start of manoeuvring close enough to the quayside to be tied up to several bollards. Only two other passengers were waiting to disembark. Looking over the ship's rail, there was no one waiting on the landing stage either to board or to meet anyone off the boat. There was no sign of the headmaster who had promised to be there when I arrived. I tried not to feel anxious. Getting the ship safely docked always took a while.

I surveyed what I could see of the town beyond the harbour and tried to absorb its features. Vadsø seemed bigger than many of the other places we had passed, which was something of a relief. I knew it was a town with various important functions, backing as it did almost immediately on to the Soviet Union. It could not possibly be the backwater I feared even though it was more than 1400 miles from Oslo. I could see how it stretched out in a long, thin line into the middle distance just like so many other Arctic towns I had seen en route. As a rule, the lines came to abrupt finality at either end. There was just tundra beyond. At first, it seemed to be the same here. As usual, the wooden houses were of similar design, in a variety of colours, although here, there did at least seem to be several rows of such buildings, not just one, and the lines seemed to stretch further than in any other place I had seen. But behind them, as usual, was the familiar bleak and rocky expanse of vast, treeless landscape as far as the eye could see. However, here, a modern church spire rose oddly, but comfortingly, from the centre of the town.

From the boat, it looked as if the church was also flanked on either side by tall radio masts: a curious sight. There was the usual, unmistakable smell of fish and there were a couple of small fishing smacks, with men busily doing what seemed like on-board maintenance work beyond the jetty, on the other side of the harbour. Otherwise, the town lay still and lifeless. There was no one to be seen. There were not even any delivery vehicles, or early birds on their way to work.

The anxious twinge in my stomach strengthened and I wondered what I should do if no one turned up to meet me. Were my southern friends, right? Had I made a terrible mistake in agreeing to come here? Was this indeed a totally different part of the world? Would all the people who lived here be utterly different from anyone I had ever yet known?

As I looked down again over the side of the steamer, I noticed two men getting out of a car from the corner of my eye. The *Hurtigruten* was going through its final docking motions tying ropes to bollards. A surge of relief swept through me as I took a deep breath, lifted my two suitcases and proceeded down the gangplank. Finally, I was leaving the ship.

'You wouldn't by any chance be Rektor Anderson?' I asked the taller of the two men.

'I'm Einar Anderson,' said the other, bending low, bowing in true, formal and correct Norwegian fashion, shaking me by the hand as he did so. His English accent was polished, and he continued to speak and act with unusual self- possession, more than was customary for many of his fellow countrymen, and rare indeed north of Trondheim.

'You must be Miss Russell. I hope you've had a good trip. Welcome to Vadsø! This is Anton Bakken. He is our English teacher.'

The taller of the two men seemed much less at ease. He endorsed what the headmaster had already said by way of welcome, but in Norwegian and rather under his breath.

'Have you any more luggage?' The Rektor asked.

It was now raining hard. Neither of the men had an umbrella but then Norwegians rarely owned such things because of the wind that invariably accompanied the rain.

The teachers stowed my luggage in the car boot. We drove from the quayside and up a central road that linked the harbour to the town, and almost before I could draw breath, stopped at what I was to discover was the headmaster's flat. To my amazement, it was only two minutes' drive from the quayside. But also, to my great relief, even in that short time I could see there really was much more to the town than my first sight had led me to believe. Several parallel streets made up in width what the town lacked in length, and there were more than just one or two sturdily built, official looking buildings. It seemed all the important aspects of a functioning community were transacted here after all.

Anderson and Bakken unloaded my luggage and ushered me inside. It turned out that they shared the house: Anderson, it emerged, lived on the top floor and Bakken, the one below – what in England is called the ground floor, but in Norway is known as the first. Once we were all inside and comfortably settled, Anderson set about making breakfast. Norwegian breakfasts always consisted of bread and *pålegg* – an umbrella word to describe what in English would be called 'fillings' - for sandwiches that were single layered and open, so not really sandwiches at all. The most accurate translation for *pålegg* is more like 'cuts of meat, egg and cheese, or anything at all edible to put on top of a slice of bread.' They were always delicious, partly because Norwegian bread was so good as many people baked their own which meant it was always fresh. *Smørbrød* – open sandwiches - were always quick and easy to make, extremely nourishing and delicious. I wandered over to the picture window and gazed out to sea.

To the left I could see the coastal steamer, which had brought me on from Harstad, preparing to depart. I watched the ropes being unfastened from the bollards and the gangplank taken up. The other side of the fjord was just visible as the mist was on the move. It occurred to me that if I could see as far beyond again, I would be looking straight into Soviet Russia. As this was at the height of the Cold War with so many Europeans worried about Russian intentions at that time, being so close and actually able to see what I had come to believe was a truly threatening place, felt both exciting and frightening at the same time. I could see the sense of building a NATO station exactly where it was. The steamer hooted twice, waited a moment or two, then seemed to heave itself away from its moorings into the middle of the harbour, gliding slowly through its entrance to the next and last town on its journey.

As it began to plough its way the 30 odd miles across the vast expanse of water to its next destination, I thought to myself, 'So that's that: no going back now.' The gradual disappearance of the steamer underlined the fact that I had severed all connection with my previous experiences in the South: maybe from much of my past life altogether, since who knew what life held in store?

***

Over breakfast at a beautifully laid table and with paper napkins, I wondered how to address my host. Normally a young man of his age would correctly be addressed just by his surname. But he was the Rektor. So maybe I should call him that? I would need to ask about that at some point, but I was too tired and befuddled to do so now. Instead, I discovered many things I needed to know about the school. Anderson explained my timetable and told me that most of my teaching would be English, but that I had been scheduled to teach a fair number of music periods too. He did not know anything about my other work - that of teaching adults. That part of my contract was someone else's responsibility.

I tried to gauge what sort of a person he was from the way he spoke, especially since he was so young. He was of medium build and height, with dark hair and a full face. This was in contrast to most of his southern colleagues who tended to be blond, blue-eyed and tall. His subject was physics, and like the majority of the rest of the staff, he came from the South - from Oslo in fact. He seemed tremendously sure of himself. It struck me that he was rather like an American businessman on the make, who might fall prey to early burn out if he was not careful. But it was clear that Rektor Einar Anderson was full of enthusiasm both about his job and his school, and that he was proud of being, at 27, the youngest headmaster in the country: indeed, that there had ever been in Norway. He did not flaunt the fact, but it seemed to me he accepted it, both as a challenge, and as a considerable personal trophy.

The Norwegian Gymnas was similar in structure to an English Sixth Form College, or an American High School, but included younger students too, so that the age range ran over four or five years, instead of the English two or three. In 1965, there were only three other Gymnas in the whole of Finnmark, an area as large as Denmark. Vadsø's Gymnas was only a couple of years old and had clearly been built as a statement of intent and influence. Its installation had given the town and the surrounding locality more gravitas. It was an area that was already well on the way to establishing itself as a self-sufficient, important administrative centre. The school served a radius of some 300 miles, so many pupils had to lodge, in and around the town. There were about 200 Gymnas students altogether in Vadsø: Norwegians mainly, including some Sami, plus a few Finns. A handful of students were in their early twenties: one was even married.

It was my turn to speak.

'Are there any out of school activities?' I asked.

'What d' you mean?' Anderson looked puzzled.

'Do the students involve themselves in clubs and societies after school hours? For example, is there a school choir?'

Einar Anderson took a gulp of coffee, made eye contact, and then slowly began to smile. 'No', he said benignly, tilting his head to one side as he spoke. 'We have nothing like that here.'

I wondered why he seemed to respond to my question so quizzically. He appeared almost amused. I could not understand why, especially since there had been a superb school choir at the Gymnas where I had taught in the South. I took it for granted that music and school choirs would be a feature of school life over the whole country. I had discovered in the year before, in Southern Norway, that it was not at all unusual for a Gymnas to have a choir.

The Rektor answered my question: 'Yes, but North Norwegians are not yet that formally musical, or too well versed in music should I say – in school at any rate. And in any case, there's only one period of music per class per week.'

I was puzzled as to how North Norwegians could be so definitely different from those in the South. 'Do you think I could form a school choir, then?' I asked. 'Would I be allowed to?'

'You could try to', Anderson replied cautiously. 'But I doubt whether you'll get much support for one.'

All this time, Bakken had been eating really slowly, thoroughly chewing every mouthful. He seemed an intensely serious human being. He had said almost nothing so far, and I began to wonder whether he and Anderson were actually friends or simply neighbours. At last, however, he found the courage to ask, 'Do you speak Norwegian?'

'A reasonable amount: yes.'

'Good. Then do you mind if I talk to you in Norwegian?'

I was taken aback by his question. When I had been in the South people had plagued me with requests to speak to them in English, even though I knew they had an inbuilt reluctance about speaking English in front of other Norwegians. They had all learnt it in school for several years and were shy, sometimes, to speak it in case they made mistakes or showed themselves up in front of their friends and colleagues. But after all, Bakken, was the only other teacher whose sole task was teaching English, and who taught it to the most advanced level. Whereas Anderson, whose subject was physics, had battled on in his stilted, but excellent English quite manfully. Apparently, he thought nothing of it.

'I don't mind at all', I said. 'But I've been home for the last six weeks, and I don't think I am even up to the standard I was before I left the South earlier in the summer. Also, I've come to see that the vocabulary and intonation up here are not entirely the same as in the South. But I'd like to be much better at it than I am, so I'd be quite pleased to try to talk with you, and anyone else, in Norwegian.'

Bakken ignored my implied plea for consideration. Instead he immediately embarked on a fairly theoretical homily about how he personally had decided to teach English. He spoke slowly and clearly, but nevertheless, it felt odd, and hardly the time or the place. Also, I was hardly in an appropriate frame of mind for an academic discussion on my thoughts about teaching English spontaneously, instead of by rule of thumb and grammar. No wonder Norwegians spoke accurate and correct, but definitely non-colloquial English, I mused, and not for the first time either!

Fortunately, at that moment there was a knock at the door. Anderson opened it to reveal the slim figure of a man probably in his early thirties, wearing a dark grey suit. His did not resemble any of the almost mythical, blond Scandinavian features: indeed, his face and dark features had an oriental, or Sami, look about them. He smiled as he lent apologetically against the doorpost, and his brown eyes sparkled. He bowed, shook my hand, and introduced himself as Øystein Hansen, the local *Friundervisning* Secretary. He was in fact, my boss. *Friundervisningen* was an organisation equivalent to the W E A - Workers' Education Association – or something akin to night school or evening classes which had become so popular in England in recent years. Lots of people who felt they had missed out on aspects of their education for one reason or another, wanted to catch up by going to classes after work. It was exactly the same in Norway. Hansen explained how he too had intended to meet me off the boat but had overslept. He readily acquiesced when he was offered some coffee and *smørbrød*. He munched away at the same time as he enquired about my trip. To my surprise, his English was excellent. It was clear, fluent and colloquial. The time was then about 7 30am.

In those days, nearly all daily work in Norway started no later than 8am. Schools ended their day at 2pm: other institutions, offices and shops and most factories also finished work for the day at about that time or soon after, so that everyone could be home for their main family meal, which was usually eaten between 4pm and 5pm. Hansen apologised for his short stay. He was anxious not to be late for work. But before he left, he invited all three of us to supper that evening.

Chapter 3

Three Arctic Musketeers

I first connected with Margaret after hearing her read her poetry some 30 years ago. We had both signed up to a series of annual, summer Christian retreats at Ffald y Brenin in the glorious surroundings of coastal, southern Wales. I remember how inspired we all were by the profound, insights of her writing. It touched and impressed us deeply.

On our free afternoon, several of us found a delightfully quaint teashop nearby. The pot of tea between Margaret and myself lasted at least a couple of hours. It was then that we first discovered how much we were both on the same wavelength. We shared in detail our separate journeys of faith and discovery about how to be genuine in understanding ourselves and relating to others. I remember we laughed so much and so heartily that other, more reserved tea-drinkers kept glancing at us with raised eyebrows. So began a wonderful, mutual friendship, which remains to this day.

In 2018 I had been thinking that I should go back to Vadsø because I wanted to see how, and if, it had changed. That year I had taken the two-day train trip from Oslo to Bodø that I had been longing to do for years, and also visited the Lofoten islands. Both experiences were stunning reminders of the stark and majestic beauty of northern Norway in all its dignified, rugged grandeur. It was not long afterwards that I knew I really HAD to return to Vadsø.

It was at this time, and between a couple of our monthly lunches in a lovely English market town roughly equidistant from where we both lived, that I decided to proposition Margaret as ideas were sown and gestating in my mind. As always, we had begun our time together by exchanging personal and family updates, so she knew that I had started writing about my time in Norway. We were almost at the point of saying our goodbyes when I heard myself say, 'Margaret, I don't suppose you'd like to come to the Arctic with me?'

My lovely friend gulped, swallowed hard the last dregs of her tea and flushed a little. No one would have guessed that this alert, wise, and full-of-fun woman was 92 years old. I knew she would be exactly the kind of companion to accompany me on this trip. She had reacted with total astonishment but did not splutter an immediate refusal.

'Good Heavens! Well! I don't know …. The ARCTIC?' She put her teaspoon down and leaned back in her chair with astonishment. 'Good gracious! I'd have to think about that,' she said. 'Wherever has the idea come from to ask ME to come with you, Molly?'

'Oh! It'd just be wonderful to have your company,' I said. 'You'd be fine! It wouldn't be like Scott of the Antarctic's trip, you know. I mean, I lived and worked there 50 years ago, and if it was possible to live there then, it will be much more possible to travel there now. The town where I lived even has an airport now, and properly built roads and many more people living there than there were - some of whom must also be elderly,' I smiled. 'There's central heating everywhere too as well as triple glazing and the weather is much less severe nowadays than it used to be because of climate change.' I paused. Margaret was listening intently. 'It might be a place that would really interest you, because it's not where elderly, American cruise tourists normally visit,' I teased. I knew Margaret would not be interested in experiencing anything like that. 'And there'd be two of us, so we could take care of and look out for each other.' I paused before adding, 'Oh! … And by the way, I speak the language. Or at least I used to be able to, which would be useful if we got into any kind of scrape. In any event, everyone speaks English - or knows it at least, and can make themselves understood.'

I could see Margaret was interested. She had been fiddling with her teaspoon for a short while. At least, she was not ruling it out as total folly from the outset.

'Let me think about it,' she said. 'I'm staggered - flattered even - that you've asked me. But I don't know if I could manage. Seriously, I'll have to give it a lot of thought. When were you thinking of going? And when would you need to know my decision?'

'Oh! Not for a while, Margaret. Well! Weeks at least. I'm thinking I need to go before school's out for the summer, and it would be great if it could also chime with the Midnight Sun period – when there's no night, or no darkness at any rate because the sun doesn't set. That would make the second half of May an ideal time to go.'

Margaret said nothing for what seemed like ages. 'Let me think about it,' she said again, but finally. 'It sounds a wonderful prospect. But I'm not sure: I just don't know if I could manage. But, seriously, I'll certainly think about it.'

I was pleased Margaret had not reacted as if the whole idea was preposterous. It would have been understandable had she done so. After all, it truly would be unusual for someone of such great age to travel such a long way on a privately organised trip rather than on a fully planned, assuredly comfortable tour. Also, I was not asking Margaret to join me on a trip to a known, regular tourist attraction. I was inviting her to go with me to a place she had never even heard of, where it would definitely be cold and potentially, a creature-comfort-free destination.

'Great! Oh Margaret! Thanks for not saying "definitely not" straight away. I've only just recently decided that I need to go back to where I used to live. I want to see how things are there now. I've definitely decided I MUST go and would prefer not to go alone. I have been wondering who I would like to ask to come with me to keep me company …. Anyway, I very much hope you'll feel you can. Please think about it really seriously. I'd absolutely love it if you thought you could agree to it. We could look out for, and take care of, each other – and, by the way, did I mention – I speak the language - which always helps.'

We both laughed at my silly bits of repetition. I had no idea what her decision would be. I would just have to wait. Meanwhile, I could at least get on with thinking and planning and decide on approximate dates.

***

A week or so later, I happened to go and see another friend, Ann, who lives near me. We often called on each other. I had met her more than 20 years ago at the same place as Margaret, although a year or so later. Once again, coming out of nowhere and with no considered thought behind it, I heard myself blurt out the same question.

'Ann! I don't suppose you'd like to come to the Arctic with me, would you? The air there is so clean and totally unpolluted. It would be awfully good for your poorly chest. I'm definitely going myself. There are things I need to do there. I badly want to re-visit where I was in the past to see what might have changed and what's still the same.'

I knew that Ann was having a bad time with a series of chest infections she seemed unable to shake off. Various health professionals had so far been unable to help her and it meant she was short of breath sometimes. It just came to me that the pure, Arctic air might help Ann free up her breathing.

'Oh! My goodness! What an extraordinary and exciting thought!' That was Ann's first reaction. But then she hesitated. 'But tell me a little bit more. I could at least think about it. When do you need to know?'

I explained I had already invited Margaret, who was also thinking about it. 'She seemed really interested' I said. 'I explained that we could look after each other. If there were three of us that would work even better! But I've not heard from her since. She probably thinks the whole idea is absolutely ridiculous!'

I could not read anything from Ann's reaction, but I was not unduly bothered. It was still early days in the planning and all I knew was that I was definitely going to make the trip – with or without any companions.

'I'm definitely going,' I said. I want to remind myself of so much that was special about being there - the whole place and the people. I know the population has doubled since I was there, and I also know that the entire national education system is different now. But I know I have to go, and I would prefer not to go on my own.' And then, I added as if it was an afterthought. 'It could be such fun, you know. We could pretend to be Elderly Musketeers! Well! actually, we virtually would be, wouldn't we? Three Elderly Arctic Musketeers! That sounds good!'

Ann laughed and I continued to explain my thinking. I would need to go before mid-June, when school finished for the summer, in order to speak to staff and students before they dispersed. I also wanted to see the school in action. Such timing would chime in with the Midnight Sun period - which began on May 17th in Vadsø. Whatever the weather and temperature, I explained to Ann, the Midnight Sun time was truly special to experience: non-stop daylight for 24 hours is not something many people would ever experience, after all.

Ann seemed to be taking it all in and was certainly not thinking of turning down the suggestion at the outset.

'Anyway,' I continued, 'perhaps you'd like to think about it and let me know? There's no immediate hurry. I could also show you maps and travel books and other stuff I have to whet your appetite or reassure you if you like.' Then, after thinking for a moment I added, 'and after all, people live and work there and go to school and bring up their families.'

I said my goodbyes and with clear 'going-now' noises I walked down Ann's garden path, got in my car and drove home.

The next morning my phone rang. It was Ann.

'Molly! I've decided I'd love to come with you to the Arctic. I've given it a lot of thought – and I'm sure I'm meant to say "yes". I sense in my spirit that I'm really meant to go with you. So, can you count me in, and could we arrange to talk further? As soon as you're able to tell me what dates I'd be committing myself to that would be great too.'

I was astonished. I had actually believed that it was unlikely either Ann or Margaret would be able to join me, and, in any event, it might be a week or so before I heard from either of them. I had even begun to come to terms with travelling on my own, which I believed I would probably end up doing.

'How wonderful! Ann, that's utterly brilliant! I'm so pleased.' I was genuinely thrilled.

'Yes!' She said. 'I truly believe I AM meant to join you on this trip. And now I've decided, I'm extremely excited. Shall you let me know when we can meet to start making plans?'

The timing and the content of the call surprised me. I felt amazed and thrilled at the same time and could not think what to say. I simply said, 'I haven't heard back from Margaret yet, and I don't want to hassle her. She's actually coming to stay for a few days shortly. I promised to give her some more information about the whole enterprise - where places are and how we would get there and so forth - so she would have more knowledge to help her make a decision. I don't want her to feel under any kind of pressure. On the other hand, I think the more she knows the more it will help her to decide. Now, I can tell her that you've agreed to come. That's bound to reassure her.'

'That sounds good. Don't worry. I'm sure Margaret will agree to come in the end. Really! I'm confident she will. Don't worry!'

A week later, Margaret rang me.

'Hello! It's me! It's Margaret! I'm just ringing to say, I'm in!'

I was taken aback. For a second or two I thought, 'in what?' Margaret continued, 'I definitely want to come with you to the Arctic. I've "ummed" and "ahhed" about it. I've seriously wondered if I'd be able to manage, but I've felt a sense of definite reassurance recently, and so I've decided I'd really regret it if I said "no".'

I knew that sense of assurance came from the same source as Ann's, and indeed my own. But even though I had known Ann would be right in the end, nevertheless, I marvelled at the knowledge that this was now really a viable project which seemed to be thoroughly blessed from the outset.

'That's marvellous! I'm so pleased – thrilled actually.' Truly, I was almost lost for words. 'Ann's coming too. So, there will be three of us and we can all look after each other, can't we? We truly will be the Three Arctic Musketeers!

Chapter 4

Shocks and Resolutions

I was 72 hours late when I had arrived in Vadsø on the first day of the academic year - at least for staff. So, soon after Hansen had gone, I found myself once more in Anderson's car en route for the school itself. It was unimpressive from the outside: it seemed rather austere and utilitarian. Classrooms for all age groups from the age of seven stretched out in one long, two-storey building. Once inside, anyone could wander from one age group's classroom area and speciality to another and stay warm and dry the whole time. This was particularly crucial because of Finnmark's extreme weather conditions. There were also several administrative rooms and areas for staff to relax. Anything at all to do with education in terms of administration or office work was conducted on the same site, under the same roof.

We left the car and walked across the schoolyard into the main building. Suddenly, I began to experience a strong, physical reaction to my journey. I remembered an elderly American aunt – used to travelling abroad – once telling me that when you had arrived in a new place, it always took several hours, even a day or so, for your soul to catch up with the rest of you. I began to understand exactly what she meant as I gradually felt taken over, not only by that numb, anti-climax sometimes experienced on arrival at a new and strange place, but also by anxiety about my new situation. Would I be able to cope? I also began to feel the uncontrollable movement of the ship under me stronger than ever. It was not pleasant: it felt almost hazardous, as if I could not be sure where to put my foot down in front of me. And then, I began to feel overwhelmed by waves of nausea. I had been travelling at sea non-stop for nearly 10 days. And, I had also been up since just before 4am. Weary and befuddled, I heard Anderson speaking to me.

'There won't be any pupils for you to meet today: just the rest of the staff. I'll introduce you and give you your personal timetable.'

He opened the door of the staff room.

'Good morning everyone! Welcome! I also want to introduce you to Miss Russell who arrived on the *Hurtigruten* this morning. She is our new English teacher. I hope you'll all make her feel at home.'

Immediately, in the typical Norwegian way, they lined up and each member of staff shook my hand, spoke his or her name, bowed or curtsied and bade me welcome. I tried to smile and responded with 'how d'you do' to everyone because I thought that would be expected, and, after all, perhaps it would be just a bit too familiar merely to say 'hello'. Again, I was astonished by the average age of my colleagues. Not one of them appeared to be more than in their mid-twenties. It was also apparent how reluctant anyone was to be drawn into any kind of conversation with me. There was none of the immediate, albeit nervous, attempt at connection I had experienced in the South. No one said how much they had been longing to meet someone from England or that they hoped I would not feel homesick or lonely. Bakken approached me again with my timetable, and in his slow and earnest way began to explain what my specific responsibilities were. I was then left to absorb them, my timetable and my new surroundings. Everyone else busied themselves as they exchanged holiday experiences and caught up with each other.

Gradually, the morning passed. Few colleagues spoke to me. Most seemed to be making sure to avoid eye contact. Although if anyone's eyes did lock with mine by mistake, it was always followed up by a slightly nervous smile. In due course, I was given a cup of coffee – very strong, black and without sugar. I could hardly drink it but made noble efforts to gulp it down while trying to think about other things. I felt it would have been rude not to drink it. At about noon, Anderson led me to his car again and we drove back to his flat. So far, he had said nothing about where I was to live. So, I asked, 'Are you able to tell me where I am to live? Could you take me there, perhaps?'

There was an embarrassed pause before he answered

'Accommodation's always a problem up here, you know', he said. 'There are so many people living and working in Vadsø now who've come from the South - there are never enough digs.'

He spoke in Norwegian for the first time and I noticed a precise, educated, Oslo accent, the Norwegian equivalent of BBC, Received Pronunciation English. As he stumbled on, I began to fear that that there was nowhere for me to live, and nothing had been arranged for me at all! He seemed truly embarrassed.

'There was a shortage of housing before that anyway. There have been real problems – ever since the war actually.'

'But I thought all institutions and employers had an obligation to find places for their staff to live when they offered them a job up here. That's what we were all told when we were all together in Oslo before we all went our separate ways around the country.'

I tried not to sound critical – or desperate. I was just longing for my own space where I could relax and have a proper shower, or bath, and change my clothes – and perhaps lie down for an hour.

'True. But once the employee arrives here, he - or she is unlikely to return hundreds of miles south again simply because he finds he is to live in a small, poky room rather than in an Oslo-sized and type flat!' The Rektor tried to laugh. But it sounded somewhat hollow to me.

I thought this quite unscrupulous, and asked again, 'Does that mean - are you telling me I have nowhere to live?'

He hesitated. ''Er, well, not exactly. We've found you two rooms near the school. And you'll be pleased to hear they have hot water and central heating.'

'Is that so unusual?' I gasped.

'It's not all that common up here, as yet.'

'But what do people do in the winter? I mean it's getting pretty cold already. How do they manage without their houses being properly heated? I thought the Germans burned Finnmark down to the ground when they retreated in 1945 and that everything was built as new.'

'Yes. They did. Most of it, anyway. But a few houses escaped being burnt. And efficient electricity and central heating came rather later to this part of the world than to the South.'

I considered my fate again. 'What exactly do you mean when you say that I can expect hot water? Do you mean I can have a bath whenever I want one without having to heat the water?'

There was another long pause. ''Er, no! Actually, I'm afraid there's no bath available. But there are showers at school which you're welcome to use any time you want,' he added hastily.

'But my boss in Oslo made it plain that it was essential for me to be decently accommodated?'

I stopped feeling desperate. Instead, I suddenly felt thoroughly depressed. I felt the need to let go in a flood of tears but held back the dam that was about to burst. I could see Anderson was obviously embarrassed. I wondered if I could make capital out of the fact that he clearly felt uncomfortable that there was nothing better to offer me.

'Will I have the chance to find something else. Now that I'm here and can do the leg work myself, I mean?' I asked, determined to press him on the topic.

'Well, actually the school is currently negotiating to buy some property from the bank which we'll be able to make into three or four staff flats. Of course, you'd be high on the priority list, and there's actually a strong chance that you'll be able to move into quite new accommodation in about five, or six, weeks' time.' Anderson did his best to sound upbeat as he spoke.

I felt slightly cheered at this news. But I had no resilience to argue about it now. It further transpired that I could not see the rooms where I was to live until after 4pm because my landlady would be out at work until then. So, Anderson offered me space to rest in his own flat for the time being. I declined an invitation to join him for lunch. The thought of food made me feel distinctly bilious. I was really tired now and wanted to lie down for an hour while he went down into the main part of the town near the harbour for his midday meal at the only place in town where it was possible to eat outside one's home. I felt relieved to be left alone. I needed to get on top of my emotions and collect my thoughts.

I must have been dozing for well over two hours when my host returned. The mist and dampness of the earlier part of the day had now disappeared and had given way to hazy sunshine. I looked out of the window, just as I had done earlier that day. I thought how strange it was not to be able to see trees and vegetation. I wondered why people didn't move away from Finnmark when they had the chance after the war. I knew the government in Oslo had offered everyone who had been compulsorily evacuated by the Germans a chance to start life again further south, but the majority by far had insisted that they wanted to return home and rebuild.

It was now so difficult, impossible actually, to imagine the street where I lived in London, let alone Piccadilly Circus or The Beatles or The Royal Family or even the simple, daily routine of hundreds and thousands of English people from the context of what now was my environment. I felt strange and out of place all of a sudden and found myself wondering if my colleagues in the staff room earlier had recognised that I felt ill at ease. I felt so tired and despondent.

Anderson put my suitcases into his car once more and took me to my lodgings. A tall middle-aged woman, the oldest inhabitant I had met so far, opened the door to us both when Anderson rapped loudly on it. She had a completely expressionless face that was chalky white, and she spoke with a strange lilting intonation. I realised that this was the first truly northern native I had heard speak so far. Everyone else I had spoken to that day must have come from somewhere in the South. I had to listen hard to understand what the woman said. Her major fear seemed to be whether or not I spoke Norwegian. Once it had been established that I did, she was greatly relieved but also took much greater care over what she said.

We were led to the back of the house to what I was told would be my personal, private entrance. There was of course no key. Nothing was locked anywhere in the town because nothing was ever at risk. Everyone knew everyone else: it would be impossible to make a getaway with stolen goods anyway, or for anyone to start living it up because they suddenly seemed to have a great deal more money to spend. In any case most people were more than content, materially speaking, even though they seemed to me to have only the most basic of possessions. Whatever the reason, an incentive to steal simply did not arise. For example, I was always able to leave my school bag in the middle of the street outside school while I ate my lunch at the hotel - even when it might be filled with camera equipment as well as school-books - to save carrying it around unnecessarily until I was ready to pick it up on my way home. Nobody ever touched it.

The three of us went up a flight of rickety, unpainted stairs. At the top, the woman opened a low, wooden door leading into a tiny kitchen. We had to duck to go in. There was just about enough room for the three of us to stand close together. On the left was another door which led off into what I assumed would be my bedroom. Anderson, clearly embarrassed by the basic, tiny and wholly unsuitable facilities, was anxious not to stay. He put my suitcases down, fixed a time to collect me later for our supper with Hansen and skipped off down the stairs, whistling loudly as if he was trying to mask his embarrassment as he left the premises.

And so, I was left. Here, I was to live for the foreseeable future. My new landlady explained how the hot water geezer worked, and how its heating was turned on and off. She was obviously proud of being able to offer these facilities, but she spoke quickly all the time, probably keen to escape from the traumatic experience of having to answer any questions. She did not seem at all bothered about whether or not I had what I needed, or whether or not I would feel comfortable.

Once she had gone, I surveyed my so-called home. Both rooms were dark and cheerless. The kitchen was a large, low room with a table and two chairs – one of which was badly broken and could not be used to sit on. There was nothing to cook on either, except one electric plate, so that all that was really possible was to boil water for a cup of coffee or tea. Soon, however, I realised that even that was not possible since the kitchen was equipped with no utensils at all except for the dirtiest frying pan I had ever seen, and a couple of chipped plates and cups. I had been assured before I left the South that my flat would be fully furnished, and so I had left all the kitchen equipment I'd bought the year before, stored with friends in Southern Norway. I sat down on the less rickety of the two chairs and wondered how on earth I was going to cope.

It was then that I really absorbed the limits of the sink. The hot water facilities, so boasted about, were equally depressing. A geezer made about two pints of hot water in about five minutes, and poured into a basin, about one quarter the size of a normal washbasin. The additional room was no more encouraging. It was small, with a sloping roof at one end. It contained a bed with a hideously, psychedelic counterpane – no bed linen, but a thick, lumpy mattress and a couple of well used blankets, and a huge, ugly desk with the majority of drawers that did not open, and a cupboard only three feet high to hang clothes in. There was also a chest of drawers with a limited amount of space, a thick-legged rocky table and two armchairs completely out of proportion for any normally shaped human body. The light from the ceilings in both rooms came from naked light bulbs. I would have to go downstairs and outside to access the only loo on the premises. I sat down on the bed and burst into tears.

I could not help contrasting this beginning with my first day in southern Norway the year before. My accommodation there had not been great either and I had had to move into a different place after just a few weeks. But, although basic, it had at least been warm and welcoming. Few houses had bathrooms, including my host's, but I had had plenty of hot water and my own loo. Also, I could at least go into the nearby town for a bath every week. Now, for the first time, I seriously wondered why I had not listened to all the advice urging me not to go to the North. But there was nothing I could do about it now, even as I began to grasp something of the reality of my present situation.

After I had stopped crying, I unpacked my most essential belongings as there was no space for more. I gradually reckoned that there must be few people my age who had the opportunity to live in the Arctic Circle for a year. It was then that I decided I would do my best to make the most of mine.

Chapter 5

Recollections

After a rest, I felt ready to explore. At the hotel entrance Vadsø's particular brand of chill greeted me as I pushed against the swing doors and stepped into the wind's Arctic bite. It was almost 3 30pm. Fifty years ago it would have been the end of the working day and I would have seen people on their way home trundling along through the slush and sludge. Now I was greeted by well-kept roads, private cars, a milder climate and newly built paths, steps and pavements.

It took a few minutes to absorb some of these changes. As I did so I was surprised by half-a-dozen cycling teenagers suddenly appearing from my right and sweeping past at speed. I looked up to see where they had come from and for the first time noticed a long flight of staggered steps leading to a monument at the top. Neither the monument nor the steps had been there in my day. I could not remember what the steps must have replaced but presumed it must have been houses. The hotel and its surroundings were also quite new, and although I had clearly remembered the view from the top, I could not remember for the life of me what would have been demolished to make the space for it.

As I climbed, cyclists continued to hurtle past me, shouting messages back and forth as they raced each other to the bottom. 'Of course,' I said to myself, 'It's nearly four o'clock! School's out. They're on their way home!'

Riding a bicycle in my day would have been difficult - well-nigh impossible. The roads were potholed and bumpy. There had been only one or two main roads from the harbour, one of which ran through the centre of the town - the site of which had so taken me aback in my hotel room since it brought back surprisingly deep emotions as well as memories. Most roads then were mere tracks. I tried to remember when the winter snow would have finally melted back then and was fairly sure that there would have been plenty still lying around at this time, in late May. That always meant underfoot was mushy and slippery as well as dangerous and tiresome to negotiate. It had always been essential, I remembered, to pay complete attention.

From the top of all the four flights of steps I surveyed nearly the whole town. The front of the administration building was now behind me, immediately across the road from the statue. I thought it seemed smaller, certainly different, from how I recalled it. I remembered how the steps up to the entrance had always seemed imposing, and I did not remember the two wings of offices which now flanked the front corridor either. But memories surfaced about some of the May 17th National Day pranks around it and I wondered how they had celebrated it this year - whether the fun was as inventive and wild as it had been 50 odd years ago.

I sat on a bench and absorbed the view. The town looked more spacious and busier than I had expected, but that was unsurprising. When I had lived and worked here, the population was just some 2,500 people. Now, there are almost 6,000 people living in Vadsø, including refugees from the 2015 trek North West across Europe who had come into Norway across the Russian border. By then, Vadsø already had a reputation for its welcoming attitude towards refugees and asylum seekers in contrast to some less-open attitudes in the South of the country.

I stood looking to left and right seeing bus stops, zebra crossings and well-made roads in all directions. The entire outlook seemed much less haphazard than I remembered. Houses were well spaced out, so the town's overall area was longer and wider than it had been 50 years ago. I could not see a single old or dilapidated building: now, everything looked well sited and cared for. Yet, curiously, in many ways, it also felt exactly the same. The heart of Vadsø was definitely still strongly beating, even though it might now be to a different drum.

The church to my left still stood proudly sentinel at the town's centre, although its surrounding garden area was now surprisingly unkempt, with weeds growing out of the few steps up to the entrance. The harbour lay way out to the right of the central main road in front of me - but I could not see a single boat either moored or moving. However, I knew it was still used because I had seen the *Hurtigruten* dock and depart earlier that same morning. To my right the street where I had lived for most of my time in Vadsø stretched out with welcoming familiarity. Every teaching day after the first six weeks, I would walk home along it, relieved that it was level from now on after trudging up the long, steep gradient towards it. I was always so pleased to get home so that I could put my feet up, make a decent cup of tea, collect some of my day's thoughts, and just doze for an hour or so.

My musings returned to the new monument. The inscription stated that it commemorated Finnish cultural heritage in Vadsø which had been substantial in the 19th century when nearly half the population were Finnish. It was an imposing and elegant construction, unveiled in 1977 by King Olav V, in the presence of President Kekkonen of Finland and King Carl Gustav of Sweden. I felt taken aback to discover how much I had not known about the overall importance of Finnish influence in Vadsø in its recent history. I had known that Finnish people had sought work and lived in Finnmark as early as the mid-19th century, but I could not remember coming across any Finnish people at all while I lived there, nor can I remember ever having had any conversations with anyone about Finnish life or influence.

I sat for several minutes thinking about how little I knew about Vadsø's history altogether. Come to that, although I knew people like Øystein really well by the end of my year, we had never talked about politics or social affairs. I did not even know what sort of work he did at the NATO station, although I knew of course that he was a highly rated and respected civil servant. I also knew all about Europe's fear of Russia's secret ambitions and just how much NATO members relied on intelligence from the Norwegian NATO station, especially any provocative developments in and around the Murmansk area and the Barents Straits. Neither could I remember anyone else I came across socially who worked at the NATO station ever talking specifically about relations with Finland. But they never talked about anything to do with their work either and I certainly never asked about it. The Cold War or Norwegian policy about relations with Russia was never mentioned as far as I could remember, unless it was to do with cultural relations - such as making music or keeping people safe in difficult weather conditions.

I talked about everything under the sun with Øystein. After all, he was my boss and something of a polymath too. But even though we became good friends and talked about most things, I never even had a conversation with him about Vadsø's history, or relations with Finland, or even how things were in Finnmark in the war. But then, no one spoke about the war; no one ever spoke of it neither in the South nor in the North. It was from other sources that I had come to know about the particularly dreadful privations and terror experienced in Finnmark. The German Occupation and the Compulsory Evacuation of Finnmark was not mentioned once while I was there.

I am taken aback realising this absence some 50 years or more later. It must all have been too recent, too utterly dreadful and painful to talk about in the

1960s, I have concluded. After all, it is only in the recent past that significant numbers of Holocaust survivors who had suffered so dreadfully have been able to talk about some of the things they had endured some 70 years ago. I have come to see just how much time, strength and courage it takes to face one's horrific past.

What also gradually came to mind as I sat, was a difficult incident in my very first week in Vadsø that until now I had also completely forgotten. A student had held up a large notice at the back of the class so that only I could see it, and only she could know about it. It read simply and starkly, 'Why Don't You Go Home?' Once she knew I had read, and could tell I had registered it, she put it away, but it was not more than seconds before another student had said in no uncertain terms that they did not want or need to learn English. It would be much more useful, she had said, if they could be taught Finnish. I remember feeling poleaxed by these incidents. I realise now that probably the whole class were in on a rebellion against learning English taught by an English person. Perhaps my being there had not been eagerly anticipated on any front!

This incident was so traumatising that I've only recently been able to recall how the event made me feel at the time and to process what a piece of such sophisticated aggression actually meant. It was a cruel intervention. And after all, this was a language class, whose students had chosen to major in English, their main subject, to an advanced level. It was not unreasonable to think they might actually be thrilled to be taught by a native speaker!

Looking back now I can see there were a number of possible issues at play. Perhaps there was a collective feeling that the decision to employ a native English speaker had been imposed by the Education Ministry in Oslo, whose boffins did not know what life was really like in Vadsø. Imposition itself might have inspired deep resentment. Or maybe being taught by a native speaker had exposed an innate, collective fear that their knowledge of the language and all things English might not be good enough. Students might fear letting themselves down, appearing foolish and unsophisticated. It would be one thing to be taught English by a skilled Norwegian teacher, quite another by a native. After all, even Anton Bakken, the one, main teacher in charge of teaching English in Vadsø's Gymnas did not speak one word to me in English the whole time I was there! As I sat, I recalled how hateful and destabilising it had felt to read the held-up notice. No wonder I did not tell a single soul about it. Whatever motivated the placard I am amazed that I can recall it so clearly now. Thank goodness relationships with my classes DID gradually change into a partnership of mutual respect and committed learning.

I sat with my thoughts, sifting through them as I wondered if I was remembering things accurately. The feelings that emerged as I sat were real and genuine. And I reminded myself that I had only just come across all sorts of records - papers, letters, photographs and articles - that brought back many incidents and experiences I had forgotten. Maybe the most important thing for me to do was to rejoice in the overwhelming feeling of joy I was experiencing simply by being back in a place that had given me so much, and to tell myself that that incident did not summarise the eventual overall deep happiness of my year in Vadsø, which was to me the most important thing of all.

After a while, I decided to walk on in the direction of the cyclists. I had rung the High School office from England and had made an appointment to visit the new school the next day. I just needed to be sure I knew where the building was. We had passed the old one where I used to work on the way in from the airport. My heart had leapt at the sight of it, even as I realised that although it looked exactly the same it was no longer a school. Now, it was apparently some sort of factory or office block.

It meant revisiting my daily walk along the top road. I would find the house where I used to live for all but my first few weeks in Vadsø. When I eventually came upon it, I stood in front of it, a large lump in my throat. So many happy emotions continued to surface to remind me of just how amazing the whole experience of living and working there had been. I turned round after a while to face the sea and take in the special view I remembered of the harbour. I had loved watching the *Hurtigruten* come and go all those years ago. The view from my sitting room - when I eventually found a decent place to live - was excellent for that. Nowadays, it is always on time. In my day, however, it had often arrived much later than scheduled, so I might well be home. I could watch it come in, load up and then sail away again. In those days, I thought of it as the only accessible link to the outside world. I remembered that I had found that oddly comforting, even though it was so increasingly wonderful to be there - certainly, in the winter months at least. I could not help thinking that it might simply have reassured me I WAS in touch with reality and the rest of the world on every front, in spite of being so geographically remote.

Eventually, I could see construction equipment and men at work, and ever more young people emerging in couples and groups from a new building which clearly was the wonderful, new school, far bigger and grander than the one where

I had worked. It was close to many new houses, including some earmarked as special accommodation for the elderly. This was all recent, as was accessibility by proper roads and pavements. Cars stood parked outside houses, and there were bus-stops here and there. Lorries carried building materials in and out and there were still more cyclists. The whole scene would have been unimaginable 50 years ago when such roads as there were, were unspeakable, and there were far fewer young people too. Significantly, back then all students seemed more reserved. These current exuberant students racing each other home from school seemed cast in a different mould from their more unassuming predecessors.

Now that I knew where the school was, and how long it would take me to walk there, I decided to explore the town's centre as I circled back to the hotel. I turned right down a street adjacent to the sea. There were many new buildings, but the central road through the town's heart to the harbour seemed just the same. I discovered that now, there were not just 'proper' shops, but other facilities too. The single, rather general, trading store that had been there in my day - that acted along the lines of a just slightly up market fur trappers' supply station in North America in the 1880s - now had several new additions. These included a garage, a large dress shop and a small department store. There were also several restaurants, a chemist and a large and well-stocked antique shop. I knew there was a library in Vadsø, built long after I had lived there. 'I should explore that tomorrow,' I thought.

There was far too much to take in on one afternoon's stroll. The whole town was considerably larger than it had been 50 years ago. But the harbour seemed much, much smaller than I remembered. There were only a couple of small boats at anchor, and although I knew the *Hurtigruten* was still a daily visitor, what I saw now did not seem to fit with any of my memories of daily busy-ness with men scurrying around and boats constantly in and out of the harbour.

I bought milk from the garage on my way back to the hotel, enough for any number of cups of tea for the three of us. I had brought plenty of tea bags from England which I knew we would need.

***

Over a leisurely supper in our hotel, we were able to unwind after our travels.

'Does this seem a rather dead and dreary place and are you beginning to wonder why on earth you agreed to come here?' I asked, once we had ordered from the menu.

'I think it's all wonderful!' Margaret said. 'Everyone is so open and friendly, and this is such an unusual and interesting place. It's not at all what I expected. I expected it to be bleak. And in some ways, it is, but it's also really alive. It's not as cold as I feared it might be either. And I'm really enjoying the slower pace. People are so warm and welcoming too.'

'I agree! Nothing more to add!' Ann smiled broadly. 'Except that I expected it to be a lot more basic than it is. 'But how are *you* feeling about being here, Molly? Are *you* glad you came? How much has it changed?'

'I'm finding it all surprisingly overwhelming,' I said. 'Well! No! Not exactly that. I'm differently overwhelmed. I feel thoroughly warmed - that's a much better way of putting it. Being here is bringing back so many happy memories. Although it has also changed a good deal and that feels strange. There are more buildings than there were, and the town stretches far wider than it did, but its natural hub hasn't changed. It's extraordinary, the way things are still just the same. I can't quite explain. I need to think about exactly what I really am feeling and what I really mean before I say any more.'

'How did you get on with your initial exploring?' Margaret asked. 'Did you manage to find where the new school is?'

'I did. And finding it took me past places that brought back many recollections. There's a beautiful, new monument at the top of the steps by the hotel and a seat to admire the view of the town. I sat for a while and so many memories came flooding back. The road looked the same, but the building looked different somehow, although I may have remembered it wrongly. What I do quite clearly recall, however, I simply *must* tell you about. But first of all, I have to explain about Norway's National Day on May 17th - *Syttende Mai* – which the whole country celebrates. It's so special because it marks Norway's complete independence at the end of the Napoleonic wars and its freedom to set up its own Constitution as a democratic monarchy that was signed in 1814. Since then, every year without fail – except of course, during the war - it's celebrated by every single Norwegian. To start with, it's absolutely de rigeur to unfurl the national flag in your garden or by your front door. In my day, every school child marched round their town with the rest of their class behind the school band playing from the front. Also, if you're fortunate enough to have a national costume, or *bunad* - which is often handed down from one generation to another and is otherwise extremely expensive to buy - it's essential to wear it. Each county displays its special, decorative emblems which are mostly floral, but quite distinctive, so it's possible to tell whereabouts in the country families have come from.'

'It's a sort of jubilee then, is it?' Margaret asked.

'I suppose you could say so, yes.'

'When I was here it was freezing cold. There was snow on the ground still, and flurries throughout the day. But everyone came out to watch the children process - even people from outlying settlements and villages. The few Sami people who lived here then also wore their National Costumes. Back then, the equivalent of Year 13 leavers, known as *russ,* would celebrate the end of their school years by instigating a variety of mischievous jokes and pranks around the town, where they lived.

'It's all different now, though. The exam system is different and pranking traditions have changed. Back then, thanking or honouring those who had taught them by teasing or playing tricks on them - was all part of the fun. Everyone looked forward to it to see what special ingenuity had been devised for any particular teacher: what clever ideas, or jokes had been thought up. Almost nothing was out of bounds. As long as it wasn't dangerous or harmful, of course.'

'We've just missed all that then! What a shame!' Margaret grinned.

'Well! no, not really,' I said. The system is very different now. There's more money about and so there's more alcohol-fuelled revelry instead. There are greater numbers of school leavers too. So nowadays, the tendency is more to hire a bus and blast the horn all through the night trying to out-blast other high schools' buses. At least in the larger towns and cities like Oslo, Trondheim, Bergen and so forth.'

'How exciting. I wonder how that would go down in the UK?' Ann said wistfully.

'Anyway, I must tell you both that as I sat in the front of the administration building earlier today, I remembered that the *russ* in my day had put the headmaster's car there, at the top of the steps. They'd covered it with all sorts of messages, which I wish I could remember. How they got it up there, I've no idea. Nor how they got it down again! And I can't remember what other pranks they perpetrated on their teachers. Although I *do* remember that the lad voted to be in charge of it all that year was a singular and particular charmer called Alf Lundeström. He did a really good job, both with all the jokey pranks and all the clearing up.'

Chapter 6

Breaking the Ice

My first week of school in Vadsø felt painful and difficult. The Rektor introduced me to my first class with an air of nervous formality I thought. When he left the room and handed over to me there was total silence. Every face looked blank and there was an air of palpable tension. I knew at once I was not welcome. A sense of panic consumed me. There was not a smile on a single face. What should I say? How exactly should I proceed?

All my classes in the South, both in schools and with adults, had exhibited warmth, openness and enthusiasm from the start. I had always been greeted with smiles and kindness – it was almost embarrassing. Gratitude came from a deep desire to know the English language well and as much as possible also about life in England. Lessons were fun with laughter and commitment to learn. Competence and confidence in learning English progressed. In turn, my students taught **me** a good deal too - about the Norwegian way of life, and what it was like to live in a cold climate at a time when the country was still recovering from the privations of war, even as they were beginning to build a sound and prosperous economy.

But, even after all these years, I well remember how difficult my first weeks were in Vadsø. Even in those classes where English was the students' main, chosen subject, I soon realised that an understanding of, and desire to know more about English attitudes and culture was different in Finnmark. At first, I half wondered if it had something to do with the fact that there were more boys than girls in every class, and they were less inclined to chat or reach out. Maybe boys were more scared of making mistakes? Perhaps the girls felt inhibited because the boys were more dominant? All sorts of possible explanations went through my mind in those first, painful few weeks.

Those whose main subjects were science only had to learn how to **speak** English rather than write it. Classes that were majoring in the humanities subjects had to be able to **write** good English as well as speak it. But it was crystal clear to me from the beginning that having to be taught in Vadsø's Gymnasium by an English teacher was generally regarded as a discourteous imposition. Refusal to connect or respond to me at the outset made me feel homesick for the truly wonderful time I had had from the beginning of my teaching in the South. It was almost as if in Vadsø students went out of their way - in two classes in particular - to make my life as uncomfortable and unwelcoming as possible. I began to believe I had made a great mistake in agreeing to be there at all.

It was immediately obvious who were the leaders in each class who were able to dominate the lessons or give a lead about how to react to me. Looking back recently, I have come to wonder if perhaps there was an actual agreement in each class to respond to me as a foreign intruder by being as unresponsive as possible. No one was aggressively hostile, but from the very beginning a definite tone of resentment prevailed, which I knew would have to be overcome. But first of all, I thought I needed to understand what it was about. I did not want to give the impression that I felt personally superior or had better expectations because I was English. So, I really did my best to grapple with **horrible**, resistant atmospheres through my first week in the classroom, at the same time as I was having to 'go home' after the school day and try to cope with my utterly, ghastly digs.

As soon as the Rektor had left the room, I introduced myself and explained that the lessons would be in English. Straight away, I could feel a wall of silent dislike. There was a total, sullen silence. No one said a word - not even a hint of objection in Norwegian. No one answered any of my friendly, social-getting-to-know-you, slowly-asked questions. I wondered at first if there might be an inbuilt suspicion of foreigners this far north, on top of a characteristic, Norwegian reserve. I knew many Norwegians in the South battled against a fear of speaking English in case, having learned it for so many years, they embarrassed themselves in front of a native English speaker. But it was increasingly clear that there was something more than that in Vadsø. Classes felt almost mutinous with a consistent refusal to answer even the easiest of questions. Even my attempts to work off piste and initiate comments not specifically about anything in the textbook, or on the syllabus, to make jokes, met with sullen silence. However hard I tried, nothing would get anyone to say anything, except an occasional 'yes' or 'no'. In one particular class, there was a much harder core of resistance and resentment. I began to believe there was tacit agreement to boycott any interaction or conversation. But I battled on and told no-one: not even Øystein.

A turning point, however, came at the beginning of the third week, during a particularly difficult lesson in which we had been studying Winston Churchill's speeches from the textbook. I wondered if I tried to stimulate a conversation about the war it might produce comment. After all, it was a subject that had always gone down well and got pupils talking in the South, even whether or not anyone present was a child or grandchild of a Quisling – someone who followed the Norwegian leader who supported the Nazis and was executed for his treachery. It was now 20 years after the war and the government had worked hard at reconciliation between various political groups at home and had reached out to what had been enemy countries abroad. Not least to be able to stand in solidarity with other European countries against Stalin's rule in Russia.

Vadsø students in particular were well aware of various aspects of Norway's political attitudes and ideas, not least because a NATO station had been established there in recent years, a mile or so outside the town. Some of their parents actually worked there. Sited as it was in a town so close to the Russian border, it was well placed to monitor potentially aggressive policies and threatening military strategies close as Northern Russia is to mutual Arctic waters. I came from England with a healthy scepticism of all things Russian, a fear almost, if I'm honest. I fully understood the Norwegian government's wish to show the Soviet Union that it was not an easy target to fool or beguile in the Finnmark North.

In the South, I had discovered that students were only too keen to discuss political issues, even in English. They were politically aware and well-read too. I hoped there might be similar enthusiasm to talk about issues in the North. However, No one ever talked about the war or its aftermath, and I never knew whether or not there had been Quislings in Vadsø. But in desperation, trying to initiate some form of dialogue and after making bland statements about all sorts of current political concerns, and then really outrageously provocative ones, I hoped to incite some sort of response in spoken English! In the South my comments there would have provoked all kinds of reactions. But in the early weeks in Vadsø there was not even a raised eyebrow.

Then, suddenly everything changed during the lesson in which we were discussing one of Winston Churchill's speeches. Out of nowhere, I heard a loud shriek of fury from the centre of the classroom. I had turned briefly, to write a new word on the board, When I turned back again, I saw that the face of one particular student had turned almost purple.

'Whatever's the matter Mette?' I asked. At first, I thought she was seriously unwell.

Mette had stood up. I could see now that she was definitely not ill, but very angry indeed and not prepared to express her rage in anything but her native tongue.

'Why do you always laugh at us when we make mistakes and why do you insist that the lessons must be in English? You come here lording it around - we don't want anyone to teach us English. We'll never use the language once we're through with school anyway, so what's the point? Why don't you go back to London where you came from? You don't fit in. We don't want you here. You keep saying things that are quite improper for a teacher to say. It's not right for someone in your position to say that Hitler must have been a fool because he forgot about the Russian winter.'

Her outburst gradually came to a halt, either because she could think of nothing else to say, or else because she could not put any more frustration into words. She also seemed to have exhausted the wave of emotion that had so far inspired her. She sat down and sobbed quietly into the back of her right hand. The rest of the class sat silent - stunned. I remember feeling sick. For a start, I had not said what she thought she had heard. No one else supported her - and that made me believe that this was not a mutinous plot to sabotage the lesson by the whole class. Mette's outburst was real and heartfelt. I had clearly pinged unwittingly on a painful nerve. I knew I had to deal with the situation and that HOW I did so was important.

Apart from Mette's sobs, there was total silence. I walked back to my desk from Mette's where I had gone instinctively to see what was to be done. I took my time. A noisy silence followed me. I decided there was nothing for it but to tackle everything - now, and head on. All grievances needed to be out in the open. So, I forced myself to talk in Norwegian.

'It seems that Mette has probably expressed a general view' I said. And I watched their wide-eyed faces suddenly change as it gradually dawned on them that I was speaking Norwegian. I continued. 'It has been obvious ever since I came that there has been an unhappy feeling in this class. I can appreciate your view that there are other languages, like Finnish, which you think would be of much more use to you than English, because the Finns are your closest neighbours. You may be right. But the fact is that your government has decided that English is to be an important part of your curriculum, and those who make the decisions about your town's policies wanted you all to have the extra benefit, almost the special privilege you might say, of an actual English teacher being here for the whole year in the flesh. So, we might as well try to work together and make the best of it. What bothers me deeply, however, is that we are not yet on the same wavelength. With respect, you imagine I say things, which in fact I don't say, and think things I definitely don't think. You forget that the situation is as bad for me as it is for you: worse even. After all, I haven't been taught your language, and you HAVE been taught mine…and for quite a few years too.'

My monologue continued, although I cannot remember what else I said. I just remember having to force myself to think all the time about what I was saying so that I did not further put my foot in it. Thus, it took me several minutes to notice that there was universal amazement. When I had finally finished stating my case, I asked them what else would they like to say, and then sat down to give them opportunity. But no one said a word. Several faces were flushed. I did not want to look at Mette, but I knew she was still close to tears. Then, after what seemed ages, the bell rang. For the first time ever, the boy nearest the door quickly extricated himself clumsily from his seat and moved towards the door to open it for me. I left the room trying hard to look both poised and unperturbed.

A 10-minute break followed every lesson so that both staff and pupils could turn themselves around. All students HAD to go outside to get fresh air. Staff, however, could swap books, drink coffee, see colleagues and catch their breath. I tottered along the corridor on legs that felt as if they were not my own. But I just managed to make it to the staff room. I sank thankfully into the nearest armchair. I felt utterly mangled and emotionally drained.

Classrooms were locked during the break. My hands shook as I turned the key to unlock the door for the next lesson. But even as I walked to my desk to put my books down, I knew that something had changed. In fact, this very lesson I was dreading - the second half of a double period, as it would have been called in England - turned out to be the first one on the right road to understanding and working together.

'Good morning again!' I said, trying to look composed,

'Good morning Miss Russell!' echoed a smiling chorus.

'Please sit down.'

I knew at once there had been something of a sea change in those few brief minutes of break. The atmosphere felt quite different. There was an unusual enthusiasm to get books open and ready. Faces looked more alert, and bright eyed. Suddenly, everyone seemed anxious to please. What an amazing metamorphosis I thought to myself. I can only but imagine the conversation that had gone on in the short break.

'So,' I continued. 'We didn't have time at the end of last lesson to discuss what's bothering you all. I wonder if anyone has anything which they would like to say now?'

An obviously elected male spokesman stood up. 'The trouble is ... er, well, we're all a little scared.' So far, he had spoken in clear and unfaltering English. 'We're scared because we don't always understand what you say - your pronunciation is different from what we've been used to, and you speak so fast!'

I had tried to speak slowly, but now wondered if in my nervousness I had speeded up my sentences without realising it. The boy went on, red-faced, but completely in control of the situation and determined to finish what he wanted to say.

'If we could ask you to speak more slowly when we can't understand, it would help. And perhaps if there are things we really don't understand, we could ask you about them in Norwegian? We...er, we were told by the headmaster when you first came that you couldn't speak any Norwegian, and we felt very angry because we didn't think that was fair.'

He sat down, and I knew that what he had said was an apology for the eruption in the previous lesson: rather perhaps even ALL the previous lessons and expressions of resistance. If what he said was true - and I had no reason to doubt it - I could completely understand the class's universal rage. I looked at Mette who was smiling up at me - in an almost naïve and childlike way, as if pleading for forgiveness.

'Thank you!' I said. 'I hope then that perhaps we might be beginning to understand each other at last. You must please try not to be so sensitive about making mistakes in English. And if you really feel that I make fun of you when you make a mistake - actually, I **don't**, but if you **feel** that I do - then you must say so. Meanwhile, I give you permission to laugh at my bad Norwegian. Perhaps you could even help me to learn your language properly?'

The whole atmosphere had changed. Everyone looked around with grins and smiles, and I felt sure there would be no future trouble about speaking English. I carried on with the formal part of the lesson, but the incident was only finally and completely concluded when halfway through the lesson I chanced to look at Mette. She was holding a cardboard placard in front of her on which she'd written, 'May I come and see you this afternoon?' Trying not to reveal her private question and at the same appear to be teaching the whole class, I nodded. The lesson continued.

This meant there were TWO occasions when messages were held up in those first weeks - both written in perfect English. Looking back now, I feel sure the whole class knew about them - indeed, they were the probable outcome of aggrieved feelings of resentment about the imposition of a foreign intruder. It was an unusually intriguing way to express their feelings and until now, I have not given any thought to how they expected me to respond! They must have known they were likely to be in serious trouble if I reported the incident.

Later that day over a cup of tea - I can't recall where - Mette said how sorry she was. It was a genuine, heartfelt and endearing exchange. Then she and I enjoyed a long and friendly talk about life in Vadsø, and for the first time, I began to feel that I was not such a stranger after all and there was even hope I might be drawn into the full life of the community. Lessons with 2R were much more relaxed after this crisis - fun even, and focussed on work, with mutually beneficial discussions about comparative life and culture in various parts of Norway and the British Isles.

This very class was joined a day or so later by one of the most interesting students in the whole Gymnas. His name was Per Johann. He added extraordinary colour to the life of the class – indeed to the whole school. He achieved just **one** English oral sentence the entire year, always insisting on replying to even the simplest of English questions in Norwegian: eternally desperate perhaps, not to make a fool of himself. He spent most of the time - in English lessons and others – appearing to be fast asleep. He had an unusual and enviable ability to shut out life and the rest of the world around him. At a minute's notice, he would just fold himself up into a ball, lean on his arms and within seconds would be in a world of his own. Later, he would re-enter the lesson with the same lack of effort as when he appeared to leave us.

He was without doubt one of the most stubborn, yet brightest and most charming of the pupils in the whole of Vadsø's Gymnas. He was blessed with brains, good looks and tremendous initiative in anything he found interesting. Yet it was impossible to persuade him to do anything he did not want to do, and in the staffroom his name always came up accompanied by heavy sighs and shaking heads. They would give way to resigned comments. 'Ah! Yes! Per Johann! He's his own worst enemy. What are we to do with him?' I liked him enormously and came to respect him for any number of reasons. As the year progressed, the respect became mutual.

From the time of that dreadful outburst onwards, life improved. I even began to feel less stressed about my awful lodgings because the classroom seemed easier. As barriers came down and mutual respect was allowed to flow, lessons became much more enjoyable.

***

At that time, all schools in Norway used the same points system as a route to further and higher education and employment. Any pupil would think nothing of arguing with staff to try to obtain the highest possible number of points to be equipped to pursue the best onward pathways. It had only happened to me once in the South - that a pupil, a grown and mature lad with impeccable manners and nearly in tears, had approached me about a lower than usual mark I had given him. I had felt stunned to have my authority challenged and to have been asked about it at first. But I heard him out and I have to confess that he was absolutely right, and I was in the wrong. I did my best to correct my mistake with the next round of marks and trust it did not cause him any obstruction to future destinations.

My first one-to-one argument with a Vadsø pupil, however, followed the return of some essays to a class whose main subject was English. The essay was Arne's - an unusual young man. His English was fluent and colloquial - partly because he had a good ear and a natural flair for words and language, and partly because he devoured American books and magazines. These were available where newspapers were sold in Vadsø, well after their USA publication date, but regularly supplied to the Americans working in the developing new oil industry around Stavanger. They were always snapped up the day they arrived in Vadsø too. Arne also lapped up every film that came to the town's occasional, cinema showings, especially if they were American, and most of them were. The Norwegian film industry chose to post translated, sub-titles in Norwegian rather than to dub the dialogue. I have always understood how helpful this was to help encourage and spread an understanding of English.

Much of Arne's vocabulary was outrageous - sometimes even crude. But he was an able student, in an off-beat, quirky sort of way. He was hampered by the fact that he had had a long spell away from school with polio and was therefore two years behind his twin brother who was hoping to take the equivalent of A level exams that very academic year. The first essay he wrote was good, easy to understand with lots of original ideas and interpretations: but also shot through with slang and shockingly crude phrases. Hence, because it was the **quality** of the English that was to be judged, I was forced to mark it down. Arne was not prepared to let that happen unchallenged.

He marched straight up to the front waving his marked work.

'What do you mean' he asked, 'by giving me such a low mark?'

'I beg your pardon,' I responded. 'What exactly are you asking me? It's my JOB to apportion the marks I give to your work based on the quality of your English, and I've written on your essay in detail the sorts of mistakes you have made and the expressions you really cannot use in an essay of this kind. As you see, I've taken great care to write down all my comments wherever relevant.' I paused as Arne stood there, obviously outraged. 'Or are you saying you cannot read my writing?' I paused. But he made no response. 'So,' I continued, 'it's MY affair, my RESPONSIBILITY, to apportion what I always think is an appropriate mark.'

'It ain't entirely your affair', the young man persisted: 'if I get lousy marks, my school record will suffer.'

I resisted the spontaneous desire to correct both 'ain't' and 'lousy' still irritated and incredulous that he could approach me with such self-confidence. 'Well,' I said. 'If you want better marks, you must try to write more formal, accurate English, Arne. As I keep telling you all, written English and conversational English are two entirely different things, and you need to be able to master them both.'

'That's all very well'. He persisted undaunted. 'But how are we to know the difference? And furthermore, while we're talking about this, how then can I get good marks?'

I felt utterly flummoxed and didn't know how best to answer his questions. He had a point, and I felt really sorry that he was forced to have had so much time out to recover from his bout of polio. So, I simply said, 'If you concentrate hard, the right language and expressions are bound to emerge eventually,' I suggested feebly, unable to cope more effectively with the problem. 'I'll try to help you if I can. You must ask questions and read English books as well as relying on American films.'

Arne was forced to yield to the voice of authority and returned despondently to his desk. But his written work definitely began to improve.

It was not long before the lessons with this class developed into a natural pattern of questions and discussion - everything from The Beatles to what an English pub was really like. What was curious, however, was the students' total belief in the literal accuracy of everything written in the textbook. All Norwegian syllabuses and textbooks were nationally controlled, so at any given time, all pupils of the same year throughout the country would be on roughly the same textbook page. The amusingly symbolic account of the two Englishmen stranded on a desert island together for more than a year, but not speaking to each other because they had not been formally introduced produced wry smiles and gentle titters in the South from pupils who were becoming Anglo-orientated. In the North however, the story was accepted as Gospel. Only by the end of the year did just some pupils think that perhaps not *all* English people read *The Times*, go to work in a bowler hat with a rolled umbrella under their arm and talk incessantly about their experiences in Poonah, or sigh with frustration about just how difficult it was to get domestic staff these days.

Five girls and five boys made up the hard-working group of late teenagers and young adults in the most senior class, facing the all-important, qualifying exams of their final school year. By dint of personality alone, the form was dominated by the presence of a certain Alf Lundestrøm. He had a strange background that I never really understood. He was what one would probably have called at the time 'a man of the world'. In any event, it seemed to me, he would very much like that to be the case. He was soundly streetwise and extremely savvy. He was a keen, popular student who worked hard. It was he who was in charge of the prank that put the headmaster's car at the top of the administration building steps that I had been telling Ann and Margaret about over supper during our 2019 trip. He was well able to express himself in colloquial English with little hint of any Norwegian pronunciation. He was also well aware of his good looks and had great difficulty in restraining himself from believing that he was God's gift to women – especially foreign ones!

I had learnt in the South not to react or be put off by tall, handsome Norwegians who wolf-whistled when one's back was turned to write on the board and winked at one from the back of the class so that no one else could see. But Alf's approach was quite different. He sat in the middle of the front row, always with his chin resting on his hands so that he had to look up at a steep angle if he were to follow any teaching from the front. He often rolled his large, blue eyes in the most suggestive of ways. His whole demeanour created a much more alarming threat to my professional dignity than just simple, blatant flirtation. I had to decide quite firmly not to be put off by his provocative antics.

'Ain't you hungry?' he asked one day when the mid-morning bell had gone which was the signal for the long break for packed lunches. It was his way of saying, 'The lesson's over, you know.'

'I shall enjoy my coffee', I replied, as I slowly gathered all my books and belongings together.

'May I accompany you to the staff room?' he asked as he oiled his way to the door to open it for me. And although this gesture had the semblance of good manners about it, I had the feeling that he was not only making fun of English manners, but also, of me.

'Thank you!' I said. 'But I really don't think I need an escort down the stairs.'

'Oh please,' he said, not in the least put off. 'I so much want us to be good friends!'

I stared at him, but he went on, 'I want you to know that if there is anything at all I can do for you at any time, I am absolutely at your disposal.'

Was he making fun of me or was this a genuine but clumsy attempt to say that I was accepted? Was he trying to make me feel at home?

'Thank you,' I said again. 'I'll try to remember that'.

I was puzzled. Normally, Norwegian pupils were scared of giving any impression of being friends with any of the staff in order to prevent their contemporaries from accusing them of trying to get better marks. Yet Alf, apparently, could not care less. I never gave a moment's thought to his real intentions or what he was really after.

Meantime, just a couple of weeks later, I was woken up about 2am by a peculiar sound coming from below my bedroom window. I got out of bed, drew back the curtain, and gazed out at the blackness through bleary eyes. There were no street-lights in Vadsø, so it took a while for my eyes to focus.

Someone was throwing snowballs up at the window. It was a second or two before my eyes rested on the bowler and discovered that it was Alf. I assumed immediately that he was in some kind of trouble and had not rung the doorbell for fear of waking up the others in the house. I pulled on my dressing-gown and virtually ran down the stairs. Finally, I put on the hall light and opened the front door. I was hit immediately by the strength of the cold. There he stood - having seen the light go on - leaning against the side of the door, grinning from ear to ear. He looked very sure of himself, and of what he wanted. I realised at once that he certainly was not in any kind of bother!

'What do you want?' I asked, taking great care not to open the door too wide.

'A chat,' he replied.

'At this time of night: You must be crazy! I thought there was something wrong when I saw you from the window, but you look perfectly all right to me. Go home, at once! People are asleep upstairs here and will not appreciate being woken up in the middle of the night. I wouldn't have come down if I had realised that this was just some sort of childish prank.'

Eventually, he went away, and later I learnt, when he came to apologise, that he had been dared to visit me in the middle of the night by his classmates to see what sort of reaction he got. He would have looked very feeble if he had refused the challenge. I dared not even contemplate how I would have looked had I accepted it!

Chapter 7

Birth of the Choir

I was surprised when given my time-table that I was scheduled to teach one music class each week. I had not known about that in advance, so I had not prepared any songs to distribute. More importantly, I did not know the specific Norwegian vocabulary for all the musical terms I wanted to use, nor who to ask, or where to go for appropriate translations. I was not sure either, of the vocabulary to use for the shape of sound I wanted to describe or the distinctions of shade and tone. I learned some new vocabulary as I went along, but what was really unfortunate was the way I pronounced some of the names of notes in Norwegian, especially those of some sharps and flats. It always caused great hilarity and I did not know why. Every time I said certain Norwegian words - which everyone in the class seemed to be waiting for - they all just fell about laughing.

What made it more difficult was that students had learnt little about how to make music in their own language, let alone a foreign one. There was no fixed syllabus, so I was forced to fall back on my knowledge and experience. And that meant I was constantly worrying about turning students off music altogether which I would have minded about a great deal, and anxious that I might lose classroom control because students might come to think I was not a credible teacher.

I had started learning to play the piano when I was four. My father was a Salvation Army bandmaster before, during and after the war – first in Birmingham and then in London. I have inherited any innate musicality I may have from him. He was unqualified by today's standards, having left school at 14 and never having sat any music exams. But long after his death in 1961, I was told by someone who knew the Salvation Army music scene in England well, that in the first couple of decades after the war, he had been widely respected as one of the best Salvation Army Bandmasters in the United Kingdom.

I went to Wycombe Abbey School when I was 12 as a boarder. I became what was known as 'the conductor' of my house. Amongst other things, I taught anthems we had to sing in chapel. Once I got to the Sixth Form, I was also commissioned to be the School Pianist and was responsible for certain aspects of whole school singing. So, I was fortunate to have had considerable experience in creating ad hoc singing groups and conducting choirs, although I had never formed a whole choir from scratch before, apart from getting up small groups, such as that of males from Marlborough College and females from my own school to sing on a joint, sixth-form trip to Oberammergau, and getting various individuals together to sing some interesting carols at various Christmas services at home.

Normally, I would have relished the opportunity to teach any form of music. But now, even had I been a native Norwegian speaker I believe my students would not have understood what I meant by phrasing and colour.

After a couple of weeks, I found myself wondering how I might go about teaching my music classes with a different approach. At the same time, the yearning to at least try to set up a choir, nagged at me. I had hesitated for several weeks, feeling set back by the Rektor's reaction when I had first suggested it. He had not exactly scoffed at the idea, but he seemed so certain that that a choir would just not take off that I felt the project might be doomed from the start. But then I began to wonder whether his reaction might be more about how HE saw the people round him in the North, especially since he seemed to have come from a particularly cultured Oslo background himself. His hunch might not necessarily be right. Or maybe his expectations were too formal or too high? Whatever the truth of it was, I knew I would never know whether or not he was right to caution me until I had explored any interest myself.

The more I thought about it, the more I liked the idea, believing it would be a smart, fun way to communicate musical knowledge and appreciation. I knew I felt much more competent and comfortable about a 'hands on' approach to music teaching than I did struggling with classroom music lessons in which we just expected to sing songs from a textbook. I also believed that running a choir might be a better way to develop relationships with students, as well as between students themselves. A great way to enhance all kinds of linguistic communication across two languages, perhaps?

I also had other reasons that encouraged my thoughts. I had come to see how little there was for people to do of an evening. I wondered if the chance to commit to something one evening a week might therefore be welcomed. Most pupils simply went home to their families after school, or to their digs if their family home was not actually in Vadsø. Some had to find places to stay in town for weeks, or terms, at a time - and spent their evenings and weekends just doing homework. There were few ways for people to have fun or get together. Reading was almost the only thing to do apart from listening to the radio, especially once the evenings began to draw in and the days grew dramatically shorter and darker. At that time, TV had not yet arrived anywhere in Norway, and Vadsø would not be one of the first places in the country to receive it anyway, even when it finally arrived. There might be an occasional football match arranged on a Sunday which involved some pupils, as well as various kinds of skiing competitions in the winter. But apart from an occasional evening film show, there was little on offer to draw people together.

Norwegians were, and still are, known to be great readers, and the town's small library provided a wide range of books for borrowing. But in spite of this great love of reading it was only open for an hour or so every weekday. Like much else in Vadsø, it relied on volunteers to keep it going. The librarian was unpaid: a typical, temporary visitor. Her husband was a civil servant, and he and his family were only living this far north for a few years. They planned to return to their southern life, especially as they both had elderly parents living near Trondheim. Meanwhile, Marit was an excellent librarian. She knew her stuff and did her best to keep increasing the stock of books. And, because Scandinavia already had an international reputation for the sheer number of books read annually per capita, getting hold of them was not too difficult. There was not much cash in Vadsø's library kitty for Marit to draw on, so it was only possible to acquire films, as well as books, now and then when they could be afforded. Meanwhile, she was generous with her time and the library came to be well used as a social hub and cultural centre, and films would be shown in a small make-shift cinema every six weeks or so. There was only one projectionist in town, however, and it entirely depended on his work schedules when a screening would be possible.

Once I began to see how the rhythms of life worked in this remote place, I also saw that there was never any shortage of goodwill or support for any initiative that helped the community to work together or enrich it. So, I felt encouraged to dare to see what would happen if I plucked up the courage to put up a notice on the board in the main school corridor asking if anyone was interested in singing with others. If they wanted to see what might be possible, I invited them to come to the school Assembly Hall one evening the following week to discuss such a project, with the possibility of forming a choir and if so, what sort of things it might sing. I said nothing to anyone about my notice. Nobody said anything to me about it either, or even commented that they had read it – apart from Rektor Anderson.

'You mustn't be disappointed if nothing happens, or only a few people turn up,' he said. 'We have no precedent for starting up anything like a choir. So, it maybe that no one comes at all. They just might not dare – because it's a new idea, I mean, and they might be reluctant to risk it. Anyway, thank you for at least being willing to take that risk.'

He had not said the project might not get off the ground, 'because you're English', however, which, if I'm honest I half feared. In view of the issues that had arisen in my classes, I almost expected to be told something like that, even though I could not think what reason might be offered by way of explanation. I was pleased he did not say anything negative like that, although I was still puzzled by his caution. After all, there had been a great choir at the Gymnas in the South where I had taught the previous year with no shortage of participants, and an excellent adult town/church choir too. I knew I would mind terribly if only a few people came of course, and certainly if no one came at all. But I told myself I would cope whatever confronted me, and I would just have to get over any personal humiliation I felt if the whole idea was a flop and hope it would be quickly forgotten.

Meantime, I had taken to heart the request to speak English much more slowly. I had put more effort into choosing my vocabulary with greater care. I could feel the initial resentment in my classes had now almost entirely evaporated. In all of them, relationships seemed to be getting more settled and comfortable. I noticed that I had also begun to relax and believed my teaching had improved greatly as a result. 'It's all about relationships' I said to myself time and again. 'How can anyone teach anything if there is no trust or goodwill between teacher and pupil? How can there ever be any kind of productive teaching without effective communication?'

I was unwilling however, to let my classes call me by my first name. Many had asked if they could. But I always maintained it was 'un-English'. They were right in thinking that the English were a more formal race than the Norwegians, I told them. Since it was my job to teach about life in England as well as to teach the language, I insisted they call me 'Miss Russell'. I would not even allow just 'Miss'. Everyone seemed to accept it as an example of the formality which they were positively convinced prevailed in everyday life in England. So, an atmosphere of respectful, friendly formality began to develop. Even though it continually felt much more comfortable in every classroom than it had felt at first, I steeled myself against any feelings of rejection if the choir project had no takers: or worse, if there were just a few, which would be even more painful to deal with, and possibly might even be difficult to turn into a meaningful singing group.

***

Ninety-six people turned up to the first choir meeting. There were even a few students much younger than those I taught. I was amazed that there were staff as well. I could hardly conceal my delight. Eventually, summoning up my best and most well considered Norwegian I clapped my hands for quiet, with as much energetic confidence as possible.

'How many of you have been in a choir before?' I asked. About a dozen hands went up. I thought that most of them must be children from the South, who were only living temporarily this far north. I could not think how they would have gained any experience of singing in a choir otherwise.

'I see. That's a goodly number. So, let's see how we can best get started. Have any of you sung in parts before?' I was thinking on my feet now, about how to cope with so many keen to sing. A few hands went up, including from a member of staff who I did not know personally, although I had seen him in the staff room and knew he taught in the Middle School. 'Great! Well, just so I know how to prepare for our first proper practice next time, how many of you KNOW you can sing soprano?'

It took a minute or two for everyone to look round at one another, seeing who would take the lead and dare to respond to my question.

'You definitely can, Grethe,' I heard one or two people say to a girl sitting at the front, who then started to giggle. I recognised her as an English stream student: a happy person, always smiling in class. I taught her but as yet, knew little about her. Tentatively, she began to raise her hand, and others quickly followed.

'That seems like a good start! Excellent! And who thinks they can sing alto – a part under the sopranos?'

Immediately, Grethe's best friend, Turild, who was sitting next to her, who I also taught and recognised, said, 'Me, I know I can. Grethe and I often sing in two parts together. We practise harmonising with each other for fun.' She beckoned encouragingly to a few others who also put up their hands. 'We can all hold a second part,' she said enthusiastically, pointing to a small group of girls, all nodding in agreement.

'And is there anyone who can sing tenor by any chance and perhaps has done so before?'

The colleague I did not actually know put up his hand straight away. 'I can. I definitely can.' He grinned. 'I'll persuade a few others to join me later,' he added.

'And what about bass: I don't suppose anyone has sung bass before, have they?'

To my amazement, I now saw that Per Johann was in the crowd in front of me. I did not remember that I had ever heard him speak before, but he even stood up and said enthusiastically, 'I love singing bass. There are a few of us who try to do that sometimes on our own,' he said, in a deep, booming voice that astonished me. 'I play the guitar and some of us just get together for our own amusement.'

'Why, Per Johann,' I said. 'I've been here for over four weeks, and I don't think I've ever heard you speak before.'

Everyone laughed, including Per Johann. But he had the grace to go a deep red as he said, 'I only speak in lessons I enjoy. I WOULD speak in yours because they're fun - except that you insist on making us do it in English!' Everyone laughed again. Obviously, they all had the measure of him. I came to see in time just how much all his fellow students respected him too.

After a few minutes, everyone had virtually re-arranged themselves into one of the four groups. I had to go on thinking on my feet.

'So, let's see. First of all, I suggest we just spend time learning to sing together and start to become a real choir by listening to each other, learning how to blend. Would you be happy to start by learning some Negro Spirituals and some American songs like 'Home on the Range,' 'We Shall Overcome' and so forth?'

There was enthusiastic response to that. 'Oh! Yes! Yes!' came from all directions with nodding heads and smiling faces of approval. 'Great! Well then, we'll start with some of those songs next time. But now, while you're all here, and to help us all to get a feel of singing together, I suggest we won't warm up as we'll usually do. But we'll just sing some rounds. Let's see. What shall we have to start with?'

'London's Burning!' Per Johann shouted from the back. One or two looked embarrassed at the obvious implication of his suggestion, since the person running the choir was English, but mostly everyone burst out laughing: as did I. I knew they would all be familiar with it because it was in the Norwegian Song Book, the only textbook I felt able to use in my music classes.

'Is that your wishful thinking Per Johann?' I asked. Everyone fell about laughing again.

Once the laughter had died down and there was order again, I said, 'What a good idea!' and hummed a note on which to start. 'Let's sing it through together in unison to start with to see what kind of sound we make. Sit up straight all of you, and please uncross your legs. You can't sing properly if you're all scrunched up. You can't open your lungs to get the breath out which is what carries the sound. Here we go then ....'

A loud and enthusiastic rendition of this round filled the Assembly Hall space. The acoustics helped to magnify the choir's efforts so that it sounded quite wonderful. It was not at all the harsh and throaty sound I feared it would be.

So, let's sing it as a round now. I suggest we divide into the four parts we've already worked out – sopranos, altos, tenors and basses. Is that OK with everyone? Just keep going until I stop you. That MIGHT mean you have to stop BEFORE your particular part gets to the end of the whole round. Your part might have to stop in the middle. But there might be a great harmonic chord on which we all finish. OK?'

I let them sing it through several times before bringing them to a halt. It was in tune, albeit a bit raspier than when they had all sung in unison, but I knew I could deal with that in time since it was obvious there were some nerves about. I knew they were all putting everything they had into the effort of singing lustily.

'Very good! Well done! And now, we'll do it again. But this time, each part will come to its own end of the round as a whole. That means that the tenors and basses especially might feel quite exposed once the other parts start to leave them, because they will be left singing on their own. But please carry on undeterred to the end.'

They did. It sounded reasonable, although the basses, fewer in number than any other part, were nervously thin when they were the only group left. But they did not give up, which was the main thing. And they were absolutely in tune in the right key.

'Well done everyone! That's been an excellent start.'

We carried on singing rounds I knew they could easily sing. Some had Norwegian words which they all knew, but the majority were in English. No one seemed to mind that. There were the odd corrections about pronunciation I needed to tell them about, but they did not seem to mind that either. Eventually,

I looked at my watch and to my amazement, discovered just how long we had been singing.

'Goodness!' I said. 'Look at the time! We've been here for more than two hours. Do you think in future you could all cope with a normal practise session of two hours which will include a ten-minute break in the middle?'

'Yes', they all chorused.

'That's not too long?'

'NO!' they all seemed to shout back.

'Very well then, I'll see you all here at the same time next week. Please make sure you each put your own chair back to where it came from and leave the hall tidy and see that you've written down your name so that I can clearly read it. Otherwise, thank you, and good night everyone.'

'Good night' came the reply: some people were bold enough actually to say that in English too.

As I was putting my own chair away, generally collecting myself in my exhausted but exhilarated state, I heard a voice behind me. It was the colleague who led the tenors. He held out his hand to shake mine and bowed, using the correct Norwegian protocol of the time as he did so.

'Bjørn Hansen,' he said. 'Pleased to meet you! I teach Maths in the middle school. I don't think we've spoken before. I'm thrilled to be part of this. Thank you so much for this evening. It's been so enjoyable. And I'm sorry I've never exchanged words with you before, but my English is terrible. However, when I feel a bit more confident about it, I'd like to try to do so. Meanwhile, if I can help with the choir in any way, please let me know.'

'Well, thank you! It's good to meet you too. And if you don't mind my saying so, you have a truly, lovely voice. Have you had lessons?'

'Some: a few years ago, when I was a student in Oslo: I really miss having someone to sing with. So, this is going to be such fun. Thank you again.'

'Well – thank YOU too', I said. 'I also enjoyed tonight tremendously. I think all those who came did so too. I hope so anyway.'

'Oh! They certainly did. You can be sure of that! Well good night.'

He bowed courteously and left.

Chapter 8

New Accommodation

September turned into October. The days were getting shorter and it felt more pressing than ever to find suitable and comfortable accommodation. As asked, I had waited patiently for six weeks to see if one of the staff flats promised by Einar Anderson had become available. But before I was able to raise the subject with him again, Øystein Hansen told me the scheme had not materialised. However, he said that there was other good news. He knew my current digs were completely unsuitable and were only ever meant to be temporary. He was embarrassed that I had had to cope, even briefly, with living in a poky, dingy and ill-equipped couple of rooms that apart from anything else, with winter approaching, were far too cold for me or anyone else, to live in, and only provided the minimum of light. He knew I needed somewhere else comfortable and suitable, and soon.

'I'm so glad you understand how much I've been dreading the thought of staying where I am through the winter,' I said. 'I've been keeping all my fingers crossed that I would be able to move somewhere else pretty soon. It's already nearly dark when I leave school.'

School finished at 2pm in those days, having started at 8am. I rarely went home before 4pm, marking books and preparing work at school before going back to my digs. And then I would inevitably go back to the staff room in the evening where it was at least light and warm.

'I have been asking myself what I would do when it's both cold and dark for the whole 24hours? I wouldn't be able to read – or even see to do much else for that matter.'

Øystein understood what I meant. 'Oh! Quite so! I sympathise. It must be really difficult - having nowhere to unwind properly at the end of the day.'

I could see he meant what he said. So, I thought I should be specific and truthful. After all, supposing another English teacher were to follow me. If I had established the precedent that the quality of living space was NOT a priority, when it was absolutely THE most important issue for a temporary visitor to this remote place where the main pastime outside work and family life was reading, I would have done poor service to paving the way for any future colleague.

So, I continued. 'The electric light in my room is hopelessly inadequate: unless I sit directly under it, I can see virtually nothing at all. And, in any event, it simply isn't warm enough where I am – even now. I've asked my landlady about it, but apparently, it isn't possible to access any more electric stream to make it warmer. I mean, there's no more power either for a standing heater or for a stronger light bulb. And I need to tell you, I'm already frozen first thing in the mornings.' I grinned. 'It's so bad, it reminds me of being back at my boarding school. Even 10 years after the war there was not enough coal to fuel its huge heating system. We woke most winter mornings to find our flannels ice-frozen across our washing baskets. You probably know what an austere reputation around the world English boarding schools have, I expect, don't you?'

'I do indeed,' Øystein said. Indeed, we had had several conversations on this specific topic. At least one every time we shared one of his fish suppers. 'You know I genuinely believed you would only have to be living where you are for just a few weeks. That's why I agreed where you are would do for just a short time.'

As I write now, I have the benefit of having found an article in the school leavers' newspaper from that school year. I had completely forgotten I had it in my possession, so was thrilled to find it, and amazed to see that Alf, no less, had responded to a reporter's questionings at the end of the school year as *russ* chairman - a later chapter explains what a *russ* is and does - a sort of 'Head Boy'. He explained the big problem in attracting good teachers to Vadsø was the lack of suitable accommodation. He also said that something MUST be done about it in order to recruit new teachers in the future.

Back then I found it a difficult topic to speak about, even with Øystein. I was trying to carry on the conversation in as light-hearted a way as possible because I did not want to give the impression that I was ungrateful for his efforts on my behalf, or that I was being snobby about what I was asking for. I did not want to imply that I was used to a better standard of life or suggest that life in Vadsø was simply not good enough. But in truth, the thought of staying where I was for a whole year had become a deeply depressing thought. The only reason I had managed to stay where I was for as long as I had, was because I was relying on the promise there would soon be somewhere else more suitable.

'I'll see what I can do right away,' he said. 'I've already begun to ask around. But I'll pursue things more vigorously now. I'm sure something will come up, and soon. Try not to worry about it!'

My instincts had been to try to find somewhere else myself. I had done that successfully the year before in the South. Then, I had asked around almost at once about what accommodation might be available, closer to at least one of the five communities where I had to teach than my original digs that had been found for me. I had found a small bedsit in one of the three towns where I did most of my work. I had wanted to ask around in Vadsø too, but the circumstances there were different. It was a more enclosed, smaller and singular community. So, I intuited it would be better to accept what I had been told in good faith and wait the six weeks as asked. In addition, I had not wanted my colleagues to think that I was dissatisfied with what had been done to find me somewhere to live, realising that it had not been easy, even for them to find suitable accommodation. Most of them were in awe of someone from England as a colleague anyway, and I had not wanted to appear to be fussy and dissatisfied. So, I had said nothing about my lodgings except in reply to any question as to WHERE exactly in the town I was living. I only mentioned the rough location: that was all. And then, I had always added how convenient it was since it was so close to the school and then managed to change the subject, since that was the only fact it had going for it. I had waited patiently for a solution, but now, it felt beyond hard to wait any longer.

So, I was thrilled when Øystein Hansen came back to me just a few days later.

'I've been asking around all the professional people I know,' he said. 'They were always a much more likely group to have space for a temporary visitor such as yourself because they're the people who mostly live in the recently built houses provided for them by their sponsors or employers. Their houses are larger than the older ones that escaped being burnt down at the end of the war - such as the house where you are living now. The newer ones have spare rooms, central heating and running hot water.' He paused. 'And actually, since you've also gained yourself quite a reputation, and everyone knows who you are now,' he twinkled, 'it shouldn't be too long before something you like will be offered to you.'

He smiled infectiously as he spoke. I had come to like him a lot. I always enjoyed our conversations because he was so well informed and amusing. There were interesting titbits of national or international news he was always wanting to tell, especially when he came back from one of his frequent work trips to Oslo.

I wondered what he meant by 'not too long', but I did not ask. The faintest prospect of real choice lifted my heart. From listening to my colleagues' conversations about where THEY lived and how awkward it was to ask for anything additional or different in the way of facilities, I had feared it would take quite a while to find somewhere else more suitable. I understood that other teachers had also found places that were fairly basic and always tiny but were nevertheless much more comfortable than my own. There was no denying that finding resources and many suitable practicalities for comfortable living were limited.

'Anyway,' Øystein went on, interrupting my thoughts, 'I've already discovered that there are a couple of rooms available in a house belonging to an engineer who works for the Highways Authority up here – planning and supervising road building and so on. He and his family live in a local authority-built modern house, so it even has central heating. You wouldn't have your own, private access, but you could be entirely private once inside. And, also in its favour, it has a bathroom, and a separate toilet, which could be entirely yours. Would you be interested in going to see the place?'

I could hardly contain myself. My ears had pricked up even at the thought of a possible bathroom and an inside loo. None of the older houses in Vadsø had bathrooms. They were the few houses, including mine, that had only been partially burned down in the mid 40s by the Germans and were perhaps well over 60 years old anyway: definitely pre-World War Two. They had since been hastily knocked together again, and half-repaired with nails and planks so that at least they provided proper shelter. But that was all. They had not been treated to any plumbing alterations or heating developments.

I had been surprised the previous year to have found the same limitations in available running water and lack of bathrooms in the South. There, in my first lodgings, I had also had to descend the stairs to the loo and use a basic, outside washbasin because there had been no bathroom. And although my accommodation there was at least on my daily bus route, it was nowhere near any of the places I taught. Fortunately, one of the towns had a public-baths building, and so, to start off with, I had gone there for a hot bath once a week until I moved into more congenial accommodation that I had managed to find in a town where I had several classes. It also had its own shower. In Vadsø there were showers at school but no similar public facilities for those who had no bath or shower at home.

However, there was at least a public sauna, which served the town and a few scattered settlements of fishing folk along the coast in both directions – East and West. As yet, most people in England had never even heard of saunas, and even if they had, might not know how to use them properly. Here in the remote and cold part of the world that is the Arctic Circle, a whole culture of its own surrounded the sauna process. I had heard all about it from a colleague who had taught in Finland the previous year on the same British Council scheme. He had explained how the whole experience worked, and just how good it was for you – healthy and invigorating. Sitting in great heat was the first part of the process. I was less keen on the second half, however. The prospect of rolling in the snow in one's birthday suit straight afterwards did not fill me with great enthusiasm. Actually, I thought it sounded extremely unpleasant – even dangerous. But fortunately, there was not yet enough snow in Vadsø to roll in. I also realised that many of my colleagues, who came from the South, disliked the idea of snow rolling as much as I did.

I had accompanied a couple of female colleagues to the sauna twice already and found the process of dry heat opening my pores helped me to feel cleaner and more energised. I was already acclimatised to Norwegians being entirely at ease with public nudity, and I was much less frightened by the prospect myself, although I felt uncomfortable at the thought of going along with it entirely. By the end of my first year in the South I was completely at ease with nudity amongst my friends. In Vadsø, I did not have a similar circle of intimates. Those I mixed with were either colleagues or students with whom I would definitely not have had a public sauna.

Øystein took me to see my potential new home. He introduced me to Jon and Bente Flyst, a good humoured, jolly couple from Trondheim. Both had been brought up on working farms, and were lovers of the outdoors, with an outgoing, robust attitude to life. Jon was first and foremost a family man, reserved, professionally conservative as an engineer, but full of fun at home. Calm and reliable, he enjoyed teasing his family. His wife, Bente, who was the most likely butt of his tender baiting, enjoyed being so, and laughed a good deal of the time. She was jovial and sociable, but more reserved than Jon with people she did not know. When we met, she was terrified she might have to speak English and visibly relieved when she found she did not need to. I later learned that she lacked confidence about anything she had been supposed to learn at school, since 'book-learning' was not her strongest suit. She and Jon had two children: Anna, who was 12, and in the top year of primary, or 'first', school located at the other end of the building from the classrooms where I mostly taught. I did not recognise her, although she seemed to know who I was. Anders was just two.

All four Flysts were gathered by their front door - an excited, curious group - to greet Øystein and myself. Anders, clutching his mother's skirt, with eyes nearly popping out of his head, was bursting with excitement. Anna held on tight to her father's hand, blushing and grinning broadly from ear to ear the whole time. She seemed completely fascinated by this new drama in her life - the prospect of having an English-speaking lady living under the same roof as herself. Grinning the whole time, she also glowed bright pink throughout the entire encounter.

I decided to break the ice, extending my hand, speaking my name as I did so which was the general custom in Scandinavia.

'This is so good of you - to even think about having a perfect stranger share your space. It's good to meet you all too: I haven't yet had the chance to meet a proper family!' I spoke as I did the rounds of hand shaking. Even Anders shook my hand although he hid his face behind a fold in his mother's skirt as he did so: his hand in one direction: his concealed face in another.

Jon did all the talking. 'You may not find what we have to offer is entirely satisfactory,' he said in a kindly, but business-like voice. 'There are two rooms upstairs we thought you might at least want to see. They may not be what you're looking for, but if you were to choose to move in, you can of course come and go as you please. We won't bother you at all. You can see our house is warm and light - really cosy, even when it's well below freezing outside. We've never been cold inside, have we, Bente?' She shook her head. 'I have to ask my wife,' Jon said in his jokey, but respectful way. 'Of the four of us, she feels the cold the most, you see.'

The six of us began to go upstairs, Jon in the lead. Once we were all gathered on the landing, he led us to the right, and opened a door that revealed a large, empty, light room. Because it was at the corner end of the house it had windows facing the fjord on one side, and out of the town and across the *vidda* on the other. The window across the fjord had a clear view of the harbour in the foreground, as well as Vadsø's island, and the Arctic fjord in the distance.

'It isn't ideal,' I heard Jon continue, as I was lost in rejoicing over the immediate difference in my quality of life the room would offer me. 'But, as I said, it's warm and we have a spare bed somewhere. We could find that for you. Otherwise, there are cupboards with hanging space and drawers – as you see.' He opened everything as he spoke, revealing oodles of space. 'Next door, there is a small room that could be your kitchen. There's an old hot plate of ours there at the moment, which works fine as a basic stove. We used to use it in our summer cabin. You see there is loo in between these two rooms which could be yours alone.' He opened the other two doors to show me the facilities he mentioned as he spoke.

Bente stepped forward. 'Obviously, I'll need to make you some curtains', she said. 'There aren't any up at the moment because we never thought we'd need to use this room. There's no separate bathroom I'm afraid. But you could use ours and have a bath whenever you want.'

I could hardly contain myself. The rooms provided all I could possibly need: warmth, space, hot water, the prospect of baths, wonderful views …. my spirits began to soar. 'When were you thinking I could move in?' I asked.

Jon and Bente looked at each other. They were clearly surprised that I was asking this question now, without going away to think about it.

'Well, I don't know exactly. I think we could be organised in about two weeks possibly. What d'you think, dear?' Jon looked questioningly at his wife to see if she agreed that was a realistic time schedule.

But Bente was looking at me and noticed the glancing flash of disappointment cloud across my face. 'Were you thinking of moving in before then? You weren't, were you?' she asked.

'Well! Ideally, I was, yes. But, of course, I don't want to put you to any kind of trouble or inconvenience.'

'Oh! No! Not at all!' Bente had taken over now. She wanted to be helpful. 'The thing is, we've only recently even thought about letting out our space. Obviously, we talked about it before we mentioned it to Øystein, once we heard he was asking around. But you've come to look at what we're offering before we've had much chance to think in detail about what might need doing in preparation. It won't take long to organise the bed. But I thought I'd have to send away for material to make curtains. There is absolutely no choice in the couple of shops up here – I guess you've already seen that? So, we thought it would be a good two weeks before we'd be ready for anyone to move in. You'll need some other bits of furniture too: a chair and table at the very least.' She paused. But seeing that the obvious look of disappointment on her prospective tenant's face was real, she turned to Jon and said, 'We could always continue to furnish it once you're here, of course, couldn't we?'

'That would be so good. I really only need a bed from the very start. Or come to that I could sleep on the floor!' I hoped I did not sound too desperate.

'Goodness me!' Bente said. 'We couldn't let you do that. Øystein told us that where you are now is very basic and was only ever meant to be temporary, so we understand how anxious you are to move. If you really mean what you say, I think we could have the place ready for you to move in and make a start - perhaps in a couple of days? I absolutely must give your rooms a good clean though, and make sure everything works properly - I mean the electric plugs and the window fastenings and so on. Let's see!' She looked at her husband. 'What d'you think, dear? We could manage that, couldn't we?'

'OK. If YOU think that's possible. Two days it is.' He turned towards me. 'You surely could move in at the weekend if that's what you'd like to do – I mean if you really think you'd like to live here?'

'Absolutely', I said. 'I can move in at the weekend if that's OK with you both. That'll also give me time to get a few basics sorted out – enough to be able to face the new week at any rate.'

I could hardly contain myself. Life would now improve 100 per cent: I could feel a lightness of heart almost at once. Øystein said he would help me move my stuff. He was one of the few people who owned a car in Vadsø because he liked to go along the coast to fish as late, and then as early in the year as possible, whenever he was able to make it along a road in fact. He always drove himself south in the summer, as soon as the roads were open for the few weeks when they would be devoid of snow, to see his parents. He thought the *Hurtigruten* was too slow – obviously, and it was too complicated to fly.

Both he and the Rektor were unusual in that they owned cars. But of course, they came from the South and would go back there eventually. Only two or three per cent of the population of Finnmark owned a car at that time, anyway. The roads were virtually non-existent at the best of times, and simply not navigable even with the compulsory winter chains attached to them - once the snow started to fall. The need of a car was limited.

Years ago, whenever anyone wanted to leave Vadsø and had no car the only way to get around was via the *Hurtigruten*. As long as time allowed, passengers could use it to cross the fjord to the nearest airport 30 miles away. There were no trains in Finnmark: none run further North in Norway than Bodø, over 800 miles further south, and only just inside the Arctic Circle even today. There were few buses when I lived there, since all the so-called 'roads' were unusable for at least eight months of the year. Even Rektor Anderson would be covering up his car and putting it out of use until next spring any day now. Soon, goods would have to be carried on sledges up from the harbour from the daily boat. The roads themselves would be so snow -covered that they would become impassable unless a driver - the single taxi driver from now on - literally followed immediately behind a snowplough to get anyone to an airport. And even this process was not one hundred per cent guaranteed if the weather was particularly bad. Travellers risked being caught in a snowstorm if, they simply HAD to get to an airport and the snow was really heavy.

However, for me, experiencing the problems and delays of difficult and impossible travel was yet to come. I was just rejoicing that I had found a new place to live. All that needed to be transacted had been done, and Øystein said he would put his car to necessary and good use by moving all my possessions from storage at school into my new home. While he was driving me back to my now temporary, miserable garret, he also volunteered to explain to my current landlords that I would be leaving - and at short notice.

'Don't worry,' he said to me. 'They won't mind in the least. They didn't expect you to be with them even for this length of time, to be honest. And they won't charge you extra for not giving notice either. They know they were lucky to have benefitted from your rent while you've been staying there, even for just the few weeks you have. They know that usually there would be no call to rent out their rooms. Well! That's how they see it, anyway. They realise that what they had on offer for you was not at all suitable!'

'Oh! Thank you so much. I must say I would have found that particular conversation quite difficult.' I felt greatly relieved.

I had sent the bulk of my luggage from the South to the North on the *Hurtigruten* just before I went home to England for a few weeks. Rektor Anderson had stored it safely for me. Now it could at last be retrieved and I relished the thought of being able to set myself up properly, with my own kitchen gear. At least I would now be able to invite people in for a cup of tea of an evening. After all, there was not much else for people to do after working hours. So, visiting each other for coffee and cake by candlelight would be the order of the day for social gatherings all through the long, dark days from November onwards.

Now I felt it was time to try to make and build relationships properly. If my colleagues were too scared to invite me, I would simply invite them. I could even serve tea instead of coffee because I had brought plenty of tea from England to do just that. I could initiate an English tea ritual and show how most people back home made a pot of tea. I could also invite my students. I could teach them English parlour games, like charades. I knew many of them would find that strange but also suspected they would probably love it once they got over their genuine reticence. These were so many promising opportunities. The prospect at last of such greater social inclusion lifted my spirits. I began to relax into the deep and satisfactory feeling that soon I would have my own, proper home – where I could actually be both warm and comfortable – and perhaps begin to feel I belonged.

Chapter 9

Undercurrents

Dynamics in the classroom improved substantially after the early days. Relationships gradually changed, becoming more warm and friendly. In general, everyone's confidence in speaking English was improving and interest in asking questions had increased. I had agreed with my students that if they ever wanted to raise anything inspired by anything we were working with, they could do so. In other words, we could take time out to learn new information or vocabulary that arose out of discussions, as long as we did not get too far behind what was nationally prescribed.

We were constantly learning new words and I always encouraged as many conversations in English as possible. At first many pupils had been reluctant to agree. They were cautious about accepting the idea in case it might lower their grades. But gradually they gained enough confidence, daring to chance their arm now and then. They realised the advantage they would gain even, in the wider world, if they could at least SPEAK English with confidence.

I had come to understand that many of my Vadsø students believed their Southern counterparts had many advantages over them in learning English. Wider and cheaper travel, as well as greater opportunities to engage with people whose first language was English was more available to them. They were also more likely to meet tourists and meet and work alongside people whose first language was English, as well as fellow Norwegians who worked in business and actually needed to negotiate and transact with people who WERE English. Not many holiday-makers ventured as far north as Vadsø. Tourists cruising on the *Hurtigruten* would rarely, if ever, get off the boat and explore Vadsø, or most other Finnmark towns, with the possible exception of Hammerfest. For a start there was rarely time before the *Hurtigruten* had to set sail again. At Vadsø the ship had to dock, unload, reload, then leave as quickly as possible. It rarely docked for more than half an hour. It always seemed behind schedule, time lost at some previous destination for one reason or another.

Some topics were sensitive of course. The question of the German Occupation was one. It had been a particularly horrendous experience in Finnmark. Since it was well before any of my students were born, no one remembered it. But even though they knew some dreadful truths that their parents and grandparents had told them, an overriding sense of commitment to a continually improving future for everyone prevailed. The emphasis always seemed to be on looking forward and outward, not back. It was rare indeed for anyone to speak about the war, or what had happened in Vadsø during those years.

However, I was to discover just how close to the surface underlying feelings about the war and its aftermath really were, at the same time as I was to discover why one of my most emotional and obviously angry students, Hannah, had appeared from the start to be sitting on top of a volcano. She always seemed to me to be about to explode with rage about something I had said, however careful I tried to **not** cause another disruption arising from misunderstanding or miscommunication. I was anxious not to repeat an outburst like that of Mette's. I had come to accept that Hannah was simply as she was – explosively tense for some reason.

Hannah always sat at the front, directly opposite the staff desk. I often sat on it when not writing on the board or walking round the classroom. I could see everyone at the same time as rest my legs. Hannah always had her head down, so I was not even sure I knew what she looked like. I wondered whether I would even recognise her if I were to meet her in the street. She rarely spoke, although answered efficiently and well if addressed directly. At times, I wondered if she was just excruciatingly shy. Or even if she was one of those obviously bright students, who set themselves high standards and were disproportionately disappointed, or angry, with themselves if they felt they could not live up to their expectations. I knew Hannah had a German father: a young officer stationed in Vadsø during the war. A colleague had told me about him in the course of some conversation we were having about how learning German in Norway had begun to grow again. It had been discouraged for a while but now, wanting trade deals and better relations with other countries meant that learning German was now acceptable and becoming important. I gathered that Hannah's Dad was widely respected for the fine person he was. He had done much in the late 1940s and early 1950s to help people in Vadsø get back on their feet.

One morning, the word 'occupation' in terms of someone's job or career came up from the text we were discussing. Some students had not met it in that context before. Someone asked if it had the same meaning and spelling as what they knew described the war years. This led to general comment about words which had two or more meanings, and then to a few, almost matter of fact, statements about the time when the country was occupied. This moved on further to recognising that it was also a noun whose verb had a variety of meanings, not least in hotel bathrooms and comfort stations. I was pleased to let the conversation run as usual, as long as it was in good English. I always encouraged this way of working because it was clearly developing knowledge and confidence, as well as acquiring vocabulary. I just corrected the odd mispronunciation as everyone talked.

Momentarily, I had turned to write something on the board when out of nowhere there was a deafening squeal of fury, followed by outrage in a stream of Norwegian expletives and accusations, the like of which I had rarely heard. I turned around in shock and saw Hannah, red-faced, staring wide-eyed and almost spitting at me, while the rest of the class sat in shocked silence.

'Hannah! What on earth's the matter?' I tried to sound calm as I asked in careful Norwegian. I realised now was not a good time to speak English.

'You're always going on about the war. You're always saying how terrible the Germans were. Your attitudes are so racist. You ought not to be allowed to say the things you do. It's not true that all Germans were bad people. Some were decent and kind, like my Dad. He's a wonderful person, and he suffered terribly after the war, just so that he could be with my Mum. He hated what was going on and didn't agree with any of it. You don't know what you're talking about. You shouldn't be allowed to say what you do. You should be reported, sacked – and sent home.'

Hannah then dissolved into uncontrollable, heaving sobs. Everyone looked visibly uncomfortable. The class remained silent. The only sound was Hannah's racking sobs. I stood shocked and amazed. But realising it to be a critical moment, I knew I would have to be supremely careful about what I said and how I said it.

'Hannah!' I spoke as quietly and gently as I could, continuing in Norwegian. 'I'm really sorry if I've said anything to upset you. Of course, your Dad must be a lovely man. He couldn't possibly be your Dad otherwise, could he? I don't know what I've said that has hurt you so much. I know I say things sometimes because I want to prompt or provoke you all, to get you talking, to contradict me perhaps, simply to speak. I admit I sometimes do that so that you might feel FORCED to try to speak English. But I'm truly unaware of anything unkind or accusatory that I've ever said about Germans here during the war, especially today – and I'm really sorry for whatever it is you think I HAVE said.'

Total silence prevailed for what seemed ages, apart from Hannah's gulps and sobs. I wondered how long that had been brewing as I reached into my bag to find a clean handkerchief. I offered it to Hannah, and she accepted it gratefully.

Gradually, her sobs began to subside. Meanwhile, no one moved although many anxious glances were thrown at me. The atmosphere felt thick with concern. I felt the full weight of responsibility to try to resolve the situation in some way. But I had no idea what to say next. I suspected all those ghastly pent-up feelings inside Hannah had been swirling around for weeks, maybe even years, just waiting to explode.

A hand went up, and I felt momentarily relieved. It was Grethe's, the choir's star soprano.

'May I say something, Miss Russell?'

'Of course.'

'May I come to the front?'

'You may indeed.'

Grethe got up, and with great dignity walked from the back to the front of the class. Afterwards, considering she was just 15, I reflected on how impressive her whole demeanour had been. She knew somehow it would be better to speak to the entire class, not just Hannah. I was astonished by her maturity and poise and listened carefully to what she had to say. Everyone could have heard a pin drop as she gathered herself.

'Hannah! I know we all tease you – if that's the right word. Perhaps we shouldn't. It's just that some of our own fathers and mothers had a really difficult time in the war years because they were either away somewhere fighting against the Germans, or because they had family connections in the Resistance or were especially vulnerable for some other reason. I guess we might all be tempted to blame your Dad sometimes for the ways some Germans behaved. And I'm sorry if we do. We all know and like your Dad. But that only makes it more difficult for us to come to terms with what actually happened back then, because not all German officers were good people like him. And anyway,' she added, 'few of us can speak coherent German.'

At least that was what I think Grethe said, bearing in mind she was speaking fast in Norwegian and I was understandably traumatised.

However, her last statement broke the tension slightly as everyone tittered or tried to giggle a bit. A mixture of 'yes', 'we agree', 'that's right' and so forth filled the silence. There was definitely a feeling that everyone wanted to resolve this crisis.

'We honestly will make an effort to do better. I will, anyway, and I'll try to take account of what you must feel sometimes. I know I can be clumsy and insensitive. I'm sorry.'

Gradually, Hannah's sobs began to subside. The girl sitting next to her tried tentatively to put her hand on her shoulder. With no reduction to her dignity, Grethe made her way back to her seat.

'Thank you Grethe! That was thoughtful, kind and very mature. Well said!' I looked round the classroom. 'I'm sure we all agree with that, and we'll all do our best to take greater care with what we say and how we behave. Does that help, even just a little, Hannah?'

Unable to speak, Hannah merely nodded. She blew her nose several times. She kept her head down even though the crisis was over, and the incident was drawing to a natural end. But such events are always difficult to emerge from. An awkward, but lighter silence continued to prevail.

'I don't think we can really get back to formal work now.' I reverted to Norwegian. 'But one thing we need absolutely to bear in mind and agree about is that we must NOT spread any gossipy information about what has just happened. Hannah must have our entire protection. We need to look after her. We really shouldn't speak of this outside this classroom. Do we all agree?'

A chorus of agreement echoed round the room, and then, mercifully, the bell rang. At first no one moved.

'Thank you everyone. How very grown up you all are! I am hugely impressed by how you've all behaved today. But now you need to get out and enjoy some fresh air – in more ways than one!'

There was a gentle titter again as everyone left in a quiet and orderly manner. Hannah was the last to leave. She waited, perhaps to protect her own dignity, I wondered, or maybe to take time to recover herself just a bit more. But eventually, she too made a move – just to stand up.

'Will you be all right Hannah?' I asked. 'In fact, would you actually like to go home now? I could walk there with you if you like. I am not teaching for another hour or so.'

'No! I'll be all right. I'd prefer to stay here rather than go home. But I don't want to go outside. Could I possibly stay here for the ten-minute break and then just go to my next class? I can't face anyone.'

'Of course, I'll wait here with you. I need to clean the board and collect all my belongings and sort out my books. I'll just get on with that - if that's all right with you. Or you could help me if you want – or just sit. Whatever suits you best.'

Later, reflecting on the whole emotionally charged incident and Grethe's great maturity, it occurred to me that she had spoken mainly in English. Had I got that right? She MUST have done I thought, because I distinctly remembered purposefully reverting to Norwegian myself right at the end of the lesson when asking for protective confidentiality for Hannah. How utterly extraordinary that I could not be clear who said what in what language!

***

It was two days later, that I was next due to teach the same class. In the meantime, I had made a bold decision.

'Good morning, everyone! I hope all's well and that you're all looking forward to the lesson this morning.' I did not wait for a response but continued without a pause. 'First of all, I've some news I want to share with you. I moved last week into new accommodation, and I want to invite everyone to come and have tea with me one evening next week.

No one said anything. Undeterred, I continued. 'I expect you'd all like to mention it at home and ask your parents if that would be all right. If you'd like to tell them my plans - I'm sure they'd be glad to know. I thought I'd show you all how to make tea like we do in England, and then how we actually serve it. I thought we could also play parlour games as they're called in England, AND, just this once I promise not to insist that you all speak English.'

I could sense the genuine relief at hearing that.

'So, will you all ask at home so I can get a rough idea of what sort of numbers I need to cater for when we meet? Now, without spending any more time on this, let's get on with the lesson. Karl! Can you remind us all what page we had got to, please?'

I believe at that moment I could sense an atmosphere of relief. Some of Hannah's tensions seemed to have been released and she behaved differently from then on. I prayed hard that something had been resolved inside her to heal her thoughts and feelings. I hoped that in some way the incident had been cathartic for her. The atmosphere certainly never felt as tense again. I could not help wondering if ANY of those pent-up feelings in my first few lessons were due to my being English. Who knows what actually drove such deep, conflicting feelings to explode? Certainly, however, it was better they were out in the open than festering inside.

I have known ever since meeting my two particular southern friends just what a terrible time both their families had in the war, even though they have only recently spoke of it in any detail. It's true that the Germans tended to treat southern Norwegians with more civility that their Northern counterparts, seeing some Arian affinity no doubt in the more blue-eyed and blonder appearance of those living in the South than in the North of Norway. But even so, my friend's father was a policeman. So, like every other serving police officer, he was rounded up at the beginning of the Occupation and shipped to a camp in the middle of Europe, leaving his wife to cope alone with three small children. He escaped eventually and rowed himself and a couple of colleagues to safety. I do not remember how. I understand from my friend that he refused, ever, to say anything about his time in the prison camp, except commenting on one occasion that the smell would always be with him: of what, he did not say.

My friend's husband is an only child. His family lived on the fjord – as he still does -with a garden that sweeps right down to the water's edge. His father had a responsible job in the local cement factory, which gave employment to most of those who lived in his small town – both then and now. As a local resistance leader, he was once arrested and imprisoned for a few weeks because the Germans thought a chemical formula he had in his pocket, was a secret code. He wore a poison pill in his lapel in case he should ever need it. Amongst many other things, he rowed escaping English and Allied airmen, who had parachuted out of burning planes and landed somewhere in Norway, across the fjord at night to make for home through neutral Sweden. As recently as just a couple of years ago, my friend also told me how terrified he had been as a little boy when any German happened to knock on the front door, for whatever reason, in case, by some ghastly stroke of ill luck, escaping allies, temporarily sheltered in the cellar of his family home, might be discovered, and his father subsequently shot. I guess it's not surprising it takes a life-time to give voice to the traumatising experiences of one's youth. Some of the traumas from those days may remain unspoken for ever.

Chapter 10

Tea Parties

I was incredibly impressed how Grethe had persuaded the whole class to respond to Hannah's outburst. It was mature and exactly appropriate. It moved me greatly at the time, and even more so the more I thought about it. I increasingly saw the courage, strength and principles these young people were made of. I had learnt a great deal in the previous year about how self-aware Norwegians were – compared to any English person I had ever met – and how important they thought it was to be so too. Here, the North seemed to give them even more personal strength and poise. Maybe, I thought, such qualities underpin the distinctive pride they take in their national freedoms. Knowing who they are enables them to believe in themselves and play to their personal strengths. In the end, this incident increased my respect for them: not least because the way they dealt with it showed great maturity. I began to believe that they would eventually risk speaking English with that same confidence that enabled them to be sure about knowing who they were.

A different atmosphere prevailed after the event, and not just around the corridors at school. More noticeably, it infused the staff room. Perhaps something had changed in me? Around town I was also getting used to being smiled at in the street by people I did not know. It seemed as if everywhere the smiles were more fulsome, spontaneous and relaxed – even though no one, not even colleagues, spoke to me in English. It occurred to me that when an opportunity presented itself, I might ask my classes why this was. After all, attitudes to speaking English had been different in the South. In southern schools I was always spoken to in English by other staff. Here in Vadsø I thought it best to keep trying to build up my students' confidence, hoping they might eventually feel more comfortable speaking English.

It was about the time I issued my English 'at home' invitation that I got a letter from my friend in southern Norway. I had written asking for suggestions about how I could communicate better with both colleagues and pupils. The post to and fro was slow in this remote area. I had sent my letter a few days before the first choir rehearsal - another vehicle I hoped might be useful in bringing down relational barriers further. My friend wrote back with helpful information I probably would never have worked out for myself.

'... I must tell you,' she wrote, 'that you need to know just how much everyone living in Finnmark was even more traumatised by the Nazi Occupation than we were in the South. The Nazis saw North Norwegians in general as inferior peasants compared to what they believed was the more naturally Arian stock in the South – blue eyes, blond hair: all that sort of thing – the kind of nonsense they set so much store by. The Nazis were much more civilised in the way they treated Southerners. For instance, where we were living in the South, if the blackout showed some light through not quite closed curtains, they would usually knock on the door to tell us about it, and politely suggest that we could put it right. But in the North, their attitude was quite different. They pretty well sent everyone to labour camps since they saw Finnmark people as inferior, peasant material, especially the Sami people, or 'Lapps' as they were called then. They saw them as a 'nothing' people – uncivilised, with no permanent homes or buildings of note, no culture, no civilisation to speak of, only fit to work as slave labour in the nickel mines. The Sami in particular had a truly dreadful time. No wonder they insisted that everyone stopped calling them 'Lapps'! After all a 'lapp' in Norwegian is the word for a scrap of paper or material. Who wants to be called a useless scrap?'

I remembered then that I had also read somewhere that Eduard Dietl, the German general in charge of Finnmark, had described North Norwegian and Finnish women as 'racial flotsam.'

I thought it was no wonder the Northerners had such a strong, resistant spirit.' They rightly didn't see why ANYONE should push them around or tell them what was good for them. No wonder some felt they didn't particularly want to learn English. And since Russians and Finns were their nearest neighbours, it made perfect sense to want to learn those languages. A new respect and admiration for everyone in the town began to grow in my heart as I began to see how difficult it must have been for Hannah to cope with certain truths and be at peace with them.

My friend's comments were timely and gave me encouragement and fresh impetus. I began to think about how to adapt my teaching and approach some topics sensitively, realising how my students' families might have been treated, and the effect that might have on how they thought about themselves. I hoped I was gaining a deeper understanding of how they still might feel so many years on from the war. Their whole county had been savagely wrecked by the enemy.

Rebuilding communities takes time. As I reflect while writing this now more than 50 years later, it seems strange to me how little the war was spoken about while I lived in Vadsø.

While I was trying to sort these things out in my mind, I was encouraged that about a dozen pupils accepted my first invitation to tea. I felt thrilled and guessed it might have taken courage to risk doing something seen as so different. That only spurred me on to play my part in reaching out, helping all of us to dare risk 'getting it wrong' in order to 'get it right'.

When the time came for the first brave group of students to visit me, I tried to make the evening as English as possible. First, I taught everyone how to meet and greet each other. Next, how to shake hands and ask 'how d'you do?' – unthinkable to answer except by asking the same question in return. Once they had stopped giggling, and had become experts at it, I served tea and cake. These were not sponge cakes with lashings of cream, called *bløtkakker* - more of a French type of gateaux than a basic English sponge - that Norwegians always served at birthdays or on special celebrations. I wanted my guests to experience normal, English teatime cakes: a Victoria sandwich, or Chocolate or Lemon sponge.

Bente had allowed me use of her kitchen oven to bake them. I had brought crucial ingredients, such as real cocoa powder, from home after my summer visit. I also had the gumption to think various ingredients might come in handy through the darkest evenings, when eating yummy cake might help remove self-protecting, communication barriers.

I waited on my visitors, serving cups of tea, explaining how to make it, English style. They were keen to understand why English people preferred tea to coffee and why they mostly used milk rather than lemon. They thought it a somewhat strange habit, in the same way that the English drank coffee with milk. Norwegians found it difficult to understand how anyone could drink coffee other than as black, or white using proper, single cream. Milk in a cup of coffee was unthinkable!

The first thing that no one knew about making tea, however, was the importance of warming the pot before adding the tea leaves, and then the boiling water. I explained just how crucial it was to let the teapot stand a few minutes before pouring out – for the leaves to infuse and brew properly before being served into cups. Most had never heard the word 'brew,' not even in connection with beer which they knew a lot about. Everyone seemed to know about English pubs which were widely admired and envied.

'Why do you put the milk in your cup first?' someone asked. 'Don't you want to see how strong or weak you're making it?'

'That's a really good question.' I put the teapot down to consider my answer. 'Yes, sometimes, if I think the tea is going to turn out a bit weak, I WILL pour my milk in after the tea, so that it's not made even weaker by the amount of milk I use. But mostly, I put the milk in first, and that's because I've always understood that that particular choice is really more to do with *class* than *taste*.'

I deliberately inserted the word *class*, emphasising it as I did so, at this natural opportunity to bring it up. Many veiled references to it were constantly raised in English lessons. A barrage of questions always followed. What actually was *class*? Was it significant? Could you change your *class*? Did it make much/any difference to your life chances? If so, what were they?

'What IS *class*? They all seemed to chorus at the same time. 'Is it like the Indian caste system? What does it mean? Does it matter? Why does it exist anyway?'

'Well! We can talk about class and what it might mean in due course if you want. But first, let me finish explaining about preferences in pouring the milk! The thing is undiluted tea leaves stain over time – especially china or pottery cups - from the tannin residue. So, for people who had servants, whose job it was to clean the cups thoroughly after use instead of just giving them an ordinary wash, they could add milk freely after the tea poured into their cups, because they would not have to do the tiresome job of working away at the tannin residue to get the cups clean. But for those who drank a lot of tea and had no servants and so DID have to clean the cups themselves, the milk was put in first so that the stains were less severe. The milk absorbed some of the acid tannin. Thus, it took longer to accumulate, and it helped keep the cups cleaner longer, which meant less work, d'you see? It's more for that reason than any other that people originally decided to put the milk in first. That's how it all started. But nowadays, since the whole culture of tea drinking has developed and there are different strengths and flavours in makes of tea even – between Indian and China teas for a start – I think the choice of which way round to do it is less complicated. In any event, many people – even English people - don't know about the origin of choice. And as you suggest, there may be other, different reasons for one's preference – including, as you said, the strength of the brew and whether or not you like your tea weak or strong. You may not want it too hot to change the flavour by adding too much or too little milk – and so on and so on!'

'Is all that really true?' someone asked. We've always thought you should use lemon in tea rather than milk. We also weren't sure whether you should put lemon in together with the milk – to do something to the flavour perhaps? Anyway, my Mum has never used milk with tea – and we only have tea on special occasions.'

'So, we're definitely NOT supposed to put both milk and lemon in our tea at the same time, then?' Several of them nodded in agreement, pleased to have this clarification.

'Actually, it's really strange you should ask because I had a colleague - Signe - in the South who taught English in the same school as me. She was keen to spend time learning how to be more colloquial and confident about what she was teaching. I asked her one day whether she would like to come for a cup of tea on her way home before having dinner with her family. Just to be friendly – you know.'

I knew I did not have to explain that this particular family had their daily meal at 4pm. Most Norwegians ate about that time in those days. By then, everyone was home from school or work, hungry and ready to unwind after the day and talk together as families. In those days, no one went out to eat. Firstly, there were few places to go except hotels, where the food was not that notable, and always expensive. Hotel restaurants were mainly used then by those who would have been called 'commercial travellers' in England, or business-men, especially hosting foreign visitors. Secondly, no one had enough spare cash to take their family out for a meal anyway - even comparatively well paid, professional people. So, the daily meal was a key event in family life throughout the whole country, planted deeply in post-war culture as I knew and experienced it. I also knew that everyone ate together at roughly the same time each day. All in all, *middag* – literally, 'mid-day' and hence had come to mean the 'mid-day' meal underpinned the national effort to strengthen family life.

(At the time of writing *middag* means the main meal of the day, or 'dinner' whenever it is served.)

'It was not long after I had first arrived in Norway. I wanted to reach out and make friends. It never occurred to me that it might be a big deal to invite anyone to my "home" and might feel a bit intimidating. It's this fear of "needing to speak English" I suppose that everyone seems to have. At that time, I didn't know any Norwegian. I didn't realise either that tea drinking was unusual. So, this was a doubly big deal I now see.'

Everyone knew what I meant. I could tell by the way they were smiling and looking at each other. In view of recent events with Hannah, however, I did not explain how much Signe loved the English or that her father had been a key member of the local Resistance and had worked closely with the British on several occasions.

'Anyway,' I continued, 'she was thrilled in one way to have been invited but was also incredibly nervous. You can imagine just how horrified I was that she put BOTH milk and lemon in her tea at the same time. I offered her both because I wasn't sure how she liked it. It never occurred to me that she would use both together. Of course, it curdled horribly before our very eyes. But I hadn't the heart to say anything because she was so nervous and seemed so anxious not to put a foot wrong. I didn't want her to feel humiliated because I said anything to make her think she had made a faux pas.'

I used this very expression, which I then had to explain to them all since they had never heard it before – although friends in the South had used it frequently. A halt was called to why sometimes you would need to incorporate untranslated words from one language to another. This would have to be a postponed discussion, I explained, since they could not keep on starting new topics to explore when anything cropped up. They surely needed to finish at least SOME topics they had started on, didn't they?

'Anyway, to get back to Signe, I actually decided not to comment on her disgustingly curdled drink, which, to my utter amazement and total admiration, she drank - all of it. Heaven knows how she managed it! It must have been horrible. I should have said something, of course. I see that now. At the time I didn't want to make her feel awkward. Anyway, where were we?'

'We were about to discuss *class*. Tell us what it means – I mean, please explain more about what you said earlier when you were explaining about tea stains,' someone asked. It seemed most of them were much more fascinated by this topic than whether or not you should choose to drink tea with milk or lemon.

'Oh! Well! *Class* certainly exists in England, but it's complicated now – and it changes, and is changing all the time. In some ways, breaking down quite quickly. But it's still significant, and difficult to explain.'

'Is it the same as being formal? Has it to do with things like not speaking to someone if you've not been properly introduced?'

I paused, wondering how best to answer and explain things that were true and helpful rather than imaginary and prejudiced. I had no doubt about the power of the class system that still existed in England, but the war had broken down many previous, rigid, social barriers and that process was continuing. Attitudes and processes were changing all the time.

'Well, no! I'm afraid it's much more complicated than that. Some upper-class people are still very formal, that's true. They don't like people speaking to them without knowing who they are – and sometimes, even other people speaking before they have been spoken to.

I paused. So many things I said would need qualification as soon as I'd said them, I realised. 'Sometimes, it also has to do with good manners, though. For instance, I was brought up not to speak to my elders before they spoke to me. My parents wanted me to listen to what was going on so that I could make a sensible contribution to the conversation when it came to it, and not say something silly or irrelevant. Or, actually, they did not want me to draw unnecessary attention to myself, Children then were supposed, "to be seen, and not heard" as the saying went. For me, that had more to do with respecting older people than issues around *class*.'

Everyone was enthralled by what I said, listening rather than asking questions at this stage. I was expecting someone to ask whether having good manners was not part of class behaviour. I knew I had already got myself into a potential minefield on every front. But fortunately, no one picked up on that.

'As I said, social structures are changing fast in England. The class system used to be based on wealth and education, for instance, and also perhaps where you lived and in what kind of home. But now, it's much more complicated than that because, for a start a lot of upper-class people are nothing like as wealthy as they used to be. Sometimes they may even be quite poor. It's spoken of as living in "reduced circumstances". There's even a specific charity to help called The Distressed Gentlefolk's Association.' I feared that eyes might begin to glaze over if I delved too deeply, so I tried to return to specifics. 'And then there are ever more people who have become wealthy through businesses they may have developed, even though they personally may come from what previously would have been thought to be an "inferior" social background. Increasingly, wealthy people who have MADE money from business enterprises or developing industries can pay for the best education for their children these days and buy large, old and expensive houses too. Such opportunities used to be available to the upper class alone.'

Everyone seemed fascinated, so I continued with the information they were lapping up.

'All education including university education, as you probably know, is free in England for anyone who is clever enough to get into one because they've passed the necessary exams to qualify for a place. So, nowadays, those who are eligible can go on to higher education and get a degree if they want to, and that opens up all sort of opportunities and job prospects. That was NOT the case before the war. And it's still not the case for everyone either. There are still families where young people have to go out to work as soon as they leave school because the family needs their additional income to manage their budget. It's a fluid situation, actually. Although it definitely IS true that old, long-established class systems and behaviours are crumbling because of changes in educational structures, and increased wealth.'

They were hungry to learn anything at all about the way people actually lived their lives in England. And fascinated, if not envious, that university education could be free.

Someone asked, 'do you mean that if you want to go to university in England and are clever enough to get in, you can go whether or not you can pay for it – and you don't have to pay the money back later?'

'Yes, that's right. Usually, the Local County Authority – or *fylke*, as you call it - where you live will support you financially. The idea comes from a general will to build the country up and make it strong and thriving again after we lost so much in the cost of fighting a war – and because education has advanced so rapidly in recent years and is believed to be the key to building a stronger, better and wealthier society. We have a chance to build a different society and move ourselves in different directions, if you will. There's a kind of new, moral pressure on people who have had advanced education to serve their communities afterwards, once they're qualified - to help make the whole country an increasingly more productive and better place, if that doesn't sound too pompous? I think your government has had the same sort of ideas.'

'It's true in one way that you can go to university here in Norway if you get high enough marks – which is why we make such a fuss about what marks you give us all the time!' Grethe made this rather rueful comment – and everyone laughed. 'We have to pay for university education ourselves. We can borrow money from the government though and pay back what we've borrowed once we start earning. And if we don't get enough points to go to university here in Norway we can always go abroad to study. But then, we have to speak English or German, and we still have to pay for it ourselves or borrow to do so, as well as the money to travel and stay there and pay all our living expenses and bills.'

It seemed no one was ready yet to go home. I tried to bring the conversation to a sensible conclusion.

'I expect when you've all gone home, I shall think of loads of things I should have said – and also worry about what I have said that may not be absolutely accurate, or I could have explained more clearly, or shown the extent to which some things are a matter of opinion and experience. There are no absolute truths about it!' I hesitated, but no one said anything. 'Well! Anyway, I may need to return to the topic sometime and clarify things further – that is, if you're still interested?'

There was a chorus of 'yes' and 'definitely', and nods of approval all round before Grethe brought the specific and focused conversation to an end.

'We definitely want to learn more. But I think probably not necessarily now since you've told us a lot of stuff that we didn't know and need to absorb. We're definitely very interested to hear more about anything to do with the way people live in England.'

I was always impressed at how mature my students were when it came to knowing themselves, and what was, or was not, appropriate. I completely understood what Grethe said – everyone needed to digest what they had been told before being able to take in anything further. So, I just said, 'That's great! I'm glad I've not bored you all to death! Now, let's change the subject. When are evenings like this going to function in English?' I underlined the question with heavy emphasis.

There was a stunned silence – followed just a few seconds later by a great burst of laughter.

This was the first of many such evenings. Sometimes the same group came, on other occasions, new people were persuaded to come. A few never came. But I was careful not to let them feel discriminated against, or that they had missed out. I did not want anyone to think that it was a mistake to choose not to come.

Chapter 11

The Sami People

I knew life had changed for the better for the Sami people since I had lived in Norway. I was not sure there would be any Sami living in Vadsø now. Not all 45,000 Norwegian Sami even live in Finnmark any longer, although many still do. When I taught in Vadsø in the mid 1960s I felt deep respect for those few Sami I met and taught. Now in the Sami towns of Karasjok and Kautekeino there are schools specifically for Sami students, where teaching is even in the Sami language – just one example of how much life has changed for them in the last 50 years, by law and in practise after the troubled wrangling with the Norwegian government in the years not long after I left.

Positive change and greater security for the Sami people followed the resolution of what was known as The Alta Controversy – a serious political row arising from the profound disagreement between the Sami and the Oslo government that dominated the 1970s. At its core was a proposal to build a hydro-electric power plant on Finnmark's Alta River, the heart of Sami country. The plan would have wrecked reindeer herds' migration-cycle routes and have seriously damaged the Sami salmon fishing industry on which hundreds of Sami livelihoods depended then, and still do today. Worse, the whole Sami village of Masi would have been flooded. The Oslo proposals prompted civil disobedience. Some Sami went on hunger strike in front of Norway's Storting – or Parliament building – in Oslo, and most Sami people refused to cooperate with the Norwegian government about anything at all, even choosing instead to go to prison.

Many Norwegians, including in government, knew little about the Sami way of life at the time. They did not realise the serious impact the proposals would have on Sami livelihoods and basic economy. As recently as the 1950s there had been Norwegians who even believed the Sami were mentally disabled. Southerners who had never ventured further north than Trondheim and who knew little about the way the Sami people lived had little idea of their innate skills and capabilities.

The row was eventually settled when the developers agreed to construct a diversion in the Alta river so that salmon could continue spawning and reindeer could continue to migrate. That river, much visited by the English aristocracy in the days of Jane Austen for its famously lavish and sumptuous salmon stocks, could continue to flow unspoilt. The Alta river remains a renowned, world famous salmon fishing site.

For many Sami, life began to change at that point, not least in the way they were spoken of as 'Sami' rather than 'Lapps' – the word for a useless scribbled note to describe a proud people had become as unacceptable a term as the word 'golliwog' became in the 1950s. My aunt made me a most gorgeously dressed black doll when I was five, which I affectionately called 'golly'. I now feel embarrassed by the memory – beautifully made and much loved though he was. Changing words IS significant.

I discovered from recent sleuthing that King Harald made a formal apology to the Sami people in 1997 for the way they had been mistreated over the years. Then, key political and administrative landmarks were officially acknowledged so that the Sami could be a people in their own right. The Finnmark Act of 2005 agreed to foster cooperation between the Norwegian government in Oslo and the Sami people in Finnmark. Ninety-six per cent of Finnmark land was ceded to the authority and control of the people who lived there – a county where land is rarely privately owned – largely so that reindeer could graze and thrive uninhibited. The government had come to understand the needs of Finnmark's scattered population, and the particular demands of the Sami reindeer herds' feeding and migratory patterns. The Finnmark Estate Agency was set up to make sure that the Act's intention was always observed. Reindeer husbandry and other small farm developments and fishing operations were preserved, continuing to flourish together alongside Sami life and culture.

It was the struggle of those days that also helped give birth to the Sami people's own Parliament. A building designed in the style of a *lavuu* – or Sami tent – was opened by King Harald in 2000. The unpaid, 39 members of this body, elected every four years, are charged to keep abreast of Sami affairs – education, language, culture and history, making sure that they are not just flourishing, but also generally known and understood. Sami MPs are responsible for counteracting misinformation about the Sami way of life and stamping out discrimination. Keeping the Sami language alive is now positively encouraged. The Sami Parliament building houses a library registering anything about the Sami way of life. A teacher training college and university for Sami students has been set up in Alta, specialising in helping to support the maintenance of the Sami language.

Aspects of Sami culture speak to me. Their way of life is founded on a desire to leave footprints here on earth, rather than take from it. The Sami choose to go with the flow of what is natural and encourage anything simple, pure and intrinsic to flourish. Two often quoted Sami sayings indicate their way of thinking: 'travel is better than rest' and 'still waters are muddy.' Such sayings help explain why only five per cent of the whole of Finnmark is privately owned. Herds of reindeer do not need farms or restricted pastures: they need to be able to roam freely over the *Finnmarkvidda.* Herds cannot be bought, only inherited, and following, or farming, the migrating herds is still a chosen Sami way of life. Some families make an entire living form shepherding reindeer, birthing calves, selling reindeer milk, meat and bones, selling objects carved from horns, making rugs, mats and coats from skins.

I have recently been struck by insights that have occurred to me as I have remembered much that excited and humbled me about the Sami. Sometimes, a light goes on about a past event or incident that I did not see at the time or need now to explore further. Even as I have been writing this chapter, I have realised that my *Friundervisning* boss in Vadsø, Øystein, was most probably Sami. I had forgotten that it was even a fleeting first impression when I met him. But the more I think about it now, the more I believe he was. His calm and mannerly demeanour, his unusual sense of humour, his amazing knowledge of fish and fishing and his capacity to make all kinds of implements and tools from all sorts of materials enhance my belief that, his high-powered job at the NATO station was even more significant because of his Sami upbringing and culture.

He certainly had Sami friends. One to whom I was introduced, called Lars, told a story that made him and Øystein incoherent with laughter. Lars began by explaining that increasing numbers of tourists were holidaying on the *Hurtigruten* in the summer, not least to experience the Arctic with its special time of Midnight Sun. Visitors were an increasing source of income for Finnmark, bringing in coveted American dollars. To contribute to and encourage developing tourist opportunities, he and some Sami friends devised an authentic replica of a Sami settlement the previous summer.

An excursion from a *Hurtigruten* Midnight Sun cruise could include a trip to the encampment.

'We thought we must charge,' Lars explained. 'After all, people went to a lot of trouble to erect the tents, which were authentic, conical *lavuu,* with proper circular floors. We also had to find healthy reindeer to tether as well as prepare a load of wooden tools, plates and bowls, and find various woven artefacts and authentic outfits. We needed to find genuine things. It took time and money to organise.'

I did not think he needed to justify the decision to charge, although HE clearly did. He was an excellent story-teller building up expectations as he went along. I knew the Sami were finding it harder to live and make ends meet, driving their reindeer herds across the Northern tundra at certain times of the year to feel off the moss, the staple diet they smelt under the snow. It was, and still is, an itinerant life style.

But times were changing. A warmer climate was melting the *vidda* snow. There were ever fewer reindeer to farm, and the lure of some of the comforts of Western Life beckoned increasing numbers of youngsters to find work outside the customs and rhythms of Sami life: even moving to towns and cities.

'We begged, borrowed, and in some cases, bought implements and tools from Sami friends,' Lars explained as we ate our supper. 'Some were roped in to clean and scrape reindeer skins or clean sheepskin rugs so that visitors could feel they had seen Sami life as it was and is now. Sami dress, especially the voluminous jackets, whose fronts, *paesh*, acted as carrier bags for all their necessities – tools, utensils, ropes, knives and so forth - also had to be begged and borrowed. In some cases, they needed to be mended or altered if they were to look and function as originals.'

He showed us photographs as he spoke. I particularly liked the one of the Sami man standing proudly in his beautiful outfit of red and blue – the complete *gakti*, or *kofte*, as it's called – with his haul from a nearby lake where he had fished through a hole in the ice. 'We had a flurry of American visitors off one boat especially,' Lars went on. 'They emerged from a vehicle which brought them from the *Hurtigruten*. The women wore high heels and were bedecked with necklaces and glittery jewellry. Actually, they must have been quite heavy now I come to think of it. Not that comfortable really.'

I noticed that Øystein was beginning to smile at this point. 'He knows what's coming,' I thought to myself. 'He must have heard this story many times before.'

'Anyway,' Lars continued, I noticed that my friend, Nils, seemed to be shaking and had covered his mouth with his hand. At first, I thought he was having some sort of a fit. But then I realised he was trying really hard not to laugh. So, I took his hand and removed him from within earshot of all our visitors and asked him whatever was the matter.' Lars himself also began to giggle at this point – as did Øystein.

'What on earth did he find so funny?' I asked.

'Well, what he found utterly hilarious was the fact that these Americans had all paid good money to come and look at us and see how we lived our lives. But we didn't have to pay a penny to see how they lived theirs. He thought it was hysterical. It creased him up. They were all hugely inappropriately dressed and not at all used to walking. They asked such odd questions. It was obvious they saw Sami life as primitive – and not one that functioned well in a civilised context. But Nils thought it was actually THEY who came from a much more primitive civilisation. Their questions and the way they reacted to the experience made it clear that it was not us who were backward, but them!'

I could not help laughing too at this point. It was a funny story after all, and Lars told it so well. I realised then how grounded and civilised these Sami were. They did not feel they were being inspected or looked down on, even if they were. It was just so funny how utterly incongruous it turned out to be for a Sami settlement to be visited by modern Americans with their extraordinarily predictable and primitive ways of experiencing difference.

I admired and respected their dignity, their mature judgement and their sense of proportion. 'How monumentally crass as well as wicked of the Nazis to have despised these people even more that they despised native North Norwegians,' I thought to myself. The sound of Lars and Nils' laughter echoed in my head for quite some time. And when I recall the memory of it to this day, even now as I type, I cannot help but smile.,

Also, I cannot help wondering what American visitors made of the fact that the town had no police force, no jail or lock up or courts of law, although there was an attorney, or lawyer, whose services were called on from time to time to deal with personal, or business contracts and probate. I have also remembered that Øystein took me one Sunday to the special Sami church an Nesseby on the edge of the Verangerfjord. It is a beautiful, wooden church that can hold 100 people or so with plenty of space for children to play between the pews and down the main aisle. And this was long before it was acceptable in the UK for youngsters to roam around in worship services. The proceedings were in Sami. The Prayer Books were published in Sami, and many of the adults who came to the service were wearing their special *kofti* Sunday best. I remember that although it was a least minus 20, the church was wonderfully warm for the service that lasted a good two hours! To my shame, I did not acknowledge the experience properly at the time for the wonderful treat it was. It was my first experience of a worship service that was completely self-effacing, respectful and genuine. Even though I knew no Sami personally, the atmosphere was warm, and I felt privileged to have attended. Belatedly, I extend my thanks to that congregation for including me on that day.

In writing this chapter, I've also wondered how life is for other minority peoples who live in the Arctic Circle – the Innuits, and the Komi, the Russian Vespians, and the Siberian Nenets. Not all minorities are as privileged as the Norwegian Sami whose lifestyle is protected by law.

***

Between the two-day train ride and the ferry across to the spectacular Lofoten Islands, my longstanding Norwegian friend and I spent a week-end in Trondheim. We attended a packed service in the Cathedral on the Sunday morning which was inspirational. The music was beautiful, he atmosphere simple and powerful. In the row in front several Sami sat gloriously bedecked in national costume. The sight alone was yet another small, well-placed brick in the wall, beckoning me back to Vadsø.

***

The third topic I wanted to find out more about was, and remains, a highly controversial concern to many Norwegians. The Norwegian government decided that Norway's 19 counties should be reduced to 11 from January 1st 2020 by amalgamation or elimination. Demographics over the country have changed in recent years. Transport problems, new roads, bridges and airports have also facilitated mobility. The population has increased from 3,000,000 when I lived in Norway, to 5,500,000 today. The Oslo government has had to make many social and administrative changes as a result. Wealth from the Ekofisk oil fields has financed many necessary administrative demands, and there will be more to come.

In the climate of change, Finnmark and Troms were told to amalgamate. Finnmark's population of some 75,000 people – the equivalent number of, for example, the population of a town like Oxford – were to join a more densely populated, culturally different, smaller in size, though much larger in numbers of people, living in the county of Troms, to facilitate more efficient, easier financial and administrative processes and improve the provision of local services.

I had been told by my Norwegian friends that the majority of those living in Finnmark were opposed to the idea. A singular county, in which only five per cent of land is privately owned, in an area the size of Switzerland or Denmark, with a range of rich, natural resources and environmental treasures, as well as a wealth of untapped mineral riches, and a road network of hundreds of square miles would not easily slide into partnership with a county hosting an international symphony orchestra, a university and a world-renowned art gallery.

The Finnmark Council – a locally, democratically elected body – decided to hold an unofficial referendum on the issue of amalgamation, in which 86 per cent of Finnmark residents voted. The outcome was a solid 75 per cent majority against amalgamation. Nevertheless, the Oslo government was determined to proceed with its plans and has now implemented them. There is talk of a review of the Finnmark-Troms amalgamation in the near future. In the meantime, many people from both counties feel this enforced partnership is simply impractical. Administrators would face problems in financing the process of keeping ALL roads open, for example, making sure ALL children got to school through the winter even if the weather was particularly bad. There will be other issues arising from fundamentally different environmental heritages and experience between the two counties. Amalgamation might stretch the application of goodwill and best practice almost to breaking point. I had never been to any part of Troms, but I knew that the geography, climate and culture there, even though it also lies within the Arctic Circle, are all utterly different from those of its Finnmark neighbours.

It is definitely not a separate country. But it makes for really awkward politics that Finnmark has its own foreign policy with Russia - certainly as far as the Murmansk and Russian Barents Region are both concerned. This reality not only means that Norway has in fact TWO policies or attitudes towards Russia – one in the Arctic and the other in Oslo. It is also at complete odds with the centre of Finnmark's gravity moves towards Troms to combine boundaries and become one county. Unsurprisingly, therefore, when the plan was fist mooted in 2016, there was fierce objection to it from many northerners.

I wanted to find out for myself how these tensions felt for those living there. Were people justifiably fearful, and what might be some generally agreed views about how amalgamation might impact life in Finnmark? A proposal such as this could not possibly have been on the cards when I had lived in Vadsø. I'm sure the very idea would have been resisted, especially by many older people who, although they might remember how the Russians had been strong allies from 1944 onwards towards the end of the war, also minded hugely about their particular identity.

Personally, I greatly fear and dislike any idea that might radically alter the special wonder that is Finnmark. Anything that might threaten its unique qualities and singular beauty feels to me immensely worrisome. However, I realise that change to life there is inevitable, not least because of its underground, unmined riches. There will surely be many political and administrative discussions and battles in the years ahead.

Chapter 12

Nailing the Itinerary

Once we had agreed to make the trip to Vadsø, we Arctic Musketeers found ourselves in a state of euphoric shock. Now we needed to plan where we would go, when, and what we would do when we got there. Before we could start to book tickets however, I needed to think about my aims and objectives.

From this point onwards, all three of us were to experience a whirligig of incidents and encounters that could only have been Divinely intended and ordained. Everything that happened was underpinned by the greatest feelings of joy and excitement and a deep sense of delight. Our trip turned out to be extraordinary. Ann and Margaret's sentences from now on often began with phrases such as, 'I've always wanted to ...' or, 'Are we really ....?' or, 'This looks amazing!' or 'Will we be able to ...?' None of us were to be disappointed. We were to be blessed and enriched beyond anything we could have imagined.

My love affair with Norway meant I could always go for any kind of visit: just being there always inspired and energised me. But for this particular expedition I would need to do some specific sleuthing and would only have a few days in which to do so. I needed to be clear about the places I wanted to revisit and explore.

In the last 50 years I have regularly been back to visit friends in the South. Seeds of nostalgic stirrings to return to the North had been sown the year before in 2018 when I had been reminded just how Arctic scenery alone was able to affect me. My Southern Norwegian friend and I had taken the two-day train journey from Oslo to Bodø and then the ferry across to the Lofoten Islands. The experience not only revived many precious memories, it also reignited my connection with uniquely stark and rugged beauty. It is almost impossible to explain in what ways the impact was so breathtakingly uplifting. The magical quality of light betrayed the time of year, just a few weeks before the start of the Midnight Sun period. The mountains were bluish-white with melting snow, set against rugged rocks and cliffs - the magnificent beauty is impossible to explain to anyone who has not experienced it for themselves.

My friend and I kept looking at each other on the bus ride we undertook from the beautiful village of Reine to Svolvaer harbour, where we were to board the *Hurtigruten* for our journey south to Trondheim, with wide eyes and open mouths. How could such awesome beauty be? Normally we would talk to each other non-stop, but we were rendered speechless by all we could see on both sides of the bus. How could the Creator have conceived of such vistas of lakes and mountains, and rugged countryside? It was an extraordinarily wonderful ride. Later, on the *Hurtigruten* over supper, we found trying to communicate our responses to what we had seen impossible to put into words. That the awe it inspired in us even affected my Norwegian friend who is used to living in such stunnung surroundings, bears witness to the particular power and moving beauty of what we witnessed.

The experience of that trip encouraged me to commit to going back to Vadsø. I could not ignore the yearnings it had stirred. I knew I needed to revisit old memories and create new ones, while I still could. I knew much would have changed in the intervening years: that in itself would be enough to explore. I also wondered if I might find the whole experience so overwhelming that I would be completely overcome. Nevertheless, I knew I should take my impulses seriously and begin to think about specific objectives.

There were two things I most definitely wanted to experience. I knew I wanted to take the bus ride across the *Finnmarkvidda* from Vadsø to the North Cape - a trip that would have been impossible in my day, since the roads then were more like tracks than today's excellent highways. In some places they were simply not there at all. People relied on ferries, snow ploughs and the *Hurtigruten* to get from A to B at certain times of the year. Today's road network, with newly-built bridges and recently constructed underwater tunnels facilitate efficient and reliable road transport. Not for nothing are Norwegian engineers deemed to be some of the greatest road builders and tunnellers on earth. Their work during the intervening years since I lived there includes tunnels constructed under the sea like the one that links the mainland *vidda* to the island of Vardø. It is three kilometres long, and some 88 metres below the freezing Arctic Ocean. But the tunnel I really wanted actually to experience was the one that linked *Magerøya*'s North Cape to Finnmark's mainland.

This furthest North, under-sea road tunnel in the world is 6.8 kilometres long and I wanted that particular journey to be factored into our travel plans. It would be right at the end of the bus journey I had longed to undertake for many years - one that would have helped Per Johann to spend a few weekends at home in term time if the road had existed 55 years ago. It would certainly have saved him his three-day skiing expedition from home to school across the *Finnmarkvidda*. From the North Cape, I hoped we could get another bus to take us on to Tromsø. Altogether, that would be a magnificent way to see something of Finnmark and enable us to be at a Sunday service at the Cathedral in Tromsø and, fly home the day after.

Apart from entirely reconstructing old bridges, new ones have also been built, such as the bridge on the E75 at Utsjoki that joins Finnmark with Finland. There is also the spectacular Kvalsund suspension bridge across the Kvalsund strait that links the village of Kvalsund to the town of Hammerfest some twenty miles to the North West of it. It has enabled traffic to access towns and other routes more efficiently than ever before. Since the county of Finnmark is an area the size of Denmark, engineering tasks to facilitate smooth and safe travel have been no small undertaking. But their arrival has changed people's lives, by making travel quicker, easier and more accessible. Spectacular engineering works have especially enhanced the quality of life for all 75,000 people who live in Finnmark.

Thirdly, I was curious to find how climate change had affected life in Vadsø, especially since it was getting milder in the Arctic Circle at an overall faster rate than in other places around the globe. I wanted to see for myself what that meant, especially for those working in the fishing industry. Perhaps fishermen had become more prosperous because there were more fish seeking warmer Arctic waters, producing richer harvests? Maybe other kinds of fish had joined the massive harvests of sardines and salmon? Perhaps the whole annual fishing cycle had changed? Or maybe those who lived there now had had to move away from the fishing industry altogether as a result of an ever-changing social and climactic dynamic?

I was unsure how I might go about finding answers to my questions since I would not have *an Øystein* to hand. He had always been able to interpret any changes or challenges to public life with clarity and wisdom. But I guessed my agenda might alter significantly once I actually got back to Vadsø. I might even feel so emotionally overwhelmed that I would struggle to investigate anything at all. Also, I was bound to encounter things I had not given any thought to and knew little about. For example, I presumed the government's county amalgamation plan, proposing that Finnmark and Troms should be one single administrative county from January 2020, would be a hot topic, and certainly wanted to find out more about that. I also wanted to know how many, if any,

Sami were still living in Vadsø. I knew that since my time there, the status, culture and general Sami way of life had dramatically changed, and, I believed, substantially for the better.

Margaret was only too pleased to leave all the organising to Ann and myself. We decided to plan an itinerary in the time between the May 17th celebrations but before the end of the school year in late June during the Midnight Sun period when, although it would still be chilly, at least the sun would be shining all the time. We thought three days in Vadsø would be ideal. I had not yet explored whether there was a decent hotel there but hoped there would be somewhere central that was comfortable, warm and had clear views.

Ann and I divided up the process of making travel plans. I found it a challenge since I had never done such off piste travel-planning like this before, apart from what had become my old haunts in and around the South East of the country within easy access of Oslo. Anything out of the ordinary, or different, such as an out of season visit to the Lofoten Islands was generally orchestrated by my Norwegian friend who knew how travel worked for everyone who lived there and needed to get about as natives, not tourists.

Ann - used to international travel because she went regularly to visit her daughter in the States - undertook to use her usual agent to explore the best offers between the UK and Norway, outside package deals. I agreed to explore internal travel from Oslo to Vadsø and find out bus and plane times so that we could get to the North Cape and on to Tromsø at the times we wanted. Ann was always structured and clear about anything administrative and excellent at making plans. It was a godsend to someone like me – not well organised, and not always as concerned with detail as I ought to be!

Increasingly, I began to see that my yearnings to return to old haunts was going to be about much more than seeing how things might or might not have changed. Trying to fathom at a deeper level why I had loved my year there so much and understand more about what it was that had so strengthened, changed and formed me, was a much more important reason to return. Of course, there were many things about visiting a town so far north in the 21st century that would make it a singular experience in its own right. In any event, I was clear I now no longer wanted just to find out what was the same and what was different in the Arctic Circle. Much more importantly, I wanted to reconnect with the Vadsø spirit of courage and love of life.

Chapter 13

Making Plans

Ann and I agreed to plan the route and sort out our itinerary.

'I'll explore the flights from Birmingham to Oslo,' Ann said at the outset. 'Just tell me the dates.'

'Great! I'll look into onward travel and accommodation,' I said. 'I've no idea how long it will take to go so far north. I'm sure there won't be direct flights from Oslo to Vadsø. I guess we'll have to stop at various places and even change planes en route. Of course, even if there are direct flights, we'll need to return to Oslo from Tromsø rather than Vadsø on our final Monday, so we can't rely on automatic internal return flights!'

We knew that we wanted to spend at least three days in Vadsø and attend a Sunday service at the *Ishavskatedralen* in Tromsø. Working our plans and timings backwards from the fixed point of the Sunday service meant we hoped to fly South to Oslo, and if possible, back to England, on a Monday. In turn that would mean we needed to get to Tromsø on the Saturday before the service. To achieve that, we wanted to take the day's bus ride from Vadsø across the *Finnmarkvidda* to Honningsvåg at the North Cape, on the Friday. We wanted to spend a night in Honningsvåg before flying on the next day, Saturday, to Tromsø where we would spend the night, ready to go to church on Sunday and fly home on Monday.

As Ann and I set to work to find the information we needed, it felt as if we were in capable and supportive hands that were not our own. We were increasingly certain about this the more we delved into trying to fix arrangements that seemed much more difficult and complicated to achieve than we had anticipated. It was clear from the outset that organising our travel under our own steam - rather than under the auspices of a travel company - especially to a little-known town, deep within the Arctic Circle and then travelling round Finnmark, was unusual, indeed unheard of. It meant we had to search for information that continually seemed inaccessible. Once our desired itinerary was agreed, we found the information we needed difficult to find. Even once we knew where to look for it, it sometimes seemed unavailable.

Before we could fix anything and Ann could book return flights to Oslo, my task was to find the bus timetable information to be sure the journeys we wanted to undertake in Finnmark were possible. We wanted to go by bus from Vadsø to the North Cape on our last Friday and then from Honningsvåg to Tromsø the next day. But it did not take long to discover that the timetable for the dates we needed in late May to the places we wanted to go to in both Finnmark and then Troms, were not available. It was unclear whether that meant there were no buses at all, or that the journey timings were not yet fixed.

Various folk I spoke to on the phone in Norway did not know when the new timetables would be published. Neither could they promise they would be the same as last year and all the years before. They always had been pretty much the same, but things were different now. As the government's plans for Finnmark's amalgamation with Troms were looming the revenue streams were in a state of flux. Hence, year-to-year planning was no longer a matter of course. On the other hand, I kept being assured that people depended on a bus service of sorts, so it was highly unlikely there would be no buses at all. Transport subsidies of all kinds would likely be one of the most important issues to be settled in the context of county amalgamation. Even so, no one could assure us we could travel when we hoped. We really needed that assurance.

A number of conversations left me feeling bewildered. The uncertainty of specifics surprised me as did the fact that several people I spoke to were keen to speak English, not Norwegian, on the phone. It made me wonder how things were in Finnmark these days? With new airports, roads and climate change, as well as all that I had read in recent days about how people were feeling and reacting in Vadsø right now vis a vis the Finnmark amalgamation with Troms, I began to wonder if life might be somewhat bleak there compared with the rest of Norway? I felt uneasy. I knew we could not just take pot-luck and hope to get around as best we could. Distances between places were so great, we needed to be able to rely on public transport to fit in with our time constraints. Although we were Arctic Musketeers, we were also elderly. We would need assurance at least that we could get from place to place as we wanted. But how could we possibly plan with no settled timetables?

It took a while to come to terms with some uncertainty. I would need to trust that buses were assured. People who lived in Finnmark would need them, surely? In any case even if it turned out that there weren't any, there were surely bound to be flights or ferries or taxis. Nowadays every town in Finnmark has an airport: practically everyone flies, especially in Finnmark where the distances are so great and the population so small.

I trawled the internet for telephone numbers which eventually led me to speak with someone in the heart of Finnmark's bus travel office, whose responsibility it was, apparently, to help produce a bus timetable.

'How much can I risk,' I asked, trying hard not to show my frustration, 'this year's timetables just being continued forward so that it will be pretty much the same anyway?'

'I can't answer that, I'm afraid. I'm not allowed to.' I was told.

'Well,' I persisted after all my attempts to persuade the lady to whom I was talking to break the rules had failed, 'could you perhaps ADVISE me? I mean would YOU risk it being roughly the same timetable from the summer onwards, as the one that already exists, or would you suspect it might be radically different? I mean if I were YOUR Mother, would you reassure me that I would be able to make the journey – somehow by bus?'

I pressed on, trying to find out what the **real** problem was. I felt sure there was a more serious issue somehow linked to the proposed county amalgamation that was due to start in January 2020.

Eventually, the lady yielded to my pleadings and explained the problem.

'The difficulty is,' she said, 'and I'm not sure I should be saying this, but we aren't really allowed to publish public, transport timetables until we're assured the funding is available to underpin the costs.'

I understood at once. So, there **was** a link to future county amalgamation plans after all? Maybe the government was already trying to influence or control Finnmark's purse strings?

'There probably will be buses pretty much as usual. In any case,' she continued, 'you can't book ahead. You have to pay as you get on the bus.'

I felt elated. It seemed that the journey I had been longing to undertake for quite some time, was now possible. Even though I knew there would be much less snow than when I lived there, I also knew that the eight-hour bus trip from Vadsø to Honningsvåg across the Finnmarkvidda would be a stunning journey.

There had been few reliable roads when I had lived there. In those days, people went from place to place via the *Hurtigruten*, or else by private boat or ferry. Otherwise, they simply skied from place to place. That had been particularly possible way back then because the *vidda* hardly ever thawed completely, and of course everyone had to be able to ski with the same competence and proficiency as they could walk. I remembered, and caught myself smiling as I recalled, being regularly overtaken by tiny two and three-year olds as I struggled to get up again after falling for the umpteenth time in one morning of my novitiate, in my early learning-to-ski days!

Soon, an email in fluent English dropped into my inbox. It was from the person I was speaking to earlier in my slow Norwegian – after all it was some time since I had spoken it regularly.

I read that there were two or three buses a day from Vadsø to Honningsvåg – **except for weekends**, when there would be no buses running.

'Help!' I thought. 'That's fine for getting to Honningsvåg on the Friday. But if no buses run at the weekend, there won't be any to get us from Honningsvåg to Tromsø on the Saturday? Or maybe Saturday doesn't count as a weekend?'

I thought back to my days of teaching in Norway. In those days, school was as regular on Saturdays as well as it was on weekdays. Overall, it was regarded as a normal working day throughout the country in every aspect of work and production. Today, however, and for at least the last 30 years, there are no Saturday schools, and few people have to work on Saturdays these days either.

I emailed the address the lady I had been speaking to, to ask. Within a few minutes I had a reply telling me that no buses ran in Finnmark on either Saturdays or Sundays. I investigated the Honningsvåg airport site and discovered no planes flew in or out of Honningsvåg or Tromsø on Saturdays either. No buses, no planes: we would be stuck in Honningsvåg on the Friday! What were we to do? I rang the online number of a taxi firm. They could certainly drive three elderly ladies the 315 miles required. It would take eight hours – driving within the 50mph speed limit and along narrow, winding roads, and including the compulsory rest stops and changings of drivers – but the cost, which I now forget, would be absolutely extortionate. It was unthinkable.

I was at my wits' end!

I sat down with a cup of tea and wondered what to do. Maybe we should reconsider major parts of our agreed schedule. But I could not see how to do this without substantially reducing our time in Vadsø – which, after all, was the main focus of the trip. I felt a bleak sense of frustration rising inside after the experience of such previous elation. I tried to stop myself from descending into a sense of despair. But suddenly, apparently out of nowhere, a thought came to me about the *Hurtigruten*. Perhaps the Southbound ship might help us. If, by some remote chance, its timings chimed with our travel plans, we might be able to get on board and enjoy a wonderful day of the most amazing scenery from a vantage point of sea and fjord rather than highway? I decided to look it up, hardly daring to believe it might solve our problem.

To my complete astonishment, I discovered it was scheduled to leave Honningsvåg at the North Cape at 05 45 on the Saturday, getting into Tromsø just before midnight that same day. The timing was perfect. It could not have been more helpful if we were to have devised it ourselves. It would enable us to sleep in Tromsø overnight, be ready to go to church in the Cathedral the next morning and fly home the day after as we had planned. It was exactly what we wanted. Moreover, it meant we'd have another glorious day, sailing in and out of remote *fjords* and islands in total comfort. Boarding at 5 45 meant we'd be able to settle ourselves on the viewing deck long before those who were doing the entire cruise to and from Bergen to Kirkenes would be up and about. We would be able to make an extremely comfortable base on the *Hurtigruten's* comfortable recliners with the most magnificent views of absolutely everything on both sides of all the fjords we would be sailing through as we voyaged around beautiful and remote islands, stopping briefly now and then at some of the world's most northerly towns and villages. We would be able to doze, drink coffee, graze and wander about as and when we wished. We would even be able to go ashore at the various stopping places if we wanted to. It was all pure gift! I stared at my laptop screen in total amazement. Within just a few minutes, everything fitted and connected. Our plans were secured. We could begin to book.

What was this other than a miracle?

***

I rang Ann and we agreed to get together to check all the details and divide up the bookings between us.

It was easy enough to choose flights from the UK to Oslo. What we needed to find out was how the timings of daily flights to the North and back would fit with our arrival and departure to and from Oslo. Then, we needed to be sure of the details of onward travel north so that we could fly back to Oslo from Tromsø at the right time to return to the UK. I was tasked to organise the flight from Oslo to Vadsø and book the *Hurtigruten*.

Gradually, we secured all the information we needed. Internal flights to the Far North were in the hands of Widerøe – the internal Norwegian airline that flies small turboprop planes, Bombardier aircraft that seat between 20 and 30 people, to the remotest parts of Finnmark. It should have been a straightforward procedure to book, but I soon discovered that every time I searched for flights from Oslo to Vadsø, the information that appeared on my screen, changed. Also, even though it still hosted the NATO station - so there would surely be people travelling to and fro all the time from Oslo - flights to Vadsø seemed to be even more infrequent than those to Kirkenes or Hammerfest. Flights anywhere further north than Tromsø seemed to be in short supply. The constant changes of information on my screen were troubling, but there did not seem to be anything I could do except deal with the information as it appeared. At some point, I would have to make a decision - and book.

The constantly changing information was one problem. Ann and I discovered that the cost of the flights seemed to go up with every passing day. We were occasionally encouraged to book at once - before the flight was full.

Another difficulty also arose, seemingly out of nowhere. I intended to put us all on the long Midnight Sun direct night flight from Oslo to Vadsø that presented itself on my screen. Even though late in the day, it would be a journey in constant daylight, and I knew that would be amazing since the Midnight Sun has its own special quality of light. So, we would leave Oslo in daylight towards the end of the day and arrive very, very early the next morning in Vadsø in time for breakfast. I had already booked us in to a hotel there and knew that once we arrived, we would have time to rest and sleep and adjust to the next 10 days of endless light. It would be an experience worth having I believed, and we all agreed.

But to my horror, even as I booked our long, internal flight from Oslo to Vadsø, to start a major part of our trip, the flight times changed in the very process of my doing so. I stared at my laptop in total disbelief when I saw how the information had been totally transformed when my booking was finally confirmed. What it finalised was a flight from Oslo to Tromsø that arrived there just before midnight and left us with a seven-hour wait before an onward flight to Vadsø early the next morning. It still described itself as one flight in spite of what was now a seven-hour gap in the middle. I remember staring at my screen for several minutes in total horror. Where would we go for those seven unscheduled hours?

However, as I sat in disbelief, I reminded myself that the three of us had already agreed that God Himself must somehow be at the heart of our whole endeavour. I did not tell Ann or Margaret about the flight problem I had encountered. I felt a strange, unusual, but strong assurance that I should not worry about it.

From the start of my planning, courtesy one of my lovely Norwegian goddaughters who lives in Oslo, I had been in touch with several people in Troms – the county – with whom I thought I might be able to chat face to face about aspects of life in that part of the Arctic. The three of us particularly wanted to know how things were in ecclesiastical circles and church life since the Norwegian Lutheran church had recently been financially dis-established. I had never been to any part of Troms, so had no contacts there. But I welcomed the prospect of any information I could glean about any aspect of life in the church while we would be visiting the Cathedral. I also wanted to know what those who lived in Troms thought about the proposed amalgamation of counties.

My god-daughter - an architect - knew I had always longed to visit the Arctic Cathedral and I knew she had several cleric contacts in Oslo. I asked her if she could put me in touch with folk while we were in Tromsø. As a result, I connected with pastor Ann Christin Elvemo, who assured me we would be welcome at a service and said we should make ourselves known after it to the pastor in charge. I emailed back to ask the name of the pastor, in case there were several. Almost as an aside, I had also asked what might be available to us for the seven hours we would have to wait at Tromsø airport. After all, it advertised itself as International – so I assumed there was bound to be some sort of hostelry nearby. Or if not, at least there was bound to be some public transport that would get us into the city. I knew I could not expect Tromsø International Airport to be like Heathrow or Kennedy. But I presumed it must have a certain standard of, or access to, various facilities at the very least.

I had not yet received a reply to this specific question. So, I continued to presume there would be somewhere we could recline and relax. And at worst, I thought, we could just sip coffee and snooze, stretched out on comfy chairs in a waiting area in the airport itself – or so I believed! In any event, I felt a strange calm about the whole thing even though I knew I would have to tell Ann and Margaret at some point how things actually stood about our journey going north.

The day before the start of our trip, Margaret came to spend the night with me. Ann, who lives just a few miles from me, was due to pick us both up to drive the three of us to the airport the next morning. After supper, Margaret and I decided we'd go through our itinerary one last time. My laptop was open on my knees so that we could check together and verify all schedules and details. I was on the verge of explaining to her that there might be a slight hiccup at Tromsø on our way north but that I was sure we'd be able to manage. Even as I was about to explain to Margaret how that might be, an unknown, Norwegian looking name signalled its appearance in my email box. I paused to open it.

My jaw dropped when I read what it said.

'Dear Mrs. Fletcher

My name is Sigmund Nesset. I am the husband of May Line Angell, the pastor of Ishavskatedralen. We have both read your e-mails to Ann Christin Elvemo. First question: Have we understood it right? Are you going to spend the night May 20 in Tromsø without any accommodation? That is not a very good idea! In Tromsø we sleep at night (like the rest of the world). After midnight it is normally very quiet here. Shops are closed, like most of the restaurants and bars. And even if the sun might be shining, it may also be very cold. Our suggestion is therefore that all of you come and stay with us that night. I fetch you at the airport Monday night and bring you there again in the morning.

All the best from

May Line and Sigmund

Chapter 14

The Angels of Tromsø

To this day I don't know what we would have done had Sigmund and May Line not offered us overnight hospitality. It turns out that Tromsø International Airport is tiny with a baggage hall and no other facilities to speak of. There was no airport hotel, no directions to the city centre – and not an official in sight. This all served to emphasise the seriousness of our plight had we not been blessed with what we all accepted was the Divine Intervention that placed us into the angelic hands of our hosts. Not only were there no facilities in the airport, it was also alarmingly noisy. There were several men with hard hats building an extension to the Arrivals Hall at one end. The sporadic noise of pneumatic drills was deafening. In between bouts of drilling, several workmen shouted to each other over loud pop music from a radio playing at full capacity. We would have had nowhere in the building to rest, and no chance of being able to relax either.

Sigmund drove us out of the airport in full daylight - it was midnight - alongside the Tromsø Sound with the famous, Tromsø bridge connecting the mainland to the promontory where the Ishavskatedralen is sited, on our right. As we drove, we watched seabirds swooping for fish from the sea.

At the start of our day, we had bussed from our hotel to Oslo's airport to hand in our luggage. We were to have an early supper much later with one of my goddaughters in Oslo's spectacular Opera House – built since I lived in Norway. We took the train into the heart of Oslo and spent the day exploring, ending up drinking coffee in one of the Opera House's bars, in good time to relax before our early supper. The Opera House sits alongside the fjord, so we had great views of boats and seabirds and activity as we relaxed in the beautifully decorated foyer, its colourful walls adorned with displays of art-work and textures – paintings, glasswork, brass designs, pottery, clay and brick.

The foyer was designed to encourage visitors to stroll, sit, chat, drink coffee and enjoy food from imaginative menus. It was open and light and spacious. As Sigmund drove us alongside this different fjord my mind registered the contrast between it and the environs of the Oslo fjord earlier in the day. The beauty of both was differently stunning.

What made an even more delightful end to the day was that our hosts in Tromsø were wonderfully welcoming. Straight away they made us feel as if **we** were actually doing **them** a favour by staying with them. Even though it was way past midnight when we arrived, they were eager to settle down and chat.

May Line's surname just happens to be Angell. I knew one of the few Norwegian words for a certain kind of *angel* was *engel* – the 'e' replacing the English 'a', which made it dissimilar in pronunciation as well as spelling from the English word. Nevertheless, we knew we had fallen into the hands of angels, and I was not willing to be prevented from pointing it out the moment Sigmund opened his front door and announced to his wife that we had arrived.

'No wonder your surname is Angell' I said, straight away as I shook May Line's hand. 'How amazingly appropriate!' I was even willing to risk being too personal to someone I had only just met because I could not help myself. 'You'll have to forgive me for pointing that out, but we all feel we have definitely fallen into the hands of angels!'

Both Sigmund and May Line protested at once that it was differently spelt and so was not actually exactly the same. But we three Arctic Musketeers chose to see it differently. I just hoped it was not too cheeky of me – or too *frekk* to actually say so. *Frekk* – which means overly bold or impertinent - is a Norwegian word of great interest and discussion. The whole of the next chapter is devoted to an attempt to explain it.

At that point, Margaret excused herself. Understandably. It was well after midnight after all and it had been a long and exciting day. While May Line was showing Margaret to her room, Ann and I took the opportunity to explain to Sigmund that she was, after all, 92!

The rest of us, Ann, Sigmund, May Line and myself, settled down to chat around the customary Norwegian coffee table in a section of the living room furnished with comfortable chairs. The whole house was open, light and exquisitely tasteful as all Norwegian homes are. The staircase in particular fascinated Ann and Margaret. It had no handrails and made the upstairs floor seem like a continual part of the open space downstairs. Tall bookshelves arranged in strikingly orderly storage surrounded us where we sat. Beautifully stacked, they made us want to browse straight away.

'Your bookshelves are wonderfully and invitingly displayed!' I exclaimed. At the same time, I was taking in the tasteful serenity that surrounded us as we sat, in an atmosphere typical of many Norwegian living rooms.

'Ah well!' said Sigmund. 'May Line was once a librarian, you see!'

'Oh! That explains it! No wonder!' I said feeling somewhat amazed at myself that I had dared to make such a personal remark. I just felt at home. I was sure all three of us did.

We talked for the next couple of hours. Among other things we learned that the two of them had met in Hammerfest where May Line had been a librarian. Sigmund came from that town and taught University Philosophy, presumably now at the University of Troms.

'My granddaughter is hoping to study Philosophy at university,' I said, trusting it wasn't pushy or conceited to say so in such illustrious company. Connections just kept on coming and it felt comfortable to make them! 'She will be really interested to hear that we've met you. She would have loved to have been able to talk with you too.'

We explained why we were making the trip so far north to such a remote and unknown place – that I was hoping it would provide appropriate information for me to finish a book I was writing. I had felt compelled to return to where I had once lived and worked to see what might be the same and what had changed. I shared that I had always wanted to go to a service at the *Ishavskatedralen* ever since it had been built and now had the chance. When I had first mentioned it to Ann and Margaret, they enthused about visiting it too. So, the three of us had booked to stay in Tromsø the following weekend en route south from Vadsø so that we could go to the Cathedral on the Sunday morning and fly home on the Monday.

'You'll all be very welcome, of course!' May Line said. 'But I need to tell you that next Sunday morning is not one of our normal Sunday services. It's our annual, confirmation service. The church will be packed with friends and relatives of those being confirmed and will be a different kind of service from usual. But, of course, you'll all be most welcome to come.'

I knew I would need to explain to Ann and Margaret what that meant. Confirmation for teenagers in Norway these days is more a rite of passage than a commitment to faith. When I had lived in Norway more than 50 years previously, it was no longer essential to have been confirmed in order to get a decent kind of job - as had been the case many years ago - but it had nevertheless become a pathway to adulthood that many families chose to follow. Substantial, valuable presents to mark the occasion are almost de rigeur these days, and young people have come to rely on large gifts of cash from close relations. After all, both advanced educational pathways and daily life in Norway are not cheap!

We talked about many topics, especially the Church in Norway. I remembered that when I lived there a local pastor would teach the basics of Christianity in most high schools. That was certainly true in Vadsø which has a beautiful church standing proudly right in the centre of the town. But May Line warned me - if that is not too strong a word - that she did not think there was even a pastor based there any longer. I was left wondering what happened there these days when a pastor was required to officiate at weddings, funerals and confirmations in particular. Perhaps I would find out when we got there.

We could have talked all night. But we knew May Line had to get up and go to work the next morning. As pastor of the very *Ishavskatedralen* itself, she had a busy week's schedule ahead never mind all the preparations necessary for the following Sunday. The three of us needed to be up early too, to be at the airport soon after 7am to complete our flight north. In any case, we were all beginning to feel that special kind of exhaustion, after a day's excitement, was beginning to take us over. It seemed to hit both Ann and I at the same time, as we found we needed sleep ourselves. Margaret, in her own room, had already been asleep for two or three hours when Ann and I finally climbed the stairs.

At around 3am now, the sun was still shining, and birds were still busy flying to and fro, singing as they went. I would have liked to have known how they managed to rest through the days of endless light – but now was not the time to ask. We drew the blackout curtains that did an effective job in keeping out the light and sank into our gloriously comfy beds with the very best of Norway's softly enveloping, snuggly duvets to lull us both to sleep.

May Line had already gone to work when we emerged for breakfast. Sigmund had been busy preparing a beautifully laid and presented meal with fresh bread and *pålegg* the next morning. He declared it was his responsibility to do so as the vicar's house-husband. He had also made a pot of tea, presuming that's what we would prefer to drink, rather than coffee. And he was right. We could not have been more honoured or better served by his careful, detailed hospitality. We chatted further on a number of topics, including a shared interest in all things William Morris. Most unusually, both for Norwegians, especially Norwegians so far north, and for many Brits too, part of the kitchen wall was furnished with William Morris wallpaper.

'So, what will you do when you have delivered us at the airport? Are you busy writing something these days?' I asked, hoping that was not too intrusive a question.

'I am.' Sigmund said. 'I'm writing a book about the Ecology of the Mind.' I felt he seemed tentative. I was fascinated, however. I could have enjoyed spending several hours talking through such a project; what it meant specifically, and what was his approach. It sounded an exciting, unusual but entirely apt topic.

'How wonderful!' I said with as much enthusiasm as I dared.

He seemed encouraged by my response. 'Well,' he said, still somewhat self-effacingly, 'you see I think it has to include God. I don't think it's possible to exclude Him from the mind.'

As we said our thanks and goodbyes and were about to pull our suitcases up the slope to the Departure building, he stopped us.

'You're all be back here next Sunday for the service, won't you?' he asked.

'That's right,' I said. 'We're staying over on the Saturday and Sunday precisely so that we can go to the Cathedral.'

'Well!' he said. 'I'd like to pick you up from your hotel and take you to it, if that's OK.'

'That would be wonderful! How very kind!' The three of us all spluttered roughly the same thing. 'How amazing! Are you sure that won't put you out?'

'Not in the least,' he said. 'I'll call you then, Molly, on the Sunday morning and tell you what time I'll be with you. You can let me know when we speak where you're staying. See you all again then!'

Overcome yet again by such kindness, and not a little overjoyed by the prospect of meeting our newly made friends once again, we spluttered our thanks –which fell largely on deaf ears as Sigmund was already edging himself out of his parking spot, waving through the glass as he did so.

While we waited for our onward flight, we could not help but wonder just how amazing our experience had been. All three of us had been profoundly blessed by this extraordinary encounter with people who none of us had literally even heard of just 48 hours ago. And we knew there would be a further, rich encounter the following Sunday which we could also look forward to.

But at that moment we were aware that yet another adventure was about to start. In just a few hours' time, we would be landing in Vadsø. I was savouring the prospect of returning to the place which had given me so much in the short time I lived there. But I also tried to prepare myself against the possibility of disappointment – just in case I was to find that some of its previous, special magic had disappeared over the years. Then I thought - that surely could not be possible … could it?

Chapter 15

Jante Law

The word *frekk* and its cultural and historical relevance needs explanation. When I lived in Norway, *frekk* described a self-effacing attitude in a self-effacing culture. But its meaning was already being questioned in a country yearning to develop and connect in a post-war world, yet not finding it easy to transition from a self-effacing past. Even today, in spite of all its wealth, confidence and creativity, issues around the '*frekk*' culture remain in Norway.

To understand what *frekk* means we have to explore what are known as the laws of *Jante* or *Janteloven*. These were described by the Norwegian/Danish writer Axel Sandemose in his 1933 novel *En Flyktning Krysser Sitt Spor* or *A Fugitive Crosses His Skis*. Although not immediately obvious from the title, *Know Your Place* or *Shame on You if You Think You're Anything Special* might be more appropriate titles to convey the attitudes and way of life that Sandemose exposed.

Jante Law describes the structured behaviour Sandemose experienced growing up in a typical small town in Denmark, largely isolated as roads, bridges and tunnels were non-existent or unreliable. Unsurprisingly, small-town mores emerged overall. Sandemose wrote about such a community in a place he called *Jante*. He describes his childhood experiences in a Puritanical, Calvinist, judgemental system, believing his experiences to be typical of growing up in similar, small towns in Denmark and Norway. Nowadays, roads, tunnels and bridges mean remote places are never disconnected from developed urban areas.

He tells his story through his alter ego - a sailor called Espen - who wants to find out who he is by re-visiting his childhood in *Jante*. He describes day-to-day events and shows how life and behaviour were controlled so that no one grew too big for their boots, or flaunted their achievements, or believed themselves to be different from, or superior to, anyone else.

Sandemose's ideas and experiences struck a nerve in Denmark and Norway - even Sweden, where life has always been more tolerant and sophisticated than her Scandinavian neighbours. The same code of conduct, checking any individual from thinking s/he is better than anyone else, still exists. Many still accept it as a code embedded in Scandinavian culture. The Laws of Jante or *Janteloven* are as follows:

1. Don't think you are anything special.
2. Don't think you are as good as we are.
3. Don't think you are smarter than we are.
4. Don't convince yourself that you are better than we are.
5. Don't think you know more than we do.
6. Don't think you are more important than we are.
7. Don't think you are good at anything.
8. Don't laugh at us.
9. Don't think anyone cares about you.
10. Don't think you can teach us anything.

I am not sure I fully understand how *Janteloven* operates in action today. Even as the world gets ever smaller, we are still brought up and shaped by the values and attitudes that surround us. Young Norwegians still talk about *Janteloven* and ponder the extent of its influence, especially as Norway's global influence grows. *Janteloven's* power may be waning, bit its influence still exists.

It seems to me that there are many similarities between *Janteloven* in Norway and some issues of 'class' in England. For example, there are definite differences between those who live in the North of England and those who live in the South. Both have recognisable values and attitudes and an awareness of class, although both have much weakened since the war.

When I lived in Norway, I do not recall ever talking with anyone about *Jante Law*, although my friend and I regularly chatted about how we wished we were not discriminated against just because we were women. I cannot say that we went as far as being fully paid-up members of what was known in those days as *Women's Lib*, but we were no longer willing to play the same role in society that our mothers had had to. This was a big deal for us in ways which were seen at the time to be extremely radical. Both of us had had excellent education. My friend had spent a year in a Californian High School. I went to a school where an entire female staff included many who had acquitted themselves with distinction during the Second World War, not least having worked at Bletchley Park and other branches of Military Intelligence. So, it was not really surprising that we were inspired to challenge many prevailing attitudes and behaviours of the time.

The ideas held by my friend and myself met with a range of reactions, many of bewildered hostility. In both countries there was also puzzlement since most folk believed that since adult women were able to vote - in Norway since 1913, and in the UK, women over 30 since 1918 - equal status already existed. Any remaining gender differences must therefore de facto be biological and fixed, and thus, *roles* were innate and finite. I see now that in Norway, response might also have been heavily conditioned by aspects of *Janteloven*.

My parents both came from northern, working-class backgrounds. My father wanted the best for his children but abhorred any idea that we should think ourselves better than anyone else just because we had had special opportunities. In line with a plethora of northern stand-up comedians in the 50s and 60s who highlighted differing social attitudes between the North and the South via humour, he taught us a number of idiotic sayings. Because many who lived in the North of England were thought to be of a much lower social and economic class than their southern colleagues at the time, his epithets included sayings such as, 'You think your body every self 'cos your mother's got a mangle,' or 'Get off me neck; me collar cost me ninepence.' Such meaningless sayings were meant to check us in a good hearted and well-intentioned way, from any temptation to get too big for our boots. 'Who d'you think you are?' was a question often put to us in schoolrooms, or at home if we had the nerve to cheek a parent or a teacher, or even volunteer a different opinion. Humour revealed the unpopularity of patronising and superior attitudes, and northern disdain of anything snobby, humiliating or condescending.

Inevitably conversations about how we fitted in specifically as women also involved discussions about the power and influence of class. People were posher and better educated in the South of England than in the North, although that was slowly beginning to change in the '60s, as were attitudes to the role of women in society. However, even as I write, it is still true to say that although social change towards gender equality continues in both countries, in the UK the Public Schools still maintain a dominating male control, providing a pool of educated talent that qualifies males to run most of the mechanisms and processes of our nation's life. Whereas in Norway there are laws that insist on gender equality in all areas of daily life and decision-making processes.

Although it is true to say that there is currently considerably more gender equality in Norway than there is in the UK, *Janteloven* still exists in Norway via the ways it subtly discourages personal bragging and encourages compliance and adherence to rules. General examples of a dislike of bragging would include the fact that even very wealthy Norwegian – of whom there are many – are unlikely to drive a Rolls Royce or its equivalent, around Oslo. This is especially true in these days of generous tax breaks for those driving cars with zero emissions, and the requirement for all cars in Oslo to be pollution-free by 2025. Compliance is infinitely preferrable to social condemnation. Even the private living spaces of the very rich, although larger than others, tend to appear similar to those of their less affluent countrymen. An overall social system that frowns on too much independence, individualism and originality supports one that wants benefit for all.

Personal bragging, self-promotion and individual assertion are all discouraged by *Jante Law* which instead fosters adherence to certain rules. That the power of it still exists, however hard to explain, is exemplified by the Swedish actor Alexander Skarsgård's recent revelation on Stephen Colbert's American, late-night TV show that, although he was proud to have won an EMMY for his role as an abusive husband in *Big Little Lies,* he could not bring himself to display the trophy in his home. That would have been seen as flaunting it, as bragging, or showing off, he said.

The French writer and lawyer, Lorelou Desjardins, living in Norway under Coronavirus restrictions, recently wrote in a Norwegian newspaper about the difference between French and Norwegian responses to government safety rules. She wrote that her compatriots in France brag about getting away with disobeying lockdown rules, declaring it would not matter if they were caught breaking Covid quarantine because they have money to pay the fines. However, she, on the other hand, has come to adhere fully to obeying the Norwegian safety rules for the benefit and safety of everyone, which she sees as crucial to the well-being of society.

Another ironic comment on the automatic power of *Janteloven* is described in a Norwegian newspaper by the Dutch writer, Rutger Bregman. He suggests that Nordic success in today's world comes 'from a well-developed ability in Norwegian society to feel ashamed - by 'success'. Norwegians have put their hearts and souls into a plethora of practical social developments and innovations in the last half century - to the benefit of everyone – health care, advanced education, engineering projects facilitating road-building through mountains of rock, and navigating deep ocean floors, and a commitment to excellence in all forms of art and creativity. And that means that Norwegians stand out and are noticed for the success for which they innately prefer not to brag!'

Today in Norway, *Janteloven* is rarely discussed in the public square although it is an issue in the academic arena. Commitment to the well-being of the whole of society is accepted as important as individual welfare. Proclaiming individual accomplishments is still not actively encouraged - although there is more of it about than there was 50 years ago, not least because great wealth has encouraged many more gifted artists in the public arena. Norway's wealth has underpinned more than just a good standard of living for all.

When I lived in Norway it was still struggling to stand tall after the social and economic ravages of war. Today it is in the top tier of wealthiest countries in the world, with many more billionaires than some other European countries. This has developed a more *me-centred* generation than hitherto, in which it is increasingly possible to enjoy financial, social or cultural success. That is acceptable as long as it does not block others from their paths to triumph nor ignore their basic needs. Bragging about achievement, blowing one's own trumpet, showing off, or giving oneself airs - not uncommon in a world where the *haves* often shout loudly in the public arena - is also not generally tolerated in Scandinavia overall, and most definitely not in Norway. Students and the equivalent of *Guardian* readers in Oslo will even still warn of *Tall Poppy Syndrome*. The specifically Australian or Japanese concept that reminds us that the nail that stands out is the one that gets hammered, thus warning against getting too big for one's boots.

Norway's monarchy – established by democratic agreement in 1814, and hereditary ever since - is widely loved and supported, not least because the king also chooses to see himself as a citizen as well as The King. He prefers to travel on the Oslo underground to the ski-lift for a day's skiing like everyone else, rather than arrive in a chauffeur-driven limousine. He will also do his duty on the Oslo Palace balcony on May 17th standing for several hours in spite of his age, while every child at school in Oslo parades past, each enthusiastically waving their Norwegian flags. The event honours people - the country's future creative seed corn - and future hope. The monarchy endorses both.

Janteloven is difficult to define: its application to daily life is simple yet opaque. The second chapter of the New Testament Book of Acts exhorts us to live together in community, *giving to anyone as they have need*. Such a principle seems to be practised in most aspects of Scandinavian life. Jante Law is definitely a factor in producing some of the humble attitudes that endorse community levelling and support. However, even though it is far from completely dead, today many of its implications and influences are changing. Achievement, success and vision are all breathing self-confidence and level headed self-belief into younger generations of Norwegians.

New Chapter 16

Sparks and Hygge

I had left my skis and boots in the South before travelling north. I had seen enough pictures of northern tundra and its bleak lack of vegetation to feel sure I would not want to make long ski- trips. If I needed them, I could ask my friends to send them on to me. It would also be possible to borrow some, I was sure. As it turned out, it was possible to walk everywhere in Vadsø.

That is, until the days began to shorten, the temperature plummeted, and the snow fell. And snow it certainly did in amounts I had never seen before. As daylight finally disappeared, and the town was gradually shrouded in darkness for days on end, it was also covered in several metres of snow. People skied from home to work, to shop, to school, in fact they skied everywhere.

Spark is an abbreviation of *sparkstøtting* - a cross between a sledge, and a *sparksykkel*, a normal, individual, snow scooter. Seats could carry the smallest of children if carefully and securely strapped in. But mostly they were used for carrying shopping bags or books or briefcases rather than people. It had been almost impossible – I had learned to my painful cost – to *walk* from one place to another. My feet slipped from under me just as soon as I stepped outside my front door whatever kind of footwear I had on, with whatever kind of snow grips attached to the soles and heels. The ice was difficult to see and treacherous to navigate. Once down, it was always difficult to get upright again. Helpless with laughter, it was also almost impossible to get a firm grip under foot. I soon discovered that no one in their right mind would undertake to *walk* or even try to. It would always be a hopeless endeavour.

Using a *spark* was the only reliable way to get about through the long winter months, apart from the skis that lots of people used. There was almost no chance of making progress in any kind of wheeled vehicle. Wheels would often just spin round, unable to grip even with the chains, compulsory by law, affixed to tyres through the winter months. I seem to remember there was one taxi in the town, however, which was available in emergencies. This might mean driving directly following a massive snowplough, that made it possible to make progress in the few seconds before the road became impassable again, just minutes later. Even if the main road in and out of Vadsø was cleared of snow it would always only be for just a short time – minutes even, before snow blocked the way again. Steps up to front doors came into their own at the time of frequent, heavy snow falls. It did not take long before the very top step of at least six, set level with the falls of snow so that their depths were level with the front door for entry and exit.

Snow that fell through the night could be heavy, with two, or three feet sometimes, deposited while everyone slept – especially in November and December. Often the first job of the day was to shovel away from one's front door what had freshly fallen so that it was possible just to OPEN the front door. I rejoiced on many a morning that I now lived in a house where I did not have to start the day by grabbing a snow shovel to clear a snowdrift even before I could get out of the house - thanks to Jon who was always up early to tackle that task.

When I had learned how to propel a *spark* securely and efficiently, it did not take me long to absorb the system that operated in the town, so that everyone could get about safely and easily. Then I believed I needed to get one of my own. So, I asked how to do that one evening.

'Where can I buy a *spark*, Bente?'

'Oh! Goodness me! You don't need to BUY one. Don't even think about it. I wouldn't know where you'd get one anyway! You just need to pick up the nearest one when you go out and leave it outside when you've got to where you're going. Someone else can use it then. There'll be another one available for you - several in fact - when you want to get home or go somewhere else. Or there'll be another one close by. There's never, ever a shortage.'

'But shouldn't I have one in the first place to start with? I mean how can someone "take mine" if I don't have one to take?'

'Oh! You don't need to worry about that! Everybody has at least one spare *spark* in their cellar: more likely several. There are more than enough in the town, believe me! No one who leaves here would think of taking a *spark* with them. They always leave them behind. So, don't worry! You'll soon get the hang of how the system operates. You'll never find there isn't one when you need it. Believe me!'

All Norwegian homes have large cellars for storing clothes and equipment, especially outdoor gear only needed for certain times of the year, such as *sparks*, skis, boots, sledges and rucksacks. The houses also have capacious hallways or vestibules immediately inside the front door with space for discarded outer clothing, as well as bicycles, skis in current use and extremely large backpacks for family day trips. Then there is an inner door that opens into the comfortable living space. They might well be called cloakrooms were it not for the fact that they were large enough to keep equipment as well as hang up removed outer garments. This was true of sports halls, restaurants – in the South – churches and hotels, in fact anywhere at all where people would gather from outside to spend time inside. Whatever the temperature outside, once through the inner door you would be comfortably warm enough to wear shorts and tee shirts or even bikinis, because all Norwegian houses were thoroughly insulated and always warm as toast. In the summer months, winter equipment would be moved to the cellar. And in the South, double and even triple glazing was often removed from all the windows and stored in the cellar until the next wintertime.

I followed Bente's advice. It reminded me about the growing practise of using bicycles I had heard might be starting in some university towns - towns without hills, presumably - at home. You simply left yours outside your destination for someone else to use. You could guarantee to pick another one up if yours had gone when you wanted to use it. It was a great system. I never experienced anyone abusing it, however casual it was.

There were no streetlights in Vadsø, of course, and *sparks* had no headlights. But even in the depths of the darkest days with no daylight, it was always possible to see where you were going because the whiteness of the snow, metres deep everywhere, lit up open spaces like the brightest of moonlight. Gleaming snow on roofs and paths to front doors of houses radiated light as did swathes of pristine snow. Personally, I did not want to go out at night much, I only absolutely had to for choir practises. Unlike my schedule in the South, I had no evening classes to teach. I was thankful for that. I found I was often too tired to venture out at night, and I also generally had work to do. AND, however wrapped up it was possible to be, it was always fiendishly cold.

It fascinated me what was possible to see without daylight. Even when daytime was exactly the same as night-time, ALL the time, it was always light enough to see where you were going and to recognise who might also be *sparking* along the street at the same time as yourself. It was always bright enough to be able to smile at someone else. I learned early on that undaunted, people went to each other's houses regularly of an evening. The lack of TV or cinema, or any kind of eatery or coffee bar, meant everyone made their own fun and used sparks as much as skis to get to and fro.

Getting about by *spark* was not only the most wonderful form of transport I had ever experienced. It had other benefits too. I did not have to take any responsibility for it. I did not need to pass any kind of test to become road worthy. There were no maintenance or insurance costs, no traffic jams, no speed restrictions, no rush hour or parking problems, or indeed any of the many issues that made travelling around by car, even in the smallest of towns and cities in England, increasingly stressful, especially at night. It was not like skating or skiing or riding a bicycle or any other outside sport one could think of. It was not as freezing cold a method of travel either as I had first expected it might be. The energy required in the act of scooting along, meant you created your own warmth as you went. There were never any unhealthy petrol fumes to breathe in from other travellers or danger from someone else's reckless driving, speeding, or generally bad road etiquette either. In fact, there were no hazards to contend with at all.

It turned out to be the greatest fun. Even if you had the bad luck to trip and fall over your *spark*, the mounds of snowdrifts inevitably provided a soft landing – as long as you could get yourself upright again after you had managed to stop laughing! Drunken behaviour would never cause an accident either since the nearest state controlled and owned off-licence, or *Vinmonopolet*, was a *Hurtigruten* trip away. Having said that however, it was nevertheless the case that some people chose to brew or distil their own alcohol. It was illegal to do so, not least because it was often extremely potent, and therefore dangerous. This was not just because Norwegians themselves knew that it was difficult for them NOT to finish the bottle at one sitting. Staggering home with a literal skinful of alcohol could be lethal, especially if a fall in the snow led to a long sleep, from which one therefore never awoke. Every so often while I lived in the Arctic Circle there would be a small article in Monday's daily paper about a person who had fallen asleep by the side of the road, and consequently been found dead because their blood had literally frozen from the cold.

The very existence of *sparks* meant that when at one of my *At Home* evenings, someone raised the question of a choir event at Christmas, I was not concerned that no one would want to turn out at a time of such intense cold and all enveloping darkness.

It was not the first time anyone had asked when the choir was going to sing in public. The timing was perfect. From the enthusiastic discussion that followed, it was obvious that many pupils had already talked a lot about this amongst themselves. Interestingly, I thought, even those who were not actually singers seemed among the most vocal and enthusiastic supporters.

'You really could put on a Christmas Concert, couldn't you? I mean, it would be possible, wouldn't it?'

Someone appealed to me directly with this question. But even though I knew *sparking* could get people where they needed to be, I felt obliged to check and ask a number of pertinent questions.

'Are you sure people would want to venture out just to come and listen to us singing? Surely most people would prefer to stay at home of an evening, in December – of all months. It's so cold and still completely dark. Wouldn't most people prefer to hunker down in the warm at home round their fireplace? Doesn't everyone feel exhausted in mid-December, what with the cold and the dark to contend with? Surely most people wouldn't want to battle twice in one day against them both?'

I genuinely did not know what the response would be. I felt I needed reassurance.

A chorus of various comments such as 'That's not a problem' and 'Not at all' all came out together. Overall, the message from everyone that night was that although people sometimes got confused about what the time was, most people still wanted to get as much out of life as possible, in spite of the piles of snow, the extremely low temperatures and the lack of light through the winter months. The rhythm of life might get more difficult, but not the desire to live it to the full as far as possible. The overall enthusiasm in the room was humbling and encouraging.

I was truly surprised by what they said. I knew just how much everyone enjoyed spending winter evenings round the *peis* so greatly loved by all Norwegians: by all Scandinavians in fact. Even newly built houses, installed with central heating also had a *peis* - the open fireplace around which families and friends sat in the evening - particularly during the cold, dark days of November, December and January. It was a longstanding, inherited and vital aspect of all Scandinavian life. To sit round an open hearth or woodburning stove, enjoying the special smell of burning wood to read and chat, drew people closer together. I had always known that it was from this habit over the many years that all the historic Scandinavian sagas had emerged. Nowadays, candles would be lit, as coffee and *smørbrød* would be served throughout the evening. At every possible social level, fellowship was enjoyed, and relationships strengthened.

But, of course, it was not necessarily the ONLY way *hygge* could be created and enjoyed. This is another untranslatable word, understood by all Scandinavians.

Like so many French words and phrases such as *tour de force* or *de rigeur*, it needs to be absorbed in its own right into English and understood as it stands in its original meaning. I could only ever explain the general concept of *hygge* rather than offer a translation of what it meant, to my English friends and family. *Hygge* is achieved via a specific way of life and has to do with living in community. As one of the deeply embedded essentials at the heart of Norwegian, indeed of all Scandinavian life, the spirit of which was not to be cowed or extinguished, even in such a harsh climate anywhere throughout the whole country, not just in the Arctic Circle, I always found *hygge* inspiring. In fact, to be cheerful against all odds was positively encouraged via *hygge*. It helped strengthen family and friendship bonds.

What I came to see and understand was that *hygge* was what it was at the centre of the choir's activities. That was why everyone in the choir had such a great time **because** *hygge* was everywhere. Loyalty to it as an entity made every rehearsal, every coming together, every event inspiring. *Hygge* encouraged and fostered connection. I came to see that it was that above all else – together with an innate love of singing - that basic *peis* ritual and culture which fostered the very kind of *hygge* that had made the choir so appealing and encouraged the enthusiasm that made it so successful. No wonder I enjoyed working with the choir so much!

Chapter 17

International Relations

Working with the choir had become one of my weekly highlights. It was enormous fun to make music with such an enthusiastic crowd of young people. It also helped forge relationships. Every singer seemed as keen as mustard to learn and work at producing the best possible sound and enjoy every practice as much as I did. By early October, after just two months since the beginning of term in early-August, everyone was learning how important it was to listen to each other as well as themselves. Hence, in good voice, the choir was beginning to sound like a proper group of longstanding. Everyone was also learning to blend and what was meant by musical colour and phrasing. The whole choir was beginning to sound like a homogenous group that had been making music, singing together for years.

The prevailing atmosphere at every practice was inspiring, and even when I felt exhausted at the beginning of a rehearsal, I always felt revitalised by the end of it. Never before had I felt so grateful for all I had been taught about how to lead and conduct singing while I was at school. Never before had I benefitted so much from the instinctive enthusiasm I had caught from my father, to encourage a group of people to make music together. Within just a few weeks, we had learned how to sing several negro spirituals, loads of rounds - some well-known, and some more obscure – some popular folk songs as well as several Norwegian songs and one or two international hymn tunes with a variety of different lyrics.

So, real social and choral progress had been made by the middle of October when the idea of a Christmas event was first raised at an *At Home*. That same week I introduced a couple of Norwegian Christmas carols at our weekly rehearsal.

Some weeks previously, after several choir practices, two singers came up to me during the break while everyone else was chatting. I was getting to know Grethe well. I already knew she was a person of some gravitas because of her wise help and kindness to Hannah. She had a great voice - strong, always in tune and clear as a bell. She led the sopranos and gave them confidence. She had persuaded the lad with her to speak to me and supported him while he approached me. I did not know Carl personally. I only knew from hearing him in the choir that he had an exceptionally beautiful tenor voice.

'Could you give us singing lessons?' Grethe asked, plunging straight in. 'I had some a while back, but I've lapsed. I'd love to have help again.'

'Well! I'm not really qualified to teach singers individually,' I said. 'I don't know if I could really be of any real help.'

'You could. I know you could,' Grethe insisted. 'You know far more about singing than we do. I know that because I've learnt so much already from our choir practices. Even if you could just accompany me sometimes and help me with phrasing, I'm sure I'd learn loads. I'd pay you, of course.'

'I couldn't accept your money,' I said. I thought I could possibly help – with general musicality if nothing else. But I was not a qualified professional, and in any case, I wouldn't want the pressure of transaction to interfere with the pleasure of working with her. 'For a start, I don't have a qualification to teach singing individually. And in any event, I'd want to be free to say that I'm not free sometimes – if I'm too tired, for example. But I'd certainly be willing to play for you and help you with technique - breathing and phrasing and projecting - that sort of thing if that would help?'

Carl was shy but singing brought him to life. His story was similar to Grethe's. He had had singing lessons in the past, but now needed a wash and brush up. He wanted to move forward and learn new songs, if possible. I said the same to him as to Grethe.

'We were wondering if you had thought about what we would do at Christmas?' Grethe asked. She looked at me as if trying to read my reaction. Undaunted, she continued. 'We know it's already been mentioned to you. We know someone's also already been primed to ask you again before we settle down after the break.'

She was right. Sure enough, a soprano, who I did not know well got up straight after our short interval.

'Miss Russell! Before we start again, could we discuss the possibility of a Christmas concert?'

Immediately, there was a hum of excited chatter.

'Goodness me! Settle down! Hush!' I was flabbergasted to see the degree of energy unleashed in the room. I hadn't given the proposal much thought – well, none at all, really.

I had been slow to see how much enthusiasm and support there was for the choir behind the scenes, everywhere - and not just in school either. In the town, people I had not even met seemed to make a point of smiling at me in the street. One or two even stopped to shake my hand, bow or curtsey according to the charming custom that I so admired. Sometimes they spoke in a stream of unintelligible North Norwegian dialect that I could not translate. All I could do was smile and say, 'Thank you'.

Inspired therefore, I canvassed further opinion a day or so later.

'We're thinking about a choir event for Christmas' I said, as I poured the first round of tea to a gathering of youngsters.

'We know. Per Johann is already canvassing support. And, as you know, no one dares to say no to him. Alf Lundeström is too, even though he's not IN the choir,' Grethe's friend Turild enthused.

'I'm quite sure they don't,' I said. 'He really is a most remarkable and persuasive young man!' They knew I meant Per Johan.

'He is indeed. No doubt about that. Did you know that he skis to school over the *Finnmarkvidda* at the beginning of every term and then sometimes back home again at the end of it?'

'No, I didn't. I know his home is some distance away, but I took it he would come and go on the *Hurtigruten* each term like other people.' I paused before asking, 'How far does that mean he actually has to ski?'

'It's just over 200 English miles from his home - Honningsvåg - to here,' Grethe went on. 'It usually takes him three days. He cooks for himself and sleeps in the open in his one-man tent. He finds his way via compass bearings. He loves it, and he's never messed up. Once there was heavy snow through one night. It took him a while to dig himself out the next morning. So, he took **four** days to get here. We were all anxious that he was late, but not really over-worried because he is such an excellent skier and knows how to look after himself in the open better than anyone else. He loves being alone too, with the vast expanse of nothingness all around him.'

I had only a vague idea how vast the *Finnmarksvidda* was. I knew it was a huge, forbidding expanse of land – an enormous, empty plateau with no sign of life, apart from the odd cabin dotted here and there. There were no trees, just a few plants and shrubs. Moss, the essential diet for reindeer, covered huge areas of ground which they could only find under the snow via smell, not by sight, which meant there was no green to be seen. Reindeer, and other small Arctic animals, such as hares and foxes, were the only creatures that thrived on the *vidda*. Fifty years ago, the whole *vidda* was meters deep in snow for months on end. As I write this chapter, the increasing scarcity of heavy snow falls remains a worry to Sami herdsmen.

Grethe continued, 'It would be incredibly easy to get lost in several hundred square miles of space which looks exactly the same whichever way you turned if you didn't know what you were doing. And if you WERE to get lost, it might take days for others to find you. Personally, I would never dare risk it. But Per Johann will never get lost.'

'Well! That's so impressive.' I was lost in admiration.

'Well, it's because we all know how capable he is that makes us respect him so much. He's a great person too. He doesn't tolerate fools. But he'll never put up with anyone being unkind, mean or selfish. We all respect him, and he deserves us to – even those who don't actually know him. You HAVE to listen to him and hear what he says. He's really kind and tremendously knowledgeable about all sorts of things.'

'I see,' I said. 'I'm beginning to understand where he gets his *frekk* sense of humour!' Grethe grinned. 'No wonder he's always able to insult people with the utmost courtesy,' I said. She laughed outright.

'Well, he's outgrown school. But he needs certain qualifications to move on with his life. So, he tolerates it and puts his all into finding out and learning what he knows he needs to know.'

Every Norwegian Gymnas accepted students of all ages at final Artium level. There were several students in all year groups of the Vadsø Gymnas who had returned to study. They needed certain qualification to continue their education, especially those who needed to move on to specific professional studies, like medicine, engineering, teaching or dentistry. I had only come across one or two such students in the South who returned to school to gain qualifications. But in Vadsø there were several in these final years.

The room had gone quiet. Everyone was listening to what Grethe had to say. They nodded in agreement as she spoke.

'You might think he's asleep in your classes, Miss Russell. But he listens to every word you say,' someone I did not even teach said that.

I thought it was truly astonishing that he was willing to take *me* seriously. How difficult life would be if he didn't. I'd have got on the *Hurtigruten* to go back home ages ago. I was beginning to see the extent of his influence. He obviously possessed strong, natural leadership qualities. He would go far in life.

I needed to make a fresh pot of tea and so excused myself and wandered into my small kitchen. While I waited for the kettle to boil, I remembered the conversation I had had with Per Johann after the first ever choir practice. I was clearing up, lost in thought about how to decide and produce what to sing. I'd have to devise everything from scratch without manuscript paper or music. I was wondering what in the world I had just agreed to, when suddenly I heard my name. Per Johann was standing beside me.

'Thanks,' he said. 'I really enjoyed that. It was great!' He hesitated. Then said, 'May I ask you something?'

'Of course.'

'Do you get paid overtime for doing this?'

'No,' I said. 'Whatever makes you think I might? Why would you even ask me that?'

'You mean you don't get paid anything at all for starting and running a choir?'

'Absolutely not,' I managed to smile. 'It's good to meet you at last, by the way, Per Johann.' He smiled. 'Please tell me why you're asking me,' I asked again.

'No particular reason. I just had a bet with myself that's all. Why *are* you doing this then?'

'I *want* to. It's such good fun. And I hoped some of you would think so too. I also thought it would help me learn more about you all.'

This was the truth, and I could see he accepted what I said.

'I thought as much – that you would be doing this out of the kindness of your heart. I'm glad I was right.'

He smiled again. And for a fleeting moment I thought he was going to hug me. And then to my amazement, I found myself suppressing the desire to hug him. For all his disguised maturity, he seemed vulnerable, but in a particularly adult way. I wondered what he had experienced in his young life that had made him so mature. But teachers in Norway were not usually allowed to know about their students' backgrounds, and I would not have dreamt to ask him.

The kettle came to the boil. I poured the steaming water into the teapot and returned to the merry party in my living room. It sounded almost as if a programme for a Christmas Concert was already in full discussion.

'Getting back to what we were talking about,' someone else contributed for the first time, 'could we set up a small group to talk with you, Miss Russell, about how to put a programme together? Grethe, you *have* to sing a solo for a start.'

Grethe grinned. It was clear she would like that.

'And then there's Carl: he's been wanting to sing O Holy Night in public for ages. It's his most special party piece. He's been LONGING to sing it – and have someone accompany him too. But of course, since it's a Christmas piece, he's never yet had the chance.'

I could feel the genuine strength of commitment and excitement from all sides. But I knew that putting on some kind of Christmas event would take time and effort. I wanted to be absolutely certain it was what everyone wanted before I went ahead with plans. I decided to raise it as a serious proposition at the next choir practice.

'What do you all think about it?' I asked, sensing the overwhelming feelings of enthusiasm in the room.

Everyone wanted to speak at once.

'We could sing as a whole choir and also do some things in groups, or solos, couldn't we?'

'There are individuals who're used to singing in public: they sing solos regularly for events like family parties.'

'There are those who'd love to sing as a foursome – perhaps for the first time.'

'It's called a quartet, I murmured, in response to so many things being said at once. No one heard me though. Correct language was upstaged by overwhelming enthusiasm from all corners of the room.

After a few minutes I took charge.

'These are excellent ideas. But before we get into all that, I'll have to talk to Rektor Andersen to see what he thinks. I'll need to sort out the best way to proceed after that. And then, I need to know if we have to book somewhere, like The Assembly Hall.

'There are all sorts of things we would automatically do in England to organise something like this. I would need help with planning about how best to do things.' I paused. 'I think we'd definitely need to form a committee, to sort out things and make plans.'

'I could get a group of people together to do all that,' Turild, Grethe's bosom pal, volunteered. 'I'd like to do that. My Dad will help too. Actually, he's already asked what plans we have.'

I knew Turild's Dad would be a great help. He was the secretary-cum-bursar for the entire school complex that included all education levels in the town. An excellent administrator, he had exactly the skills and experience that made things happen and run smoothly. He knew everyone too, and who to ask about what.

Turild spoke again. 'We could liaise with you about everything – and in any case, you'd probably want to join us as we sorted things out, wouldn't you? I think we'd really need you to do that.'

Once again, I was amazed how mature these youngsters were. As a complete outsider, it seemed to me they had so little. Their southern counterparts had sports grounds, parks, cinemas and increasing numbers of shops and cafes on their doorsteps. Here there was little on offer to support any recreational or social life. Even so, they had an enviable community spirit. What their parents and grandparents had been through during the war must surely have helped make this next generation strong, positive and outward looking perhaps without even realising it, even though no one mentioned the war socially the whole year I was there. I was particularly impressed by the way they encouraged each other to play to their strengths and use them. AND they also knew what each other's strengths and gifts were.

A day or so after this conversation, Turild's Dad approached me as I sat in the staff room.

'Excuse me Miss Russell. Could you spare me a minute to talk?' Sven Pedersen gave his name in the correct Norwegian way and bowed from his waist. He was not exactly tentative but slightly flushed with cautious embarrassment. 'I have a favour to ask.'

'Of course, what can I do for you Herr Pedersen?' I stood up as he spoke. He had made no attempt to sit.

'I think you know I organise one or two things in the town. My daughter might have told you. Well, the thing is we've arranged a cultural event in 10 days' time, in the Sports Hall. Anyone with any musical talent or dramatic skill will perform. We have a town band, for example, and they will play. And there is someone who always recites monologues. This year, we've persuaded someone from Hardanger to play the Hardanger fiddle. Perhaps you've heard of those?'

'I have indeed, and I've been to a special event where several of them played at once – last year in the South. It was wonderful.' I was excited, even before I knew what Herr Pedersen was going to ask me.

'Well, there are various items, as I said. It's a family fun event. It's given us an opportunity to invite some Russian friends to sing for us - or with us - too. We were helped by the Russians in the latter part of the war, you know, and have a special kind of cultural relationship with contacts in the city of Murmansk. Anyway, there's a male quartet coming from there to sing.' He paused. 'And the thing is, we, I suppose I mean ... I, wondered if you would sing a couple of British folk songs for us, perhaps?' He blushed almost crimson at this point.

Although I had only been in Vadsø a couple of months, I already knew there were longstanding connections between Murmansk and some Finnmark towns. It was a commonly held view was that the name 'Murman' was a russification of the word, 'Nordmenn'. So, it would be natural to have some sort of cultural contact between the two towns. Pedersen went on to tell me that a College of Arts, including a Music Department had been opened a few years before in 1958.

Coming from the UK as I did, I was understandably cautious about the Soviet Union. At the same time, I was coming to understand that some Norwegian towns in the North, including Vadsø, hosting as it did a NATO station that was vital to Europe, although wary of Soviet policies had a more positive view of Russians than I was used to. I felt I should try to learn from that even though I felt uneasy. After all, here was a marvellous opportunity to build bridges. And weren't all things cultural meant to be bringing people together? I knew I should try to be positive.

Much, much later, as I was writing this book and was in touch with a Tromsø journalist who had written a brilliant book which I had read about the German razing of Finnmark in 1944 and 1945, have I managed to get anything like a real grasp of affairs. I realise now that I was not alone in my reservations. There was anxiety in Norway in the 1960s about their Northern border with Russia, and a fear by some that the Russians might try to infiltrate the West via Norway's back door.

'I'd love to sing.' I said. 'It sounds a marvellous event. I'm flattered to be asked.'

'Oh good. That's so kind. Perhaps we could speak again in a day or so – when I've more of an idea how the whole thing will be coming together? Perhaps you could think about what you might like to sing in the meantime – a couple of English folk songs, perhaps?' He stressed the word 'English' as he asked.

The thought of actually meeting some real, live Russians, being in the same room as them and even, maybe, shaking them by the hand, felt an extraordinary prospect on many levels. I knew it was significant. I had known how close Vadsø is to the Russian border before I had even been asked to go there. Moreover, several of my Vadsø colleagues had been across into Russia on permitted day trips already. Such visits were encouraged between the two countries. I had written to the appropriate authorities to ask for a visitor's visa to cross into Russia too, but had been refused permission because I was not Norwegian and would have needed more time to have my particulars checked so that I could obtain a visa. When I mentioned the Russian visitors to the Flysts, they too were thrilled.

'You're bound to be introduced to them all,' Bente said as we chewed the cud together over some strong coffee to revive ourselves in the middle of a long, dark day. 'Why don't you ask if you could bring the quartet back here? You could suggest you make them a cup of English tea as a sort of cultural exchange?' She roared with laughter at the thought. I noticed she often roared with laughter as a nervous reaction after making a helpful comment which she seemed to fear might be overly bold and daring.

'Bente! That's a brilliant idea. On the grounds of international friendship alone, Sven Pedersen is bound to consider your suggestion. I'll pop into his office tomorrow and ask him.'

'Are you sure?' Bente asked. 'Won't he think it rather *frekk* to ask? I only suggested it as a joke.'

Pedersen thought it an excellent suggestion and said it would add an extra cultural dimension to the whole venture – visiting a Norwegian home, experiencing English tea served round a Norwegian *peis*. 'It will be a rich, cultural exchange indeed! It all helps to build good relationships and break down barriers of mistrust,' he said. I asked if he would like to join our tea party, but he politely and charmingly asked to be excused. He did not say why, but I suspected he might feel awkward at such an unusual social event.

I thought our Russian visitors might be used to strong vodka and that it would be their drink of choice in the winter months. So, it was just as well that no one would be in a position to serve alcohol at Bente's. Throughout the country, alcohol was only sold in government owned and controlled shops, called *Vinmonopolet* which were open for certain hours each weekday. Since there was no *Vinmonopolet* in Vadsø in those days, only a two-day *Hurtigruten* trip to Kirkenes, would produce sophisticated bottles of alcohol in those days.

I cannot remember how the Russians actually arrived at the Flysts' home or who accompanied them. Whoever brought them did not stay for tea. I cannot even remember if Øystein was with us although he was likely to have been. The concert would not have been his style, but fostering international relations certainly was, and he may well have been there too. However, I can clearly remember that it was an extraordinary experience. The Russians spoke no English or Norwegian. None of the rest of us spoke Russian. Yet we related to each other in an effective warm and friendly way. It is amazing how much can be communicated through sign language and laughter alone.

Tea and cake were served exactly as they would have been in England. *Hygge* round the *peis* was Norwegian. After feasting over afternoon tea, warmed by the open hearth, the quartet sang to us again - in Russian. What could be a more genuine cultural experience than that? The Murmansk quartet even had a tape of their songs which they presented to me in style, accompanied by a stream of Russian that no one understood but took to be hugely friendly, judging by the wide smiles, low bows and vigorous handshakes. In addition to recently recovering the tape, I have also found – to my joy and delight – a note of their names which they themselves wrote down for me. I do not know where those four young men are. They may even have passed away by now. But I recall that event as I write with feelings of warmth and joy, simply because it was delightful to make music together and share hospitality in a welcoming environment in which we were all just human beings having fun and enjoying each other's company. And could they sing!

Here are the names of those four singers plus their manager that I recently happened to come across and did not know I had kept. I write as they have written themselves. If anyone reading this book happens to know anything at all about any of these gentlemen, or their families or their descendants, I would of course be thrilled to hear from you! My email address is:

mollyfletcher7@gmail.com

Nikitin Igor,
Murmansk pzoesd Kapitan
TARAN, 17, kb 51

Tshugunow Ewgenij,
Murmansk,
Lenin Street 4

Jurkow Juri,
Murmansk,
Profsojusow-street
1, kb.53

Syssojew Wassilij,
Murmansk,
Musical scool NL

Borissow Wladimir,
Murmansk,
Milizejskaja street,
3, kb 42

Chapter 18

All Things Fiscal

Per Johan's question about whether I was paid overtime needs a contextual explanation. My time in Norway between 1964 and 1966 was a couple of years before the large-scale discovery of oil from the North Sea Ekofisk field in 1969 went viral, as the say. The Snøhvit Barents Sea 5,500 miles of gas pipeline had not been laid either. Neither were fully operational until after the turn of the Millennium. Today, these resources of oil and natural gas provide the largest share of Norway's annual income as the main contributors to her overall, considerable wealth. Recent figures indicating how much money the country still accrues from the 1960s oil discovery, show that in 2018 the quantity of oil recovered each **day** was in the region of 1.8 billion gallons. In 2017, the total value of Norway's oil exports alone was approximately 442bn kroner. In addition, the country also exports vast amounts of gas, including to the UK, as well as large quantities of lumber, a variety of minerals and sea food and a considerable quantity of fresh water. This puts a hefty balance of payments in the black for 5,500,000 people. The Norwegian government itself has substantial holdings in all its prominent industries. That fact alone helps cap the numbers of possible super rich individuals and is a policy that underlines Norway's overall attitude about what it means to live in a society to which everyone contributes, and in which everyone is cared for.

For 50 years or so from 1945, elected governments had been politically central or to the left, and government policy prioritised support for high quality social and welfare needs. There are plentiful funds to ensure that everyone can have access to the best health care and be well provided for on all social and practical fronts. Everyone is also well-educated and highly literate. Support for the social glue that encourages overall harmony and happiness reveals the Norwegian state's belief in, and commitment to, maintaining responsibility for all its citizens, even when under severe pressure such as during the years following the world-wide collapse of banks. Comprehensive funds and forward planning to meet social needs – schools, surgeries, hospitals, care homes, transport - is also extended to immigrants.

In 1966, however, life was totally different. I remember the first time I was asked how much I had paid for something when I pulled out from my handbag a gold-plated, Parker, fountain pen that had belonged to my father. Two or three people standing close by all said 'ooh' or 'aah' or 'goodness me!'. The student himself, Hans - it was an adult class - was clearly impressed and equally unabashed.

'That looks expensive,' he said. 'How much was it?'

'I don't actually know,' I said, taken aback and feeling uncomfortable to be asked such a direct and, what would have been thought in England to be an inappropriately intrusive, even rude, question. 'I inherited it from my father.'

'How much would he have had to pay, then? How much did it cost to buy it in the first place?' Hans asked in formal English, enraptured by the pen as he continued to stare at it in my hand.

'I don't know that, either.' I said. 'He had it for as long as I can remember, and I never thought to ask him.'

Hans wanted to know more. He took the pen from me and twirled it round between his fingers. 'Is it usual to own a pen like this? Do many people in England have one?'

I remember feeling extremely uncomfortable: anxious about his close examination of my Dad's beautiful writer and embarrassed at being asked about how much it cost. I did not know what to say, especially as I knew Hans would never knowingly offend anyone or deliberately cause them discomfort. And after all, what did it matter what he was asking? He wasn't doing anything wrong or unkind. Nevertheless, I felt really ill at ease.

'Well! Most people use fountain pens. It's necessary in schools, for instance' I replied, 'where everyone is supposed to have an ink pen to write with, especially at exam times and for formal essays. But there are many firms who produce a range of styles and quality. You can buy cheaper or much more expensive ones, depending, I suppose, on how often you will use it and for what exactly. This one writes really well, which is why I used to borrow it when my Dad was alive if I needed to write something in my very best handwriting.'

I knew I was rambling as I struggled against my inappropriate feelings of indignation and confusion.

Working through and overcoming my reactions from my own cultural reserve helped me to see that what Hans was asking was simply a way of re-connecting with the commercial world. Norwegians had only recently been in a position to start doing that, even as they were emerging from their own reconstruction programmes after the War. It would have been the same for Per Johan. He knew how tight family incomes were in Finnmark in the mid '60s, and how people would be glad to learn about extra work that paid well. He also knew that wages were higher at that time in the UK. How could he have known how his question would have been received in England? His question was not at all improper. He would be one of the last people ever to deliberately make someone else feel uncomfortable.

Today, Hans will be enjoying the benefits of personal wealth and reliable services. He will also be able to get about more easily than he did nearly 60 years ago. Nearly every small town has its own airport, so he could currently fly from the South to the North any day of his choice. If he wanted to drive, he could reach the remotest of places on decent, well maintained roads with brilliant bridges of any length, the longest of which is taking individuals and heavy loads from one place to another across the deepest of rivers and gorges every single day. Sixty years ago, he would have had to rely on ferries to get from island to island in most parts of the country. Today, tunnels, hewn out of rocks and mountains and dug under the sea connect the most unlikely places. Billions of kroner have been poured into the building and upkeep of roads, accommodating transport of all weights and sizes. The advanced engineering skills that have facilitated the building of roads, are being taught and learnt all the time by expert Norwegian engineers. Norwegian road builders rank among the most skilled in the world.

Today, the Norwegian economy could not be more different from how it was in the mid 60s. In addition to enjoying well paid jobs, Norwegians are now favoured with a high standard of personal and social security, free and accessible health care as well as life in a highly civilised society in which music and the arts flourish, emphasis is put on style and quality for all shapes and sizes of buildings, and travel inside and out of the country is popular. Few, if any, people are what could be described as 'poor'. Wages are high; unemployment, low. In 2020, a typical Norwegian salary was 612,000NOK Norwegian Kroner – approximately £52,000 – which would make an average monthly salary in the region of £4,300, although some especially in the far North of the country, would earn considerably less, and many in the developing industries would earn considerably more.

Prosperity today stems from several important background factors. Firstly, a series of Labour Laws from 1892 to 1936 laid the foundations to ensure that any work force would be treated fairly. This established and relied on a culture of trust between employers and employees that ensured pay differentials would always be fair. A mind set of equality of worth established this trust between employers and employees that has lasted over the years as the background to all employment negotiations in all fast-developing industries.

Secondly, since 1947, Norwegians have been able to borrow money from the state to pay for all avenues of further and higher education. This has meant that when the oil and gas discoveries were made in the 1960s, there were already educated engineers, accountants and technicians ready and able to cope with what was necessary to develop businesses, understand technology and ensure that a whole generation of technicians and engineers was ready and able to take things further at a rapid pace and to deeper and wider levels. Able and educated people were absolutely ready for new and interesting tasks. They were also keen to innovate with their substantial knowledge of technology. Money borrowed for further and higher education had to be repaid over time. But the wealth enabled by the oil and gas industries meant that repayment was not as heavy a demand on normal, personal finances as it would have been in many other countries or at many other times.

However, personal income tax – between 30 and 45 per cent for many professionals and business-people – is high. Purchase tax on luxury goods and alcohol is also considerable. Excellent health and social security services have to be paid for, as do the guaranteed comfortable lifestyles for seniors and investment in the well-being of future generations. Currently, as also mentioned in a previous chapter, the government can claim that each Norwegian citizen has an endowment of around £200,000 – if available state funds were to be equally divided between every single citizen. In spite of high levels of income tax and the fact that luxury goods especially are extremely highly taxed and therefore, expensive – currently, the Forbes List ranks Norway as the second most expensive country in the world after Switzerland, and fourth on the world's highest salaries list after Luxembourg, the US and Switzerland again – the standard of living is rated as one of, if not actually the, highest in the world.

Prosperity also spills over into many other aspects of life. Nowadays, most families can afford at least one car: often two, and increasingly, one per person or more. The government wants people to buy cars with zero pollutant emission and so taxes those at a lower rate than other cars. Parliament has decided that by 2025, all new cars must be electric or some other kind of zero pollution-emitting vehicle. Even though such cars are expensive, more than 55 percent of Norwegian car owners already possess emission-free vehicles. Many people own, or at least have access to, a family ski cabin. Many also have a summer cabin by the sea which they probably built themselves as a family project in the years after the war. Whether or not they live by the sea a goodly number also own boats. Climate change has altered the fishing weekend habits of 50 years ago, especially in the Arctic Circle where temperatures are rising at worryingly fast speeds for fishing overall. But it has not dimmed the Norwegian love of boating.

A much wealthier Norway has facilitated a huge investment in all forms of the arts, especially music. One of the world's first orchestras, the Bergen Philharmonic, was founded in 1765, with just 40 players. Ole Bull himself, also from Bergen, was its principal violinist for a large part of the nineteenth century at the same time as Edvard Grieg - another Bergen citizen - was composing at his creative height. Robert Schuman, no less, described Bull's playing as possibly even better than Paganini's. Grieg, working with excellent musicians of the time, developed ideas and themes from early Norwegian folk music to be played by classical orchestras. His Peer Gynt Suite is one of the best known of such works. Just like other contemporary nationalist composers, equally inspired by the life and beauty of their own countries, his compositions were encouraged by his love of nation and a deep sense of patriotism.

In 2018, Norway – from a population of a mere 5.5m – had no fewer than 16 fully performing orchestras, including The Arctic Symphony Orchestra, homed between both Tromsø and Bodø. Hardly surprising then that in 2011, there were no fewer than 85 applicants for the post of trombone player in the Oslo Radio Orchestra. Unsurprising also that as recently as 2017, an 81-year-old violinist had to pay the equivalent of £2,5m in income tax alone – and not just because he had sold one of his violins for £100,000 pounds, but rather because, being a really good player in the entertainment business in Norway today can earn a musician a great deal of money – even after a huge tax bill.

Not all Norwegian music-making today, however, is of a full blast symphonic or classical repertoire. Two current, unique examples of innovative and thriving musical creativity can be found in the annual Chamber Music Festival at Risør and a recently founded, new choir, known as *Nidaros Domen's Jentekor* based at the Cathedral in Trondheim. Risør is a tiny fishing village, on the coast to the South of Oslo, long known for its singular beauty and love of boating as well as its reputation to be a delightful place to live. Since 1991, however, it has also hosted a Chamber Music Festival each June in its tiny, white, wooden, baroque church, built in 1647, with space for just 450 people. Originally inspired by the internationally acclaimed, Norwegian pianist, Leif Ove Andsnes, the best of soloists and chamber players from all over the world are only too delighted to go and play all kinds of chamber music, both classical and modern. Tickets are sold out, months beforehand.

The equally inspirational, but quite differently innovative *Nidaros Domen's Jentekor* was founded in 1992 in Trondheim, under its conductor, Anita Brevik. This incredible choir is made up of girls between the ages of 12 and 18, who manage to produce the most sublimely pure, and homogenous sound. On a recent trip, I was privileged to experience the transporting delight of one of their concerts in Nidaros Cathedral itself, where the acoustics enhance the purist of pure sounds from the whole choir together as well as in smaller group combinations and solos. An accompaniment, if required, was provided by percussionists, drummers, a guitar player and a Cathedral organist. This unusual combination managed to create something acutely special and new.

All kinds of civic buildings have also needed recent investment. The administrative building to house the dealings of the expanding oil industry was completed in 2012. The Stat Oil/Equinor office building is often described by critics as the best office building in the world. Two and a half thousand people work in 66,000sq m of a building that looks like a giant game of Jenga on the banks of the Oslo Fjord.

Architecture is booming as an industry in Norway. With money now available and on the scale that it is, innovative design can produce whatever is truly desired, no matter what the cost. In the last 30 years, Norwegian architects have been able to use their considerable creative gifts to design public buildings which are more than just fit for purpose. The Opera House in Oslo, where people are encouraged to walk on and ski down from the roof, is most usually cited as an example – renowned for the specially wonderful acoustics inside as much as the various family attractions on and around its exterior.

This striking building completed in 2008, seats over 1,300 in its auditorium. But it has many other functions apart from hosting operas, ballets and other concerts – both inside and out. There are places to sit and chat as well as eat. Outside as well there are spaces for a variety of outdoor entertainments and visitors are positively encouraged to visit it for social reasons as well as to experience all the outstanding operatic productions. A variety of art projects function inside; plays and stand-up entertainments outside. It is designed to be a place to meet others, sit and relax and be inspired. As the largest Norwegian building to be constructed since the 12th century, the new Oslo opera house dominates one side of the inner-city, Oslo fjord.

Another Cathedral completed in Alta in 2013, which won a prestigious prize for design in 2001, could not be more different from the Cathedral in Trondheim, built in the classical Romanesque Gothic style with its foundations laid in 1070. Alta's Cathedral is sculpted to reflect the shape of the Northern Lights, and from some angles, even looks like a submarine. It is a far cry from anything constructed even by any Norman or Gothic predecessors who built many places of worship, awesome in style, size, concept, use and accessibility throughout Europe. But nevertheless, Alta's Cathedral is highly regarded as a place of worship. Similarly, in that it conceptualises and reflects aspects of the Scandinavian environment, the Vennesla Library in Agder, looks like the inside of a whale's ribs. The divided wooden cubicles provide comfortable spaces to sit and read. Another civic building recently completed - in 2009 - at a cost of 1.7 bn kroner - is Kristiansand's Concert Hall in Kilden which serves both as an arts centre and as a base for the Kristiansand Symphony Orchestra.

Per Johann, Alf Lindstrøm, Grethe, Karl, Sissel, Elsa and many others whose names, though changed, are mentioned in this book as well as all those who are not, will have lived through these years of change. Now, they will surely look back on their lives and may well rejoice with their children and grandchildren that today there is peace and choice and a decent standard of living throughout the country. Maybe they and many others who I taught nearly 60 years ago, were swept along by adventures that began with Ekofisk and continue to this day with organisations like the Arctic Barents Programme, which helps preserve and develop the Arctic environment. Maybe some of them are living in America or China or Australia. Wherever they are, they all, together with their families and contemporary friends from days in Vadsø will look back on lives of enormous development and change. Grethe, Hannah, Carl, Thor, Alf, Arne and many others – whose names have all been changed because I do not know where they are in the world, so have not asked if I can write about them - and many, many other gifted, resolute and mature youngsters at the time, must surely have played their part in Norway's amazing development. All those wonderful youngsters who sang so enthusiastically cannot have failed to have made their mark over time, and also made and left a difference in their communities. Perhaps they have even sometimes reflected on their good fortune to have been school-students at a time when their government was keen for future generations to be equipped to branch out in life and explore whatever it and the world had to offer them?

1. Me with my aunt - swimming in the *fjord* at Flåm on my first visit to Norway in 1953.

2. The steps from Vadsø's only hotel to the Finnish Monument, erected in front of Vadsø's Administration Building in 1977.

3. Vadsø's School Complex in November 1965.

4. Half of the Vadsø School Choir at the Carol Concert in December 1965.

5. Honningsvåg – from where Per Johan skied across the *Finnmarkvidda* to school – seen from the *Hurtigruten*, February 1966.

6. Docking at Vadsø's ice-bound harbour, February 1966.

7. An ice-bound fishing vessel in Vadsø's harbour, February 1966.

8. Outside Marcus Svenungsen's cabin on the *Finnmarkvidda*, late February 1966.

9. View from our bus ride across the *Finnmarkvidda*, May 2019.

10. Environs of our Honningsvåg glamp site, May 2019.

11.Vadsø school leavers ready to parade on May 17th, *Sytennde Mai,* 1966.

12. A comparatively tiny tributary river thaw, May 1966.

13. Myself and my choir friend wearing *bunad* in Iceland, May 1965.

14. Entrance to Tromsø's
Ishavskatedralen, May 1966.

15. The organ loft of
Tromsø's *Ishavskatedralen*.

Chapter Nineteen

The Joy of Carols

Rektor Anderson gave thumbs up to the Christmas project when I went to see him about it the next day. He was also gracious enough to apologise for doubting the whole idea of starting a choir.

'I must say,' he said, 'I'm astonished that the choir has already come so far. Of course you must go ahead with a Christmas event. I feel totally embarrassed every time I think about the cold water I poured on your suggestion when you first mentioned it. Just think, if I'd managed to put you off, and you'd never put up your notice, we'd certainly not be having this conversation.'

He grinned awkwardly. But I thought what he said showed real generosity of spirit.

'I too am amazed at the choir's enthusiastic spirit,' I said.

Practical conversations began at the next practice.

'It seems we ARE going to put on a Christmas event!' I said. There was a roar of approval.

'No one HAS to take part if they would rather not,' I continued. 'But I hope you all will feel you want to. It would be great if everyone was included. In any event, please keep coming to choir practice! Don't feel you have to drop out.'

'Can we suggest items?' was the first question, closely followed by 'Can we propose solos or duets - that sort of thing?'

'Of course: the more suggestions we have, the better. But we'll have to have a process of agreement and programme construction.' I was thrilled by the enthusiasm and energy. Every face seemed alight and created an atmosphere that inspired me too.

'I'd like everyone to feel consulted and included,' I said. 'Even if you're reluctant to sing as the event draws closer, perhaps you'd prefer to help Turild and her Dad with some practical jobs. At the very least, please tell people about it and come to the event yourself and support us, if nothing else.'

I promised to choose carols I thought most people would sing well and enjoy.

'We might need some extra rehearsals nearer the time,' Per Johann said. 'Some of us might also need help with our individual parts. Could we schedule time in with you – if we need to?'

'Of course,' I said. 'I'll gladly help with that. Could you let me know what's needed, Per Johann?'

'Sure' he said, and grinned while many titters went around the hall. It was the way he said things, and the beguilingly charming way he always smiled at me every time he spoke that fascinated and entertained everyone else.

The genuine buzz of excitement about it all was impossible to miss. Even those who seemed cautious now might feel more confident and enthusiastic in due course, I thought. Meanwhile, it seemed as if the whole choir developed what I can only describe as a new spring in its step!

Preparing for a formal event meant I hardly noticed the all-pervading darkness from lack of daylight for the next few weeks. Suddenly, there was much more to do. Additional mileage in teaching content also presented itself from some of the practicalities that arose. With the one class that was not scheduled to do an exam that year or submit to any formal assessment, it was agreed, at their suggestion, that they would abandon the textbook for one whole week, so that their lessons could be entirely devoted to learning all the special vocabulary that would occur around the process of putting on a such an event. They wanted to know how to translate everything from 'stacking and un-stacking chairs' to 'designing and printing programmes, and the processes of selling tickets'. What was the differences between a hymn, a song and a carol? What was the accurate vocabulary for describing aspects of music written on staves? How could different sorts and styles of music be described? How would tickets be sold in England. What was a 'box office'?

Everyone in the class had a role to play in the mock organisation they set up. We went through all the procedures with new words they would need to know. We aimed at accurate intonation, inflection and pronunciation when the students had to ask and answer questions in English. As a result, everyone in the class gained confidence in speaking whole sentences and developing conversations. It became fun to plan how to invite people, to describe what interaction there might be between the organisers and the performers, acting out conversations, getting them as close as possible to how an actual English person would speak. The students loved it. Everyone agreed to put the maximum effort into catching up with the national curriculum immediately after the week we had set apart for this different learning programme.

I knew I was taking a risk in deviating from the proscribed *pensum*. But I put it to the class that the exercise would help them so much in building up their confidence, that they could easily do three weeks' work in two afterwards. I agreed to mark them on their individual oral contributions at the end of the week, because that was the formal grading which was required all the time. I lured them with the bait that the harder they tried, the more they would learn and the higher their overall mark would be. Those who would need as many 'S's in their final mark as possible welcomed the whole idea. 'S' stood for *saerdeles*, which meant the work was excellent.

At that time, the science stream was not expected to study any further written English. But oral English was a key subject in which to gain top marks in those days. Today, in 2020, the curriculum is entirely different, and I no longer know exactly how the mark system is devised. However, I do know that English remains a key subject at all levels of Norwegian education.

The many mannerly tags I taught them in particular intrigued them all.

'You can't just say "D'you want a ticket?" We wouldn't speak to anyone we wanted to buy something from us like that. We'd say, "Would you like whatever it is," or at more sophisticated levels, something like "Could I interest you in ... or persuade you to buy ... whatever it is". You need to use the kind of common idioms that English people use if you're to sound as English as possible.'

Most of the class found this an intriguing approach to buying and selling. A few members of the class found it pernickety 'nonsense' as they called it, and completely unnecessary.

'What does it matter if we don't get the idiom exactly right? We only need to make ourselves understood, don't we?'

It was Thor who had always had serious reservations about learning any oral English since he was determined he only wanted to know enough of the language to be able to read articles in Scientific Journals and Official Papers. He found learning to speak English boring, a waste of his time and also, for him, incredibly difficult. He had no ear for it at all, struggled with pronouncing certain words, and was not interested in getting the intonation right.

'Well! That's definitely a point of view,' I said. 'But supposing at some time in the future you want to go to an important science conference in England, for example. And let's say you especially want to spend time talking about a particular topic with an Englishman, or an American, who happen to be well known experts in the field you're also interested in. Wouldn't you want to know the very best about the language and the way it's spoken in England and America to have relevant conversations with them and to get the best out of your trip? I think it's quite unlikely you would find such a person was fluent enough in Norwegian to talk over the subject matter with you in any way that was meaningful and constructive.'

There was a chorus of 'Yeah!' round the classroom. Even Thor was forced to smile. He waved his hand to support his comment, 'you win!'

'Well, I don't want to "win" Thor. I just want you to see that I'm not at all interested in wasting your time.'

He grinned again. 'As I say, you WIN! You're right, if you prefer? You always are, actually. But that doesn't mean we can't argue with you, does it?'

I was about to go on, when he interrupted me again.

'I suppose if I were English, I would now say "I'm sorry for being so rude?"'

'You certainly would.' I replied, adding, 'especially if you were a pupil and I was the teacher.'

So, Thor got up from his desk, walked to the front, bowed, took my hand, kissed it dramatically, and said in correct English, even if the pronunciation was distinctly Norwegian, 'I'm very, very sorry, Miss Russell, and I ask for your pardon.'

Slightly embarrassed, I said, 'Now you're just being altogether too French! You've not exactly been spared from the guillotine! But apology accepted.'

Everyone clapped and laughed at the same time.

I knew that this was an unconventional way to get through the work I had been assigned, but if it inspired the pupils to dare to speak – which increasingly it seemed to – if it increased their confidence and extended their vocabulary and helped them to use English spoken idioms, I could not help but be in favour of it. 'They can only sack me and send me home, after all,' I thought to myself. And somehow, deep down, I knew they would not do that! Meanwhile, everywhere was buzzing about the upcoming Christmas 'do'. The enthusiasm was almost palpable.

***

Plans for the event moved along nicely. Per Johann – who else? – had gathered together three others to form a quartet. Grethe was the soprano and her best friend Turild, the alto. They were used to singing together for fun anyway. I was already impressed by the way they had learnt to improvise harmonies together —never having been taught how - they just seemed to manage naturally. Clearly, they both had a musical ear. Per Johann wanted to sing the bass part and had persuaded his good friend Hans Frederik to sing tenor. Hans Frederik had a beautiful, tenor voice and was a quick learner. He only needed to spend half an hour or so with me to be certain of his tenor line and had no trouble holding it against others. It was such fun working with them all. They had such positive attitudes, were so delightfully authentic, with a seemingly unending source of untapped ability.

'We're all so excited about doing this,' Per Johann had said. 'We just love singing and haven't had the chance to do so in such a big group before. It's just great. And we all want to do the best we can.' Then he asked, 'Which pieces, or *carols* d'you think the quartet should sing?'

'Well! What about Silent Night for a start? That would sound really powerful, simply sung by just four voices, don't you think?'

Per Johann liked that idea. He also suggested a Norwegian cradle song - a Christmas carol that many Norwegian children learnt when they were little. We both thought it would be equivalent to a lullaby like Away in a Manger.

'If I bring a copy to show you what it is, d' you think we could sing it?' he'd asked. He was full of enthusiasm. And his attitudes were infectious. It was almost as if he alone had the capacity to infuse everyone with the conviction that they COULD do something rather than that they couldn't. I was continually amazed how encouraging everything was, how engaged the choir members became in getting everything 'right'. I was also pleased that Per Johann had found a role for himself in which he could shine as well as take responsibility. From what I kept on learning all the time it was obvious that when it came to the ways of the world and issues of simple survival, most of the youngsters I taught seemed to know much more than I did. And yet, I knew they respected me and understood that I had things to teach them that were worth learning. Per Johann had believed that – and his positive influence around school was enormously infectious.

Gradually, a full Christmas programme for the choir came together, and with everyone's agreement was eventually finalised. At some point, an occasion presented itself to ask Turild's Dad's men's group to contribute to the event as well.

'Why don't you join us?' I suggested in the middle of a meeting. 'Your group could also sing some Christmas carols, couldn't it?'

It was obvious Turild's father was pleased to have been asked. He went bright pink, straightened his papers several times while it seemed he was trying to get hold of himself and think what to say. Eventually, he cleared his throat and said, 'I'll have to ask them. I can't speak before I've consulted them. But I could do that at our next practice – the day after tomorrow. I could let you know what everyone thinks.'

'That would be wonderful! I so hope they agree. Please tell them how much we'd appreciate it if they felt able to sing. And, if they're willing, could you also ask them for suggestions about what that might be? There could be a couple of slots, both with two items, for example – or, whatever you think is best.'

I hoped I was striking the right tone. Turild's Dad, Sven Pedersen, was such a kind and modest man; I did not want to offend him. And I certainly did not want to imply that I knew more than him, or even as much: I knew it was definitely the other way around.

As the day approached for the Christmas concert, excitement in school was almost palpable. Two or three extra practices had been scheduled for all participants and at one of these, Grethe, raised her hand in between rehearsing one carol and another.

'Miss Russell,' she asked, 'what should we all wear?'

I was so glad she asked this. I had been wondering about it and when and how it might be best to raise the issue since I did not know what formal clothes any of them might have – if any. Just in the very asking was the implication that it should not be the usual, sensible, warm, practical outfit worn daily to school. Her question was followed by a flurry of enthusiastic suggestions.

'Black suits for men and black skirts for girls,' someone said.

'With white shirts and blouses.'

'The men and boys must wear ties – dark ties, classy stuff.'

'Shoes, no boots - properly cleaned and polished.'

'What about hair styles? And jewellery? Can girls wear necklaces, hair ribbons, bracelets? And what about boys' tiepins?'

One after the other, questions came thick and fast. The enthusiasm to look decent and special took me by surprise. I clapped my hands for silence and a general 'Shush' followed my request to be heard.

I thought it best to be business like. 'Hands up all those who think it should be dark suits for males and black skirts for females with white shirts and blouses.'

It seemed to me that every single hand went up.

'Do we all agree about that then? Would anyone find it impossible to honour that? Well, actually don't feel you have to tell me now in front of everyone, but no one must feel left out because they only have a red skirt or a purple suit!'

Everyone laughed.

'Don't worry Miss Russell.' It was Grethe again. 'We'll all help each other. We've definitely got enough of the right clothes to go around, haven't we?'

There was a resounding chorus of 'yes'.

My Maths teaching colleague Bjørn then interrupted in impeccable English. I had long since realised he had lied when he said his English was poor! 'I suggest the men in particular MUST pay attention to their shoes. They must be dark and properly polished. Are we all agreed, gentlemen?'

Thrilled, obviously, to be called gentlemen, most males in the room simply grinned and nodded.

'D'you all think wearing any sort of jewellery – necklace, chain, tie pin or whatever, should be allowed as long as it isn't too shiny or too showy?' The response was via sounds of approval all round. 'So, are we all agreed, then, about what should be worn on the night?'

Heads nodded vigorously once again, and another practice session was over.

The great Christmas event was scheduled for the week before the end of the Christmas term. The singers were excited, beautifully turned out and obviously keen to do a good job. To my astonishment, the capacious school hall was full to bursting, and not just with proud parents. The press also turned up in the form of the culture correspondent of the Finnmark Daily News. A young, male journalist approached me at the beginning of the evening as people were arriving and asked a few questions in a nonchalant, casual sort of way about the event, about me and the music. I hoped he had not been MADE to come and that he might even enjoy it.

I was stunned by every item. There were carols for everyone to join in with here and there, which they did, lustily. Grethe and Jan Erik sang their solos beautifully, and the well-blended quartet sang their hearts out, with some inspired dynamics – phrasing, light and shade, change of pace and so forth. Per Johann winked at me when they had finished their contributions – as if to say,

'I told you we could do it! Didn't you believe me?' His friend, Hans Frederick, who I also taught, winked at me too, as he clasped his hands together and shook them in delight. 'What a pair of charmers they are,' I thought to myself as I smiled back. They had sung exceptionally well.

To have such a large number of youngsters standing before me singing their hearts out to do their absolute determined best was a moving experience that I will always remember. I had worried that when it came to an actual performance their nerves would take over. Not a bit of it! Everyone watched me the whole time: there were no wandering eyes, no mistakes – total commitment. To me it felt truly awesome.

Since the journalist who spoke to me at the beginning of the evening was not from Vadsø, I thought he was just familiarising himself with what he needed to know before he found a seat. So, I was utterly astonished to read what he actually wrote after the event.

'No one had expected much,' he had written. 'After all, there had been so little time for a choir to establish itself and learn the carols to sing. But everyone in the hall, who had come with little expectation, including myself, should be ashamed of themselves. The performance was amazing. The singing was accurate, well blended and clear. It was an impressive achievement,' he had written, 'to inspire and build up a choir to that level of achievement and performance in so short a period of time.'

I was overcome when I read the article a couple of days later. But what blew me away most of all at the event itself, was the magnificent bouquet of flowers I received at the end of the evening. Flowers were terribly hard to come by in Finnmark, and each stem was devastatingly expensive. If you were lucky enough to be invited out to dinner or even coffee, it was the best of good manners to take a single stem to your hostess in gratitude, which would then be placed in the centre of the dining table. A single rose was a wonderful present for any hostess to receive since a single stem cost about three times as much as a whole bouquet of flowers in England at that time. To be given a whole bouquet there and then, by the choir members themselves, was an extraordinary thank you. I was utterly overwhelmed and completely dumbfounded. The journalist's write up ended with a sentence declaring that the flowers I received at the end were richly deserved.

What thrilled me most of all, however, was the relational distance that had been travelled between the time I had first arrived in August, and now - mid-December. There was an astonishing difference in the overall atmosphere.

The change that had occurred from the reluctance of everyone I taught to accept me because I was teaching English rather than Finnish or Russian, to the warmth shown to me now all the time, was enormous and I did not underestimate how important that was. More significantly, I had learned so much from these youngsters and their families. Their kindness and simple goodness made them truly great individuals, totally unspoilt by any kind of envy or resentment of what they might be missing out on in comparison to the rest of the world or even to their southern compatriots, never mind what they had to endure in terms of climate and remoteness. It was a privilege to be amongst so many amazing individuals who, because they were so brilliant at living it themselves, were showing me so much about how to become whoever we are each individually, truly meant to be.

Chapter Twenty

Dicing with Death?

I had decided well in advance.to go home for the two-week Christmas break
It had taken several weeks for the airline tickets to arrive in the post, but I was
duly booked on flights through to London from neighbouring Kirkenes, Vadsø's
nearest airport. Three colleagues were also flying south for Christmas, so when
the time came to face the challenge of getting to the airport through meters of
deep snow, the prospect was more of a fun expedition than a potential feat of
endurance.

Getting to Kirkenes airport turned out to be an adventure in itself. Our first
problem was how best to get there. The *Hurtigruten* was not viable. It was too
slow, inconvenient timewise and docked nowhere near the airport: we would
still have to work out how to get from boat to plane. In the end, it turned out
that the most sensible, the quickest, and the most direct route by far, had to be
by road.

However, the roads in and out of Vadsø were almost permanently closed
during the winter months. The depth of snow was so considerable that it was
difficult and expensive to shift it in a way that would keep a road open for a
daily flow of traffic. In any event, there were few vehicles those days able to take
advantage of a road open in the winter. It was generally thought unnecessary
even to try. Fortunately, although well outside the town, Kirkenes airport was
on the Vadsø side of it. It was definitely the best option to access the airport
by road from Vadsø. The only way to do that, however, was literally for all four
of us to be driven by taxi **directly** and **immediately** behind a large and slow,
snowplough.

We began our journey at four in the morning. Fortunately, we had no idea
what lay ahead. A drive of about 80 miles, which in the summer would have
taken an hour and a half, took the best part of four hours in mid-December.
Since it was snowing hard when the taxi left Vadsø, we saw new flakes, thick
enough to close the road directly behind us just as soon as our taxi had driven
through. Our driver had to keep moving to ensure we would not be so far from
the tractor that we were left stranded - a perilous fate that would have been!

Fortunately, the driver knew exactly what he was doing. He had made the same journey in similar conditions before and seemed to enjoy the challenge. He also knew exactly what his plough could do and was used to working with our taxi driver. They made a good team. The plough driver turned round every so often and gave us all a reassuring grin and a thumb's up. Eventually, we arrived at the airport safely and in good time.

Our flight south was due to leave at 9am, but our plane was nowhere to be seen. We learned from a friendly telephone clerk that it was delayed by heavy snowstorms en route north, and we would not be able to fly south until mid-morning at the earliest. Meanwhile, a uniformed official appeared and opened up a cordoned off area that served as a kitchen. For the next couple of hours, he made us copious cups of steaming hot coffee and kept us all awake and cheerful with his lively chatter.

We chatted, dozed and read while we waited. Eventually, we heard the soft, distant hum of an engine as our plane finally approached the tiny airport. Three crew members exited it on landing, and there were three passengers. The captain, the co-pilot and a single flight attendant joined us in gulping down even more steaming coffee, completely undeterred by their delay, talking and laughing with us all: apparently not much bothered by the bad weather conditions, which I found encouraging.

'How far are you all going?' the captain asked eventually when we were all chatting in the tiny lounge over our warming brew.

'Trondheim, Oslo,' came three of the answers since two colleagues were both hoping to get home to the capital, albeit at opposite ends of the city, that day.

'And you?' he asked me.

'Heathrow', I said, simply.

'Oh! Wow!' he said. 'Well we'd better get started as soon as we can then and do our best to make your connection. But I need to warn you that the first part of our flight will be pretty bumpy. There are massive snowstorms to negotiate over parts of the *vidda* as well as high, blustery winds. We'll get through, though', he said with a wry smile, 'although you need to know that it will be quite uncomfortable at times. Don't worry. You'll be quite safe. We'll get your luggage stowed and take off as soon as we can - at least, when the winds we need to fly through look as if they have abated and we can be certain to make it. Don't worry,' he added again with a reassuring smile. 'I promise we never take off unless we're certain it's safe to do so. Our bosses in Oslo wouldn't allow us to anyway. Safety always comes first.'

For the first hour of the flight our small, turboprop plane – with a 20 to 30 seat capacity - was tossed and buffeted by high winds, but nevertheless managed to navigate its way through heavy snow showers and squally weather until we had left the Arctic Circle altogether and its severe conditions. The further south we flew, the smoother also the flight became. In the same way as a long-distance train journey our plane made stops at key points on our way at Alta, Tromsø, Bodø and two or three smaller towns. None of us minded that it took most of the day and part of the early evening before two of my three colleagues and I arrived in the capital. Our third had left us at her hometown of Trondheim. We all felt weary but were thankful to have made it.

I waved au revoir to my two companions. It had been good to have had company so far. In addition to many other things, I had discovered that Marianne, who taught in the Middle School on the Vadsø campus, was also Rektor Anderson's girlfriend.

Conversation had been easy, and I had learnt much about some of those I taught or knew. I welcomed information about their lives and experiences: how they coped with long-term illnesses, for instance with no easily accessible hospital. I had thought a good deal about Arne in particular – my argumentative student who had queried his low grades, because of his colloquial, slangy language. I thought about just how difficult it must have been for his parents to have him even diagnosed, let alone treated, for polio in the early days of his illness. There were other families I heard about too who had to make long, expensive, time-consuming trips to Oslo for specialised hospital care. The government helped with payment for travel, but sometimes parents needed to be away for several days, or weeks, at a time leaving other children and spouses to cope in their absence. Everything I learnt from my fellow travellers only served to increase my respect and admiration for the people I worked with and amongst.

It was too late to connect with my scheduled flight to London when we landed in Oslo, so the airline put me up for the night in an hotel. Far too exhausted to cope with the formality of eating in the public dining room, I asked for my supper to be served in my room. As I unwound from the day, I realised my body was tense after the trauma of parts of our flight, and I made a conscious effort to try to relax.

The following morning, after a good night's sleep, I flew on to London and reached my destination after two long days of weary travelling and a couple of short nights' sleep. A milder climate and the experience of daylight alone were rejuvenating, however. It had been a new experience to fly through such exceptional weather in late-December. But then, I was surprised how bizarre it felt to go Christmas shopping in London the next day, crossing roads heavy with traffic, gazing up at ornamental streetlights and a plethora of Christmas decorations strung up everywhere across busy main roads. The contrast with the singular, unadorned main road, deep in snow with no traffic and no lighting at all in Vadsø's time of total darkness, could not have been more extreme.

Everything felt seriously strange, easy and accessible compared to the environment I had left behind. There was light, transport, shops, people, noise, luscious spicy smells and busyness in all directions. Nevertheless, it was good to spend time with friends and family, who were longing to hear all about the students I taught and the colleagues I worked with.

My time in London revived my spirits and renewed my energy and focus. By the New Year, I felt rested and refreshed by the stimulus of a different milieu and encouraged by finding new music and teaching material. As I prepared to make the 1600-mile journey back up North, I was looking forward to getting back to the people to whom I had begun to feel so preciously attached.

***

With my previous experience in mind, I was prepared for delays going back to Vadsø. But there was nothing about the return trip that I could either have predicted or prepared for.

It began with an unremarkable flight from London to Oslo. I had planned to arrive in Kirkenes two days before the new term was due to start. I judged I would need at least one full day to re-adjust to the harsher climate of Vadsø after the milder weather in England. I knew I would want to rest after my long trip and be sure I was ready to start a new term's work. I also knew I had plenty of time in hand before flying onward, from Oslo, so was unhurried as I got off my flight from London and entered the terminal building at Oslo's Fornebu airport.

So far so good. I went through passport control without a hitch. But before I settled down in the airport lounge to wait for my next flight, I joined the check-in queue to make sure all my tickets were in order and my luggage would be safely transferred. It was then I realised that my transfer was not going to be at all straightforward. From snatches of conversations I overheard and from the looks on various faces I began to understand that my day was not going to go at all according to plan. Although it took a while before I knew exactly what was happening.

Eventually, it was my turn to speak with the check-in clerk.

'All flights north are delayed,' he told me 'The weather is very bad further north, and your plane has not even arrived yet. It's been held up in transit somewhere on its way south. But don't worry. Delays are fairly normal at this time of year. We'll get you going just as soon as we can when the airport authorities believe it's safe for everyone to travel. As soon as we have news, we'll announce it on the tannoy. And yes, when it comes to it, of course we'll transfer your luggage.'

I knew then there would be plenty of time for a hot drink before my northern flight took off. It would be back to coffee now. There would be no more tea until I could make my own brew back in Vadsø. Unperturbed, I settled myself down with a cup of coffee to wait for my flight to be called. I found a cosy seat in the warm and comfortable airport lounge and settled down to read my book. I was also able to see the planes out on the tarmac and could keep up to date if I wanted to. My book was absorbing, however, so I hardly noticed that one hour passed, and then another, although I looked up now and then and saw that nothing much had changed - the same planes were standing exactly where they had been when I first looked out. On the other hand, however, I noticed that inbound flights from abroad were coming and going all the time. They seemed to be landing and taking off at regular intervals as might be expected.

Another hour passed. I began to feel restless. I had finished my book now and was anxious for news: or at least an update. No internal arrivals had been announced over the tannoy, so I made my way to the information desk for an update.

'Can you tell me yet when the next internal flight north will be leaving?' I asked.

'Ah! Yes! Soon, I think. We are about to announce something. There's a flight going north to Trondheim that hopes to take off within the hour – and your name is…?'

The young lady with the information was pleasant and wanted to be helpful. I gave her my name, asked where my luggage might be and how I would know when I could get on a plane that would take me further north even than Trondheim. Could I also be sure of a seat?

'The weather is bad, we understand. I'm not sure anything can fly further than Trondheim today. But at least we'll get you as far as that so that maybe tomorrow you can complete your journey. And don't worry, we'll make sure your luggage is on board and with you at all times. And if you need to stay overnight somewhere, the airline will put you up in a decent hotel.' The information attendant smiled broadly. 'The weather's often bad at this time of year. We think safety is SO important that we never take risks. But again, please don't worry. There are usually gaps in the bad weather which we're always ready to take advantage of.'

Just as she finished speaking, her phone rang. I lingered hoping there might be news. There was.

'Well,' the attendant smiled at me. 'I gather the plane to Trondheim will leave in half an hour or so. So, if you like to sit down again and listen out to be called, I'm sure you won't have to wait too long. We'll sort your luggage out, as I said. You won't need to do anything about that. Please just wait until your flight is called. It's the only one going to Trondheim, so you can relax – you'll definitely be able to get on it. It isn't full.'

I felt reassured by the calm confidence with which my needs were heard. The attendant had been right. Within the hour, I heard the Trondheim flight called and soon I was on it. I was pleased to have been given a seat by the window so I could admire the snow-covered landscape below, especially as smaller, inland planes flew lower than big, international jets. It was stunningly beautiful everywhere. The flight was smooth and entirely untroubled by any sudden, windy squalls or blinding snowfalls.

At Trondheim, everyone disembarked. The plane was definitely not flying further north, we were told. It was late in the day now in any case. I quite understood that hours of further flight through the night into the early hours would not be on the cards. I walked with a sense of growing resignation into the terminal, where to my delight, sitting in the airport lounge and waving to me as I made my way to wait again for further news, were my three colleagues. Marianne, Kari Ingrid and Mads, with whom I had made the initial trip to Oslo from Vadsø before Christmas.

'Hello, hello, hello!' It felt wonderful to be greeted so warmly, thinking back briefly to my formal greeting by colleagues at the beginning of the school year last August. Now, all four of us greeted each other with smiles, hugs and handshakes, as well as floods of questions about how each other's Christmas and New Year had been. I learned that my colleagues had started their travels from

Oslo, before I landed from London. Kari Ingrid, who lived near Sandefjord, had been home for Christmas and had then gone to Oslo for New Year. It had been sheer coincidence that they were all booked on the same flight north and had got as far as Trondheim where they had all been stranded for seven hours.

Marianne said. 'We've been waiting for your flight to arrive because we were hoping that we could join it to fly on further. But then we all realised it was too late to be going anywhere else today. Just as we were coming to terms with that, you appeared!'

They had learned that the weather was truly dreadful further north. Marianne had phoned the Rektor and explained what had hitherto been their predicament, and that they would not be able to get back on time for the new term. The message had been passed on apparently to all those who needed to know. So, I felt I could relax a bit, believing I could be sure that Einar Anderson would know I was included in the delayed party. He would want to know where Marianne was and that she was all right. She was bound to keep him informed and updated.

All of us were told that a bus would take us and our luggage to a local hotel. We would be given vouchers for an evening meal and breakfast and further information about our onward travel the next day. We had a jolly evening meal together, but tired out after uncertain waiting meant we did not linger to chat afterwards. We needed rest and sleep.

The next day, we woke to see it was snowing hard. It was a gentle, soft snow, however, and the wind had dropped. By midday, it was extremely cold, but the sun emerged, making us all feel that long distance travel was not so onerous after all. Even if it was only for a few hours before darkness descended again, we hoped we might be able to make some progress further north. Sure enough, after an hour or so, the hotel receptionist paged us to announce our flight would proceed. An airport bus arrived, our luggage was piled in and we drove off to our waiting plane.

'We'll fly first to Bodø,' the pilot announced while we were strapping ourselves into our seats. 'After that, we'll have to see what conditions are like', he said. 'I'm afraid the outlook and the forecast are not all that promising at the moment. We won't fly unless it's safe to do so. We cannot ensure safety if ice might collect on the wings. But we'll see how the weather is in due course. Meanwhile, we'll at least make **some** progress. Please fasten your seat belts and obey any instructions as usual.'

A minute or two later, the plane taxied to the runway, turned, waited a few seconds and then hurtled down the runway and took off. At once it climbed high through the clouds and into the darkness of the earth's curve. Chatter between all four of us, sitting next to each other across the aisle ebbed and flowed for a while. We were all pleased to be on our way. Gradually, however, conversation slowed and finally came to a complete halt when our small plane began to rock from side to side. At first the movements were minimal: not really different from any normal request time for passengers to fasten their seat belts because of turbulence on a usual fight. But then the movement of the plane became a good deal more severe. It was just once or twice to begin with, but nevertheless it was more extreme than any of us were used to. It felt scary after a few minutes and became increasingly difficult to take what we were experiencing in our stride. I began to feel really concerned, and from the looks on their faces, I was sure my friends did too.

'Maybe this is just a more violent form of turbulence,' I thought to myself. But after a bit, I had to admit I actually felt terrified. The plane seemed to swoop, lose height, and veer briefly off course, now and then. Gradually, the length of time between considerable movements grew shorter and the swooping and veering seemed to grow longer. My stomach rose and fell accordingly. My hands were wet with perspiration, and I found myself gripping my seat as if my very life depended on it. I thought what was happening must be like how it would feel to sail through huge boulders on the open sea. I admitted to myself I was afraid. Actually, I began to feel very anxious indeed. I even feared we might not make it. And from the drawn, white faces of my travelling companions I knew, they were frightened too.

'We're experiencing heavy turbulence at the moment.' Someone said over a loudspeaker in the cabin. 'We'll be landing in about half an hour, and it will be rough until we do, so please don't leave your seats – for any reason. Thank you!'

The cabin fell silent. No one spoke. When I had the courage to look round – mostly I was frozen in fright – I saw that no one was reading or talking. I knew that everyone else was frightened too. I did not dare even to look out of the window because I was terrified of what I might see. In any event, I did not dare to risk moving any part of my body in case it added to the violent movement of the plane. It was an irrational thought, I knew, but my heart was pounding so hard I was afraid everyone on the flight could hear it, and probably see it thumping too!

I began to wonder what the landing might be like. As we approached the ground, would the turbulence be more or less severe? How forceful would the wind be at ground level? I tried to occupy my mind in attempting to reason that out, even as the plane began to feel increasingly more like a breakable toy than a heavy, solid vehicle, fit to carry considerable weight, as it rose and fell and rocked from side to side, swooping and whirling, often all of a sudden and at great speed. To terrified passengers, there were good reasons for feeling the plane might possibly be out of control.

Finally, and thankfully, I felt the pilot begin his descent. This was many minutes after we had all been asked to stay in our seats, I thought. But I could not confidently judge anything about our situation while ever it continued to feel as if the rhythm of movement did not change much at all. At least twice, I believed the plane flew up again after going down, accompanied by an extra roar from the engines. Or so I thought. But gradually, it was obvious we were definitely descending and getting closer to the ground. Not that it was an entirely smooth landing in the end, but it was certainly much less wild than I had feared it would be. I had never been so thankful as I was when I heard and felt the wheels from the aircraft's undercarriage scream against the tarmac after a few bumps up and down, as they hit the landing runway. No one applauded. The silence in the cabin was deafening. When someone opened the door, the noise of the wind outside was even louder. But somehow, it was also welcoming, especially to know we would soon feel firm ground beneath our feet in spite of the freezing temperature somewhere between minus ten and minus fifteen.

The pilot emerged from the cockpit, putting on his cap, trying to smile as he did so.

'Sorry about that everyone,' he said. 'Turbulence this far north is not easy to fly through. We weren't actually in any kind of danger, but I'm sorry if it felt a little rough and uncomfortable. Anyway, welcome to Bodø!'

Since Bodø lies within the Arctic Circle, the four of us knew that from now on, we had left the joy of daylight behind, however brief during the daytime it had been. Now, it would be dark again the whole time: we had returned to perpetual night which lasted a few more weeks yet. Earlier everyone had hoped to be able to fly on - at least as far further north as Tromsø, but once we hit the bad weather from which we were now trying to recover ourselves, we knew we could not face a further flight unless conditions drastically improved.

Bodø is just 50 miles inside the Arctic Circle and 200 miles or so west of the Swedish border. Its other claim to wider civilisation is that it is the most northerly train station in Europe – or was then. Train travel to Bodø is possible from many other places in Scandinavia and as far south as train travel is possible, with access also to the whole of Europe and the rest of the world. Thus, it seems and actually was even 50 years ago, more of a cosmopolitan centre than many other Arctic towns and cities. It was and still is generally full of people from a diverse milieu. The hotels even then rose to the need for comfort and rest for weary travellers after long journeys, and once again we four itinerant, weary pedagogues were put up overnight in welcome warmth and comfort.

'Why don't we not eat until later,' suggested Marianne. 'Why don't we change the rhythm a bit and go and see a film first instead? There actually is a cinema here and I for one wouldn't mind losing myself in a film and recovering my general equilibrium after that very scary ride we've all just had. What d'you say?'

We all thought that was a great idea, so off we trundled to see 'Dr Strangelove' in English with Norwegian subtitles. I thought it really odd to see Peter Sellers in a wheelchair in charge of nuclear buttons, instead of larking around being hilariously funny as Inspector Clouseau. The others had not come across him as an actor: they were not devotees of The Pink Panther and had never heard of him as a film star or as a comedian. The film gave us all a lot to think about concerning atomic and nuclear power though, and we chatted happily about it together over and after supper. It was not until we had finished our meal that anyone mentioned the next day. None of us suggested what might be next – on any front. However, we all realised that now, after a long and fraught day, it would be a good idea to try to get some proper sleep.

We woke next morning and found the winds had dropped, although the temperature was still a long way below zero. Overall calmer weather prevailed, and it promised to be a more settled kind of day than the previous one. The hotel receptionist saw us gathered together at breakfast and explained that we would be flying at least as far as Alta that day. After that, she could not say what further progress might be made. Affected by mountainous terrain, and the way in which that and the bleakness of exposed tundra might or might not influence the winds, who knew what the weather would bring until we were actually up in the air and flying further north?

We took off at mid-morning and I hoped there was a real chance we would be able to reach Vadsø that evening.

All was well for the first half hour or so. But then the plane began to wrestle with sudden turbulence again, even worse than we had experienced the day before. At least that was how it felt - as if the plane began to fight the external conditions in a kind of wrestling or boxing match. Now and then, we were literally flung in completely the opposite direction before finding and returning to our scheduled course. The engines changed the pitch of their roar now and then, as if to catch their breath when huge squalls struck them head on. One side of the aisle seemed to be flying higher than the other. Sometimes, the plane jerked so forcefully to one side or another that the books and magazines that people were trying, or pretending, to read were snatched from their hands and dashed to the floor. After a while, a horrified, silent stillness fell once again over the whole cabin. I did not dare look round at anyone else or catch anyone's eye. I was afraid lest I might inadvertently communicate my own fear to others and was reluctant to add anyone else's to my own. The huge, iron bird rose and fell and rocked and rolled, losing height and then gaining it for what seemed like hours but was probably only one hour at the most. Intermittently, the wind seemed to rush the plane now and then with great squalls of loud, thundery effort.

'Any minute now, we'll all be done for,' I said to myself, over and over again. But miraculously, the plane flew on. There was no message from the cockpit for some time. No one spoke in the cabin either. But eventually, the captain's voice was heard at last.

'Well! We seem to be through that difficult patch now,' he said. He was trying to speak calmly, but the slight tremor in his voice as he spoke was obvious to everyone. 'We may hit another spot of turbulence, but it should not be as severe as those we've already weathered. It's about 45 minutes to landing. Please stay strapped into your seats meanwhile – as a precaution.'

The relief in the cabin that it was not long until landing was palpable. People turned to each other and tried to smile - forcing it a bit, I thought. I tried to breathe deeply and decided to concentrate on doing that although it was not easy. My three friends nodded and tried to smile at one another. Kari, Mads and Marianne looked particularly white-faced, I thought. And it was not at all surprising since it had been a very, very frightening experience to fly through such terrible weather conditions.

We were ushered quickly into the small terminal once we finally landed. It was terribly cold, and the wind was bitter and cuttingly sharp across the tiny stretch of tarmac we all had to negotiate, but the airport buildings were warm and welcoming. We were all offered hot coffee immediately, and an air of surface bonhomie prevailed for a while as all the luggage was unloaded and brought inside. Eventually, after an hour or so, a young, airport official approached us all.

'Welcome to Alta,' he said. 'I gather your flight was a bit rough, so I hope the coffee has revived you. I need to tell you that there are no onward flights – which won't surprise you. It really isn't safe to be in the air for the next couple of days. So, we're going to put you on the *Hurtigruten*, going north round the North Cape to your various onward destinations. It doesn't call here, however, so first thing tomorrow morning we'll need to organise you on to a bus which will drive you to the nearest port of call to pick it up travelling in the right direction. Meanwhile, we'll install you all in a local hotel with vouchers for supper and breakfast. Please help yourself to coffee, as much as you need, and please try to relax while you wait.'

'Well', someone said, 'at least that will be a different sort of rough ride! Sea billows instead of hurricane winds!' But no one laughed – or even smiled.

The fact that the camaraderie between myself and my colleagues was strengthened, however, was a real boon in these trying circumstances. The more time we spent together and braved it out, the greater the bonds of friendship strengthened between us. Even so, this time we spent a quiet evening together, greatly sobered by our experience of the last two days. We all retired early knowing there was to be a prompt start the next morning.

We boarded the *Hurtigruten* around seven the following day. We had expressed some degree of anxiety to each other about how scary it might be on heavy seas, but our fears turned out to be largely unfounded. The movement on the *Hurtigruten* turned out to be much less severe than we had all feared. We were now in a group of eight passengers, seven of whom had set off from Oslo on the same plane and had met up with us in Trondheim. Four others needed to be dropped off at various destinations going north: the four of us, further on to Vadsø, remaining to the end. But at least NOW at last, we would be moving closer and closer to where we needed to be, even as we slept – or tried to – through the night.

Kari, Marianne and me, were given berths in the same cabin. Our colleague, Mads, was assigned a different, all male berth. There was food available if we wanted it, but none of us felt much like eating. I excused myself from all further socialising for the duration since I needed to lie down. Even if I could not actually sleep, I wanted to rest, stretch out and try at least to doze.

I felt exhausted. I drifted off now and then into light episodes of semi-consciousness as I came to terms with what I had experienced so far since leaving home in London a couple of days previously. This would be my fourth night in transit. Could that really be possible? My mind recalled various encounters and events of the last few days and tried to think forward to our final arrival. Surely, it must be in prospect at last? It really could not be long now? At least we would all four be able to walk down the gangplank when we finally docked and perhaps even all four of us would then be able to *spark* home quite easily – even with all the luggage between us. Finally, in the middle of my daydreams, I managed to fall into a deep sleep.

The next thing I knew, Marianne was shaking me to wake me up.

'You need to get up. They're only serving food for another half an hour and you really should eat something. We've been waiting for you to join us.'

We sat down together to enjoy a civilised meal, relieved that we were through the worst and nearly home again. Or so we thought. We chatted away to each other until late, wished each other good night and agreed the time to share breakfast together the next day. We had no idea what time exactly we would get to Vadsø, but we suspected it would be some time really early the following morning.

We met as agreed next morning. As we all slurped our way through final cups of coffee, we were approached by one of the ship's stewards.

'Good morning!' he said, attempting a smile. 'I need to explain to you all how we are going to deal with your disembarkation.' He paused. We all gave him our complete attention. I was simply expecting him to tell us our estimated time of arrival and any other necessary information.

'We cannot actually sail into Vadsø harbour,' he continued. 'It's our day to visit it on our return south, not going north. It would take up too much time to add a detour to our schedule today. We're already somewhat late, you won't be surprised to hear because of excessively rough seas that slowed us down before you joined us'. My attention was diverted at this point. I was trying to make sense of what I had just been told and translate it into what I feared might be coming next: more delay, perhaps? Or, would there be another boat to transfer to – or, what, exactly? I had run out of any other ideas to imagine. I heard myself saying, 'I'm sorry. Excuse me, but could you please repeat what you just said?'

'Of course: we shall drop anchor OUTSIDE Vadsø where you will be met by and transferred to a waiting motorboat which will take you right into the harbour, and to Vadsø's jetty itself.'

'And how will we get into the motorboat from this ship?' I asked. I was hugely puzzled by the prospect. It made absolutely no sense to me at all. How could there be a gangplank from such a large ship to such a small motorboat?

'By climbing down the side,' the steward answered in a matter of fact voice.

'Climbing down the side? Of the *Hurtigruten*? Whatever do you mean? How on earth will we do that - "climb down the side"?' I asked. What I was hearing seemed to be utterly incomprehensible.

'We'll use a rope ladder, of course.' The steward was still matter of fact and unruffled.

It was a good deal colder on the *Hurtigruten* than it had been on a plane. The cabins were warm, but the minus 20 freezing temperatures cut through like a knife every time we walked outside from them to the restaurant or the lounge. I had thought my boots and woollen tights on top of warm underwear as well as my tweed skirt, three-quarter length warm coat and furry hat would see me through airports and across tarmacs. I knew the act of trudging up to my small flat from the harbour would warm me through and would only take 20 minutes or thereabouts. But whether or not I would be warm enough descending down a rope ladder or fearing that any normal robust sailor might try to look up my skirt was the very least of my worries at this point. Admittedly the *Hurtigruten* in the 1960s were smaller than those that are the cruise ships of today. Nevertheless, the side of it would need a rope ladder of some several metres in length I thought. Surely that could not be what the sailors were proposing we must negotiate now?

'A rope ladder? D'you mean we'll each have to climb down the side of this enormous *Hurtigruten* on a rope ladder to a smaller, waiting motorboat bobbing up and down in rolling, heavy seas? How on earth will we do that? It's not even safe, is it?'

I began to feel consumed by panic at the thought. How would I manage to complete this manoeuvre? Even the sturdy *Hurtigruten* had felt at times like a hand-made, papier mache, floating vessel in the last 24 hours. What on earth would it be like descending to, by comparison, a flimsy, tiny toy-like motorboat as the massive waves rose and fell all around us, transferring from one to the other in the dark and freezing cold? What would happen if I lost my grip, or footing? I could not help noticing that my companions were also looking a bit dubious at this point.

'I'm not sure I can manage that!' I said simply.

'We'll help you, of course', he said. 'You'll be absolutely safe. Please don't worry. It will be another hour or so before we'll be ready for you to disembark, so there's no hurry. We'll help you with your luggage too, naturally.'

I had to admit that his manner was calm and reassuring. 'Don't worry!' Marianne said. 'They honestly would not even think of letting us off this way if they weren't sure it was absolutely safe. They will help us, honestly, they will.'

'Yes, I'm sure they will. But you're all tremendously tough and fit Norwegians. I'm not anything like as resilient as all of you in circumstances like this. I'm not sure I'll actually be able to manage.'

My thoughts turned to my southern friends as I spoke. The previous year, I had gone boating with them every weekend on my friend's husband's small fishing boat. I had learned a great deal about boats and sailing and a lot about the water and currents and weather conditions as well as where fish could be found for stocking the freezer and where it was safe to drop anchor overnight. I believed I had become quite proficient in coping with many of the particular demands of understanding, and actually enjoying, boating. But watching someone else skilfully manoeuvre in and around southern islands and fjords was different, very different, from descending down the side of a huge passenger ship to a waiting motorboat on swelling seas in the middle of an Arctic winter of well below zero temperatures and in total darkness and in a skirt!

When it came to it a short time later, our luggage was assembled, and we were duly called with a 10 minutes' warning. We had been watching the ship get closer and closer to Vadsø's coastline for a good half an hour as the harbour itself and the dot of an approaching motorboat came into view. As the dot grew larger, it kept disappearing from sight when waves in front of it had risen higher than the boat itself. My legs felt like jelly.

Eventually, and with the utmost confident nonchalance, a sailor threw the rope ladder over the side. He whistled as he did so. The motorboat drew right up to the *Hurtigruten* so that their sides were touching. There were two men in the boat: one held on to the wheel while the other anchored the rope to one of the boat's rowlocks before Mads agreed to be the first to descend. He made a kind of grimace as he turned to go down the ladder backwards. It was as if to say, 'here we go: nothing for it now!' It was a long way down, but it took him less than half a minute before he stood and waved from the boat. Kari Ingrid went next, trying to smile to put a brave face on things as she descended carefully, one rung at a time. Then it was Marianne's turn, to be followed by myself. Before Marianne started off, she clasped my hand.

'You'll be absolutely fine. You're so very much braver than you think you are, you know. We all keep saying that to each other all the time. You should be proud of yourself. You're a truly gutsy lady! You'll be totally safe. You'll see!'

I was not sure what she meant, but I knew it was all intended to be encouraging and I certainly wanted to be brave. The sailor on the *Hurtigruten* then took me firmly by the hand and placed my first foot on the rung of the ladder. He made reassuring eye contact as he did so, smiling. He did not let me go until he was absolutely confident that I was totally secure, some two or three rungs down. There were at least two more rungs to negotiate without the possibility of any help before the sailor on the motorboat could grip my ankle and hold my legs as I placed them on the final few rungs below. But just before the *Hurtigruten* sailor let go so that I could descend to the unaided rungs, he said, and in English with slow and firm reassurance, 'You'll be fine. Just take it steady. You're nearly there! Don't pay any attention to the huge waves. The motorboat is really, really safe: it's virtually unsinkable. And more importantly, the two men in charge of it are the most brilliant, experienced and competent sailors in the world. They really, really are!'

Once in the boat, I was shaking so much with fright I could hardly turn round to step into the centre of it. But I made myself look up to the helpful sailor, who was watching me. He waved, and then put both thumbs up, signalling that all had indeed gone well. He waved again for several moments before the *Hurtigruten* hooted to announce its departure, and clearly began to move away, back further out to open sea.

The last 15 minutes or so of this tremendous journey from London to Vadsø were, in many ways, the worst. It felt so exposed for a start. Not only was it dark, it was terribly, terribly cold: at least minus 20, and that was a raw shock in open water. Secondly, there was little shelter in the tiny motorboat, and the wind felt really powerful. Thirdly, the waves were enormous, although I had to hand it to the man in charge: he knew exactly what to do to make progress in such dreadful conditions. He knew how to USE the huge waves so that the motorboat could make progress to the harbour by harnessing their immense power rather than being confronted by them. Feeling very cold indeed, exposed to the elements and up against a fierce and mighty rolling sea, I felt utterly terrified. But, incredibly, the motorboat got ever closer and closer to the jetty, which appeared to stretch longer and longer still the closer we got to it. At some point I noticed our luggage was also in the motorboat, although I had no idea how it had got there.

There was only one more ordeal to face: ascending the slippery wooden steps of the jetty itself. That would be tricky. This was not least because my legs were shaking so much, I was not sure I could control them sufficiently to tell them what to do. In addition, because I feared the wooden jetty steps would be icy, I dreaded this final test of my courage and stamina. I definitely did not want to slip. This time, I was let off first, helped by the sailor who had secured my last footings into the motorboat. Another man was waiting at the top of the steps to help me up and on to firm contact with the jetty. He smiled broadly once he had made sure I was standing upright in complete safety.

'Welcome back Miss,' he said in English.

Chapter Twenty-One

A New Year

I just managed to be sufficiently organised for school the next day to get through the few hours necessary before the Sunday when I would have a whole day to recover fully from my adventures, or rather, ordeals. My first class was Alf's, for which I knew I would have to be both prepared and composed since everyone knew about our travel dramas. Together with his nine colleagues, he was agog to hear every detail of our eventful journey.

'We're all glad you're safely back – and longing to know if the rumours are true,' Alf asked. He didn't make a single eye roll or attempt a wink.

Alf had quietened down since my early days in Vadsø. If we passed in the street, he would still wink and revert to an adolescent flattering routine, but he had become less flirty and more respectful: more serious, mature and mannerly. He no longer tried to embarrass me by oozing oily charm whenever he had the chance, trying to put me off my stroke with the inane flattery of my early weeks. Exams were only weeks away and he was working hard.

His class was lovely to teach. We always had good rapport, and enjoyed excellent, interesting discussions about local and international politics. Everyone's English had improved enormously which helped them to express many sophisticated and well-thought through attitudes and ideas with fluent confidence.

I had missed two days of teaching in transit. Once he realised his class would be the first to be able to hear from my own lips what had happened to the four of us, he was thrilled. Indeed, his entire class was excited to be the first to hear what our journey back to Vadsø had been like. Alf especially welcomed the opportunity to be able to tell vital, key information around the whole school!

'So,' he said, once the door was shut, and everyone was sitting down, 'we want to know everything: each specific, tiny detail'.

'About what exactly?' I asked, trying to sound nonchalant as I pretended to access my notes from my bag.

'Your journey from London, of course,' he persisted. 'We've heard it was long and difficult. It must have been, since it's taken you four days to get here. Is it true that you had to climb down the side of the *Hurtigruten* for the last bit - to make it into the harbour?'

'Yes, it's true. Good heavens! Was it only yesterday? I seem to have lost track of time. It took so long to get back. And yes, it *was* a difficult journey. But I wasn't alone. All of us found it hard, and it was good to have each other's company.'

Everyone was listening to every word.

'What was it like in London?' Elsa, asked.

Elsa, hard-working and able, was also a gifted pianist with whom I had spent time the previous term. I had brought back some new music for her. But this was not the time to mention that.

'You do come from London, don't you? That IS where your home is, isn't it? Please tell us what it's like there at Christmas. Don't let's work normally today. May we just talk, in English of course, about our vacations? We could learn lots of new vocabulary and idioms!'

'Well! Maybe just this once we could,' I said. 'But EVERYTHING must be in English. No lapses into Norwegian. Understood? Agreed?'

Everyone nodded. All lessons were in English now with this class - the top school year within which ages ranged from rising 18 to 23. This was the most senior language class in the Gymnasium. Both written and oral English were elements of their advanced level curriculum since they were majoring in English and Norwegian. Three students had returned to school after a couple of years out in the world because they needed the *examen artium* qualification, the equivalent to a collection of A Levels, for further progress to ultimate qualifications. One of them, Rastus, was a married Sami in his early twenties, whose first language was Lappish. He wanted to study at the Technology University in Trondheim and needed his *Artium* qualification to do so. He worked hard, as keen as mustard to be fluent in English.

Rastus was a classic example of a student fluent in five languages – Lappish, Norwegian, German, French and English. By law, the Sami had to know Norwegian before they started school at seven. Rastus would need his second language, Norwegian, for further studies in the rudimentary basics of scientific and engineering vocabulary he would encounter lower down the Gymnasium in French and German as well as English, before ultimately specialising at this level. When I think how I struggled to pass O Level French, I can only but applaud his sheer tenacity. Not for the first time, living and working in Norway challenged my English attitude to learning other languages. We are so lazy by comparison.

I often felt this class saw me as a purveyor of superior information and wisdom as well as language. I kept reminding myself the extent to which their art of harmonious living, caring for, and knowing about their peers, was so different from the culture from which I came. Mine was more inclined to hold others at the end of the sugar tongs rather than engage in close connection. These Arctic students had more to grapple with and master than I ever did. I took for granted many things that challenged them, such as easy access to libraries, transport that could take me to interesting places to enhance my knowledge, and my state funded university education. It felt ironic that several classes seemed to think I had much to give them when I knew I received more than I gave all the time. Whenever I taught Alf's class, I was especially humbled by Rastus' approach to life – his genuine humility and gentle grace.

'Well! To answer your question, yes, I come from London. Its central shopping area along two juxtaposed roads called Oxford Street and Regent Street were buzzing with Christmas sales and events – as they always are in December.

I was concerned not to sound like a travel agent, but everyone looked rivetted, so I continued.

'The shops put up spectacular Christmas decorations strung across from one side of the street to the other and display festive windows too. There's a special atmosphere everywhere. Groups of carol singers sing to raise funds for various charities and collect donations from shoppers passing by - who join in for fun sometimes. A small Salvation Army band generally plays too. There's a prominent Salvation Army Centre in Oxford Street itself, which fosters great musicians. Some of them also work in London so can play carols in their lunch hour, sometimes with singers from nearby churches.'

Norway has a different concept of raising money for charity because of its smaller population and its commitment to a comprehensive welfare state. But their charitable giving has always been spontaneous when there is need, for example when there is drought and famine in Africa or floods in Bangladesh or there is destitution in war zones. There may be special appeals occasionally, but people do not stand on street corners with collecting boxes as they used to do in England at that time.

'Are there lots of department stores?' Elsa asked. 'I have an uncle in America who told me about them. He thought there were some in London too that Americans had started.'

'I expect your uncle was referring to a store in Oxford Street called 'Selfridges'?

'Exactly! That's right' said Elsa. 'You've reminded me.'

I continued.

'Rebuilding many stores and shops has taken a while after the London blitz. New ones have also appeared since then, built on sites finally free of bomb rubble. At Christmas most stores employ a Father Christmas for children who queue up and tell him what they'd like for Christmas. There were lots of people doing their last-minute shopping when I was doing my own. It was hustle and bustle everywhere.'

'Hustle and bustle?' someone asked. 'What's that?'

'Don't you know that phrase? It describes a lot of busy, hectic activity – like in a restaurant kitchen.

I wrote the phrase up on the board. 'It's important to learn to spell it correctly – with the 't' as well as the 's',' I pointed out.

'At least we've all have learned a new expression today.' Alf remarked. 'We could always use it as an example of the value of not sticking rigidly to the *pensum*! We'd never have learnt it if we'd had the lesson we were supposed to.'

'Probably not,' I said.

'What did you mean when you said that children queue up to see Father Christmas?' Rastus had at least one small child, so I presumed he would be especially interested to know.

'You know about hanging up stockings on Christmas Eve, don't you?' Everyone nodded. I continued. 'Well, in England, children have got used to getting toys they want at Christmas, from a fantasy character called "Father Christmas".

'Since the war, gifts for children are put in hung-up stockings on Christmas Eve, supposedly by this mysterious Father Christmas. It's certainly been the tradition in England ever since I was little. Small children believe there really IS a Father Christmas.

'Because department stores want people to spend their money, they employ a dressed-up Father Christmas for children to talk to. He wears a red suit with white trimmings and always has a long, white beard. Children sit on his knee and whisper in his ear what they'd like for Christmas. The stores hope that parents will then buy what their children want from adjacent toy departments. It's all part of our English, Christmas ritual – to see Father Christmas in a department store and tell him what you want. And it's horrible when you get older and find out there's no such person, and it's your parents who fill your stockings on Christmas Eve! I felt really upset when I discovered that Father Christmas didn't exist. A lot of childhood magic disappears at that point. Christmas is never the same! I realise now how important all these rituals were to me because there was a sense of increasing availability after the war with money to buy the many new things that could be bought.'

Everyone was listening with rapt attention. Living in such a different culture and circumstances, far away from a city like London meant they hung on every word, keen to glean as much information as possible.

'Does it snow in England?' Sissel asked. Lovely Sissel hardly ever spoke, but when she did, her engaging smile and her perfect pronunciation were a delight. Her commitment to accuracy and learning was second to none.

'Sometimes; not invariably. When I was just home it felt extraordinarily mild in comparison to here. But your homes and buildings are always beautifully warm however freezing the weather. In England, it can be as cold indoors as outside – especially in London. Since the awful smog of 10 to 15 years ago, strict rules apply about what fuel we are allowed to burn.'

'Electric fires, instead of burning coal or coke, are expensive. When power stations were short of coal after the war, there were regular power cuts for a two to three hours at a time. Demand for electricity was high: coal, the fuel to fire up the power stations was in limited supply for several years. There are hardly any power cuts now, just the occasional breaks in supply from overload, when there's high demand for power – such as meal-times. In general, winter in England often **feels** cold, and IS. We have to wear warm clothes inside our homes as well as outside. Even so, we don't need the same level of protection outside that you need here. It's never anything like as cold in England as it is here. But ironically, you are truly warm indoors. We are definitely not! Am I making sense? Is this the sort of thing you want to know?'

Alf spoke again as everyone nodded. 'None of us have been to London, or England. And we were only saying recently that none of us know anyone who has. We're all DESPERATE to go there whenever we get the chance. We really want to know the sorts of things you are telling us.'

'Oh! How nice: but why England? Surely you would all prefer to go to America?' I was genuinely surprised by their apparent Anglophile enthusiasm.

Sissel spoke up.

'I think it's because England's not that far away – at least from southern Norway, and we'd like to see how good our English really is, D'you think we'd be able to make people understand us?' She blushed.

'Of course, you would. Whatever makes you think otherwise?' I was genuinely surprised.

'Well, we don't speak like you, do we? And speaking for myself,' Sissel continued, 'I'd really like to go to England anyway because of what my parents have told me about the war. Our King fled to England from the Germans and remained in charge of our country, running our government and working with the Norwegian Resistance from London, in exile, didn't he? We've always been told that that he was really courageous to refuse to submit to German Occupation as a puppet King, and only got out of the country in the nick of time. That is the right expression, isn't it? My parents told me that that gave many Norwegians courage and hope. And your Royal Family supported him, I believe. That's true, isn't it?'

There was so much Sissel said I wanted to pursue, but I was not sure how to. I just smiled and said, 'He did, indeed. And our monarchy has always been great friends with your royal family. They have the same ideas about monarchies in democratic societies. Which reminds me that I should also mention the Special Christmas Tree your country sends to mine every year, installed in the middle of Trafalgar Square in central London. You know about that, don't you?'

They did not, so I explained.

'The first tree you sent us in 1947 was a present from the City of Oslo to thank the British people for their help during the war. My family moved to London that same year and my parents took us to see the very first tree that same Christmas. And when I was home just now, I went to see this year's – or rather, last year's, tree. You always send it at the beginning of December. It stays decorated in Norwegian style with 500 white lights until Twelfth Night on January 6th. Then it's mulched down for recycling. It's always a Norwegian Spruce that's around 20 metres tall. And what I LOVE is how its smell reminds me of Norwegian forests. I love just standing in front of it, breathing that in.'

Everyone was rivetted, so I continued.

'Anyway, I've always known how wonderful Norwegian people are and just how beautiful your country is, because I came here with my aunt when I was 11. That's when I knew I had to find out what the whole of Norway was like rather than just the West coast where she took me. It's different from what I thought it would be like, even after learning about the Vikings at school!'

Everyone burst out laughing. Alf chimed in. 'Vikings mostly came from the South anyway. We're the only Norwegians who have always known how to behave properly. We're the primitive PROPER Vikings, those of us up here in the PROPER North, I mean.'

There was more laughter.

Questions then returned to my return journey from London, which I described as accurately as I could, making a good story of it, filling in bits of vocabulary. I admitted how frightened I had been on a couple of flights, and that I had been terrified when I had to climb down the side of the *Hurtigruten* to the motorboat. I praised the way I had been treated by the *Hurtigruten* sailors, however, and said it had been great to get to know other colleagues as the four of us were thrown together. It was a fruitful conversation, and a good lesson even if not part of the *pensum*. Everyone learned new things. Most importantly, talking informally meant we had a productive and positive exchange of what we thought and felt – quite apart from many new and unusual words. I think everyone surprised themselves how fluent their English was.

***

Øystein Hansen called round after school. He wanted to see that I was all right after my travels. But he also had other things on his mind. He smiled his twinkly smile when I asked him if he would like a cup of tea. He constantly teased me that it always seemed to be the 'right' time for one.

'English style, with milk?' he asked.

'Exactly!' I replied.

'I'd love it', he said. 'Will you be pouring it out of a teapot as well?'

I knew he was teasing, and I played along. 'Of course,' I said, pretending to curtsey at the same time. Øystein smiled again. He did not want to ruin the jokey exchange but could think of nothing else to say, except 'goody, goody' - another expression I had taught him.

'You must be tired after your extraordinary adventure. Are you?' He showed genuine concern when I relayed the details of my return travel as briefly and accurately as I could.

'Thank you for asking.' I said, before adding, 'I AM weary, actually. Ideally, I'd have liked another day to recover before going into school. But I guess I'll catch up with myself eventually. I found the last bit at the end, really scary. I'm not surprised the trip has exhausted me.'

'Don't overdo things this week,' Øystein advised kindly. He took a few more sips of tea, then said. 'Actually, I want to talk to you about something else. This is not just a social visit, although I WOULD like to invite you to supper tomorrow night. If you're not too tired.'

'I'd love to come. I'll make sure I'm NOT,' I said, settling myself back into my chair to give him my full attention. 'You've been fishing while I've been away then ... but surely not, on reflection. No one fishes at the moment through the ice, do they?'

'You're right. It'll be fish from my freezer I'm afraid. So please don't tell!' He winked as he smiled. 'I just thought I'd have a small supper party in defiance of the cold and dark and introduce you to one or two people I think you won't have met before.'

'That's really kind. Thank you! I'll look forward to that. What language will we speak?' I asked as I sipped a few mouthfuls of refreshing, steaming, hot tea.

'I think they'll all want to show off their English. I haven't said that they don't need to speak it. But they might want to.' And then he added with his naughty sense of humour, 'If they don't know that you know Norwegian, they may well say some things that you'll be glad to know without them knowing that you do.'

We both giggled.

Then Øystein became serious. 'I'm afraid I have some news which you may not like,' he said. 'I have to resign as *Friundervisning* Secretary. I only took the job on in the first place because I was supportive of the idea for Vadsø to benefit from having an English teacher here. It was a new government initiative, and I believe in the project so wholeheartedly that I promised Oslo I would help to bed it in. But the workload from my job here is getting bigger almost every day. So, since things seem to be working well, I really need to hand things over to someone else.'

I knew Øystein was a top civil servant who worked at the NATO station, although I did not know what he actually did. I knew the station had been set up in Vadsø by the Norwegian government to show the Russians that Oslo was seriously committed to NATO. English taught in school had never been his responsibility, and my adult classes seemed to be working well, so he rarely had to liaise with Oslo about them. His counterparts in the South, where *Friundervisning* had been running smoothly for several years, had many more adult classes to support. The year before in Skien I had had adult classes in four different locations, as well as just one or two hours in a couple of schools and three different industrial plants to monitor and connect with. Øystein had done a great political job in helping to establish *Friundervisning* English in Vadsø.

'I understand. But I'm really, sorry to hear it none the less. Will someone take over from you then?'

I felt genuinely sad I would not be working with him any longer. He was a great support. He never interfered but always encouraged and sorted out difficulties diplomatically. He always knew the right person to talk to – such as when he found me somewhere to live. I gathered from his colleagues how much he was liked and respected by his bosses in Oslo too.

'Yes. There's a young woman who's really keen to do so. Her name is Mette Haraldsson - a sailor's wife. She's here at the moment, while her husband is currently not at sea. They are living here, rather than at home in the South, to stay with his mother who wants to get to know their three-year-old son. She's full of energy, speaks excellent English - although she knows she won't have to speak it all the time – and is keen to work with you. She's so enthusiastic, that the day after she heard the post might be coming vacant, she sought me out to ask how to apply for it.'

'I see. That bodes well then, doesn't it? It's good to know that someone actually wants the job.'

Then, almost as if he could read my thoughts, Øystein added, 'Mette most particularly wants to try to build up the adult work and she has some ideas she would like to run past you. Perhaps before I hand over to her officially, all three of us could meet? That way, I could introduce you to each other to smooth over any unfinished business.'

'An excellent idea,' I said. 'Why don't you both come here one evening soon? You can introduce us, and we can chat over tea.'

'I'll get back to you then. Meanwhile, I'll see you tomorrow evening, and don't worry! It'll all be fine – just a different person dealing with the paperwork.'

I knew that we would remain friends. I admired how he made up for the lack of social events and culture in Vadsø by throwing supper parties. He introduced me to a wide variety of interesting and lovely people. He was also a good cook - always of fish, usually freshly caught. He liked introducing people to each other, and inviting colleagues who, like him, were also exiles from the South. After a few glasses of *brennevin*, the illegal, homemade, powerful, but always delicious, alcoholic brew that Øystein made regularly and always kept in stock, everyone would unwind and chatter away as if they had been friends for ever. Behaviour was always impeccable: never any riotous or drunken conduct. So, I always looked forward to his supper parties.

A few days later, Øystein introduced me to Mette.

I drew a sharp intake of breath when I first laid eyes on her - a typical Norwegian stunner. She had style too. She chose colours that not only suited her, but also flattered her glorious, blonde hair in ways that were different from the almost uniform, Norwegian female appearance. She hardly ever wore trousers, for instance. Instead she floated along in long, beautifully cut, woollen skirts over her boots, and draped scarves around her neck that echoed her overall colour scheme. To start with, I could hardly take my eyes off her. She had an elegant way of moving her whole body and hands in particular ways that I found utterly fascinating.

'How do you do?' Mette asked as she extended her hand to me. She continued in flawless English, 'I'm so pleased to meet you. I've read all about you in the newspaper when you first arrived, and I've followed everything you've been doing since. And I'm absolutely thrilled to have this job; I can't wait to get started.'

If I had not known beforehand that Mette was Norwegian, I never would have guessed. Because of her lack of any kind of accent and her fluent use of vocabulary and idiom, I could not help but think she **must** be English.

'How do you do indeed?' I replied. 'Your English is amazing!'

Her father had been a military attaché at the Norwegian embassy in London, so she had spent several years in England when she was growing up. She had even gone to an English school, for a few years. Her parents insisted that only English was to be spoken at home because they wanted their children to be bilingual. It was not until the whole family returned to Norway, when Mette was about 10, that she changed to speaking Norwegian.

The evening continued in a kind of 'Nor-glish'. It turned out to be the first of many occasions in which I could not recall which language was spoken or when, in all the months to come. The most important thing that emerged from it, however, was that I knew Mette and I would be able to work really well together. At first, I thought she might want to take over my adult classes. Øystein had been a great support but was entirely back seat and laissez-faire which suited me absolutely. But I need not have worried. The more we talked and the more time we spent together it was clear that Mette wanted to work with me in just the same way as Øystein had done. She had time to do so too. She relished the opportunity to polish her English – in the same way that I wanted to improve my Norwegian. She also wanted to be friends. She began to drop by for the odd half an hour or so just to chat or talk through some teaching plan or other.

At the end of our first meeting between just the two of us, she said, 'I hope you won't think me rude, but your room is very sparsely furnished. There happens to be an old sideboard in the cellar of my building which doesn't seem to belong to anyone. I wondered if it would be of use to you. It needs a coat of paint. I'm sure it would be useful for storing things, as well as putting things on, so I thought we might paint it together and talk through any bits of business as we do so.'

First of all, it was rare for any Norwegian to say they hoped they weren't being rude, so I was genuinely surprised by that. Secondly it was unusual to suggest spending time together in doing something practical *in*doors instead of *out*doors such as a skiing, hiking or taking a boating trip. It sounded as if I could make really good use of the furniture she described, and I liked the idea of a practical task in view. Though how on earth a *sideboard – of all unlikely furniture* - could be stowed away in the cellar of a house together with a load of outdoor equipment, in Vadsø of all places, I had absolutely no idea.

Together, we managed to move the sideboard, strapped across three *sparks* from Mette's home to mine. Jon and Anders Flyst then helped us get it upstairs. Anders did not actually do much: he was only little, so how could he? But Jon kept on telling him what a great help he was, so he just beamed as he made sure he kept as close to his father as possible, in case anyone spoke to him. He watched in wonder, his little eyes agog at yet another drama happening in his home. He wanted to see and be part of everything!

Bente had done a superb job with the curtains in my quarters. She was right that there was no choice of material in Vadsø, but she had somehow managed to scoop up two fabrics in bright greens and oranges and to hang them so imaginatively – one shaped as a half-moon and the other as a rectangle – so that at least I could be private and unseen from the street. Mette suggested we use two shades of green paint to echo the curtains. Where she managed to get the paint from, I had no idea. The piece of furniture itself was useful too. It was like a typically English dining room sideboard with cupboards and drawers. I was glad to have the use of it to store piles of papers as well as cups and saucers. I could also put things on top –work to be marked, schoolbooks, trays of tea, and best of all, my record player. It was particularly special to me since the same aunt who took me to Norway in the first place had given me this record player for my 21st birthday. Now, I would no longer have to bend down to play my records on the floor – which I invariably did to help me unwind after my day. (I remember that Ray Conniff's singers were my inspiration at the time.) The sideboard greatly improved my quarters It was a most useful acquisition – and it looked good too!

As we painted together, Mette chatted away, wanting to hear how *Friunder-visning* worked in Vadsø with the adult classes.

'What are you doing in your groups?' she asked.

'We're working through a book of short stories I used in the South,' I told her. 'But we've not got far because as soon as any part of the reading touches on anything at all interesting, we find we just go with whatever that is. We learn all sorts of new words that way, as well as many English ways of doing things, and in what feels like no time at all, we find the time's up. Why d'you ask? No one has complained, have they?'

'No! Absolutely not! I just wanted to know, that's all.'

'Since you've raised questions about those groups,' I asked cautiously, I've had some thoughts over Christmas that I want to talk over with them. I'm thinking about the possibility of organising and running an English Evening in a few weeks' time. I haven't mentioned it yet, but I will when I see them next. I want to find out if there's any interest in the idea and if so, if they would take on the necessary admin to make it happen. So, it's just as well you asked.'

'That's a wonderful idea.' Mette stopped painting and held the brush with the bristles pointing upwards for several seconds before realising that the paint might dribble back down her wrist and on to her hand. 'Woops' she said, automatically choosing an English expression as she righted her brush.

'Can I be involved? I don't suppose I could actually come to your next class, could I? I promise to be positive and not say a word unless I was asked.'

I laughed. 'Of course, you can come. I'd love you to. It would be good to introduce you and explain that you've taken over from Øystein anyway. Your feedback would be much appreciated'

We worked energetically at the painting after that to get the task done, sharing ideas as we did so. By the end of the evening, we had pooled a number of thoughts about how an English Evening might work. We wanted it to be entertaining as well as an opportunity to share aspects of English culture. I felt encouraged. Mette's input was timely. I could hardly believe my good fortune to be given yet another excellent colleague to work with. Whenever we met from then on, we were never short of topics to discuss – whether or not it had anything to do with the English Evening.

Chapter Twenty-two

The English Evening

In the South, I only had six periods a week in schools. My classes consisted mostly of adults: daytime classes with factory or chemicals plant workers on site, housewives in community centres or private homes, and evening classes for professional people - engineers, teachers and retirees on school premises. Bosses and managers preferred to meet in their board rooms. The curriculum – if it could be called that – for each class varied according to need. I was asked to encourage confident, conversational English with accessible topics and colloquial management styles, using ordinary every-day idioms as much as possible.

However, in Vadsø, I only had two adult classes - entirely of housewives aged between 20 and 80. Highly motivated, knowing much about life and keen to know more, they were a joy to teach. Conversations invariably morphed into discussions about life, inter-personal communication, bringing up children, cultural behaviour, with frequent references to values and attitudes - and always in English.

I thought about these classes over Christmas. I knew everyone enjoyed them and wondered how we might progress in the New Year. I began to wonder if I might persuade them all to help with what I wanted to call an *English Evening*. There were more dark days to come in the New Year before the sun put it even the briefest of daily appearances, so I thought an evening event might be well-received. Ideas swirled in my head and I decided to discuss them with both groups.

'I'm so pleased to meet you all - to let you see my face.' Mette smiled as she met the first of my groups. I wondered if she knew how beautiful she was as I registered the looks on various faces. 'Just so that you know who I am if we meet in the street.' She swept her eyes around, taking everyone in.

'*Friundervisningen* in Oslo had been unsure whether there would be any interest in learning English outside the school curriculum so far from their usual sphere of operations. So, it's great there are a couple of classes in full swing.' She paused. 'I can tell by the looks on your faces that you enjoy them. Am I right?'

Fru Lium was a doctor's wife whose husband was working a five-year contract in Vadsø. She was well-educated, courteous and kind. They had temporarily moved north. I wondered if they, including their two daughters found life challenging. Not because they were snobby or aloof, but the extreme cold and darkness might mean they had little time or energy for entertaining. Perhaps they also missed going to concerts, plays or films available in Oslo?

'For me,' she said in flawless English, 'this class has become one of the highlights of my week: especially now, when it would be so easy to get depressed because I mind the lack of light. Our sessions together have taught us a lot. Also, we're all more confident in knowing and speaking English, aren't we?' She looked around at radiant smiles. 'More importantly still, we've all become friends.' She looked around again. Everyone nodded even more vigorously in agreement.

Someone else said, 'The classes are fun. I enrolled because I wanted to become fluent if I could. I want to know what to say when my husband brings his English work-colleagues home. We come from Stavanger where we often have English visitors to host for days at a time. When we return there, I want to be able to look forward to such English visits, instead of feeling anxious.'

I knew there were few decent hotels outside Oslo. Overseas business-people working with the developing southern Norwegian oil economy in particular tended to stay in the homes of their Norwegian counterparts. Coming and going at that time with the emerging oil industry meant there were many British and American personnel working in towns on the west coast and speaking English. Larger towns had good hotels, and restaurants, mainly for commercial travellers who needed rooms and charged everything to expense accounts. Otherwise, staying in hotels or eating out was a rare treat for most people. Both were expensive and heavily taxed. There was limited choice and no concept of 'cuisine'. Holiday hospitality was developing along the west coast and around the most visited fjords mostly for tourists, and accommodation was appearing apace. In Vadsø, and similar small towns however, there tended to be just one small hotel with a restaurant offering minimal choice. I do not remember how often there were guests in Vadsø's hotel, but the restaurant served many working professionals every day. Most of us teachers ate there, for example.

'I've learnt such a lot. We all have. 'And we've been taught things we wanted to know about too – like how to make a pot of tea and bake a Victoria sponge. So, we have choice in our coffee-break - we keep TRYING to remember to call it a tea-break and we really WILL one day. Anyway, there's always someone who brings an ENGLISH cake. We take it in turns. We light a candle, which is the

Norwegian way and it's dark here, and it's just like having a party – except that we speak English, learning as we go along.'

'Obviously, I've paid each and every one of them to say these things,' I said to Mette, who, for a moment looked shocked before everyone burst out laughing.

'Goodness,' she said, 'I thought you were serious for a minute. You really had me there!'

Another member of the class spoke up. 'Because we've all got to know each other, we really DARE to speak English and so we've become more confident and fluent. We're learning new vocabulary and idioms, and things we knew nothing about, as well as the difference between ENGLISH and AMERICAN English.'

'That's good to hear. I don't suppose you could give me examples, could you? My *Friundervisning* bosses in Oslo need to know that the North is not as cut off as many southerners think it is.' Mette spoke in her flawless, enchantingly phrased English. 'Anything I can tell them to reassure them would be helpful.'

'Yes!' This was a bold response from someone who had not spoken yet. 'What I was so pleased to learn about, that I had never heard of before, was English Pantomimes. If ever I'm in England over Christmas and New Year, I shall make a point of going to see one. They sound quite different from any other form of entertainment.'

'And we'd no idea at all how to make a pot of tea, or how to serve it,' someone else said. 'We thought we did, but we didn't have the first idea! I don't like coffee so I'd love to own an English teapot and a proper kettle. I would much prefer to plug in to an electric socket instead of boiling water on a hotplate. It isn't easy to pour boiling water from a saucepan into a teapot. It's heavy, clumsy, and potentially dangerous, especially when my hands shake because the pan's so heavy.'

The conversation turned towards the idea of an English Evening. 'What a great idea!' was the immediate, excited response. They could hardly wait to start. Suggestions flowed. A basic plan began to materialise.

A date was chosen in early March. It would still be dark, but with some daylight for a few hours or so, morning and evening, heralding the return of Spring. Complete darkness in Vadsø runs from November 26th to January 17th. But for a few weeks either side, minutes of increasing light, morning and evening every day began to alleviate total darkness. A fun evening event to look forward to at that time would hail longer periods of returning light.

My suggestion that the evening should start with a light-hearted talk about what it was like to be a Norwegian journalist, temporarily working on a newspaper in London was welcomed enthusiastically. Gunnar, a friend of Øystein's to whom I had been introduced at one of his suppers, was the person I was thinking to invite. He had been seconded to Fleet Street from his Oslo newspaper for a few months. He promised to tell some funny stories about his experiences. When I asked him to do it and enquired about the sort of stories he would tell, he assured me he had loads that were hilarious, and at his own expense.

'For example,' he said, 'there was the occasion when I asked a young lady if she would like to come and have a bath with me, when I really meant a bathe. And actually, I should have simply asked her if she would like to join me for a swim. We'd discovered from friendly conversations around the office that we both liked swimming. So, I said I thought it might be nice to go together sometime. She was terribly embarrassed, and I felt mortified when she explained what I had actually asked. I had no designs on her at all, I assure you! And anyway, I knew she had a serious boyfriend in the army. The fact that he was currently overseas made matters much worse for a while, once I understood what I had actually said! But eventually, after some embarrassing days, we agreed it was quite funny, and I was totally forgiven.'

The more I pictured the scene and the conversation that might have transpired between a shy, reserved, young typist in a newspaper office and a glamorous, forthright, Norwegian hunk, the more I laughed. I liked the way Gunnar told the story too. He had an understanding of how to plant oral footsteps towards an hilarious climax. He knew exactly how to build and milk it at the same time.

'Then there was the time when I thought I'd like to shop in Harrods,' Gunnar explained. 'I had heard that you could buy anything at all there, from a drawing pin to an elephant, and I wanted to see for myself what this famous department store was like. So, I wandered in one Saturday morning. I must have looked a bit lost because a floorwalker came up to me and asked if he could help me. I thanked him and told him I wanted to buy some *nikkers*, by which, as you know, I meant *men's specially designed knee breeches for skiing*. I thought the English was almost the same as the Norwegian, since I had heard the word like it spoken often enough. So, you can imagine my embarrassment and total confusion when he actually led me to the *Ladies Lingerie Department* and introduced me to a sales lady who, he said in the politest language possible, would assist me further. I don't remember exactly what I said to her, but I CAN remember that I've never made my excuses so hastily or dashed out of a shop so quickly in all my life. I thought everyone in the street could see how red-faced I was and thus assumed that I must be guilty of some terrible misdemeanour.'

I was convulsed with laughter once again. It was utterly brilliant, I thought. He was a good story-teller and I believed his funny experiences would go down well with an audience, whether or not they spoke English fluently.

Another tranche of the programme was given over to some music, of course. The male voice choir wanted to be included again. They promised to sing some English songs. Then, since I had picked up various copies of madrigals I had sung at school while I had been home for Christmas, I tentatively suggested to Per Johann that his quartet might like to learn to sing one or two at the English Evening. He was delighted by the idea.

'What on earth are these *madrigals?*' he asked. 'I've never heard of them.' I played one or two through so that he could judge what they might be in for. At once he said how much he enjoyed the sound, although he thought the words were really weird!

'They're written in sixteenth century English, that's why they're weird as you call it,' I explained. 'Per Johann, if you had been a courtier at the time of Queen Elizabeth I, you would have been expected – as part of your manly duty, as well as your deference to your Queen – to sing music like this at sight, of an evening, when everyone socialised at Court by singing and dancing after supper. You'd be expected to be able to do that in just the same way as you would have been able to read words in English and Latin, fight duels and also fight for your country's honourable success. It would have been thought *very, very UN-manly* not to be able to sight-sing when required, especially if the reason why you couldn't, was that you actually couldn't read music.'

'Ah ha! Well we'll have to rise to our manly duty then, won't we? And pretend we're at Court! Don't worry Miss Russell we'll do you a brilliant job. Just you wait and see.'

Per Johann could always be relied on to enter into the spirit of things. I knew he meant what he said and that I could leave him to get on with recruiting his friends and learning the music.

Nothing daunted, within three or four weeks, with the minimum of help from me, this inspiring quartet learnt *The Silver Swan, My Bonny Lass, she Smileth, Now is the Month of Maying* and *All Creatures Now are Merry Minded.* They produced a fantastic sound when they were confident and sang out. They found it extraordinarily amusing to sing old English words with - *eth* on the end, and to learn about *lasses and lads*. 'It's all grist to the learning English mill,' I thought to myself.' All four of them lapped it up and felt proud of themselves – justifiably so.

'You jolly well SHOULD all be proud of yourselves,' I said to them after a practice one evening. 'These madrigals are not easy to sing, and you make them sound wonderful. You blend so well together. You must keep going as a group if you can – when you've left school. You have huge potential.'

Grethe, the wonderful soprano, asked if she could sing a couple of solos at the event.

'I'd love the experience – if you don't think it a cheek to ask?'

She actually asked using the Norwegian word *frekk* – the meaning of which is explored in a previous chapter. Grethe was genuinely unsure if it was appropriate to ask. In those days, especially in remote Finnmark, Norwegians believed the English had extremely rigid codes of conduct to which everyone unquestioningly conformed. I had many an interesting conversation with students trying to be realistic about what was, and what was not true about both their culture and mine. I always told them it would NEVER be a problem to ask. Even when *frekk* could mean anything from a charmingly daring question to brazen impudence, Grethe's request could not have caused anyone's eyebrows to rise.

'Let's go and find somewhere to chat, Grethe,' I said moving away from the public hall where so much was going on, down the corridor to an empty classroom. We sat facing either side of a desk.

'Is it the experience of singing in public you're after?' I asked, in as kindly a tone as I could. 'Is that why you're asking me and wondering if it's out of order to do so?'

'Well, yes. It is. I didn't know whether I SHOULD even ask you, because although you've encouraged me, I don't know if I'm any good. I talked about it with my parents. I asked them if it would be *frekk* (that word again) to even ask, and they said I would only find out IF I asked. They said you would soon tell me if I was out of order.'

I admired her integrity - and was touched that she trusted me enough to ask.

'Grethe,' I said, 'you have a lovely voice, and it's a privilege to work with you. If you were to sing you would experience what it feels like to perform in front of people. So, of course you can! Had you anything in mind?'

Grethe grinned sheepishly, relieved.

'I have. I'd like to sing two Schubert songs. I know he wasn't English, but 'Who is Sylvia' is popular in England, isn't it, and after all it's from a Shakespeare play. It is, isn't it? My Dad said it's from a song in 'The Two Gentlemen of Verona.' Is that right?'

Amazed, because I was certain few English people had even heard of 'The Two Gentlemen…', never mind that the popular song came from that play, I nodded before adding, 'that's right.'

'And then I'd really like to have a shot at 'The Erl King'. I know that's not English either, but the whole idea of the story it tells is from a Scandinavian, well Danish really, fairy story, or folk lore. And at one time, English kings were Danish, weren't they? And I could at least SING it in English, couldn't I?'

Amazed again, and not a little daunted by the prospect of having to manage the piano accompaniment to the latter, widely known to be fiendish, I simply said, 'You're right, it is, you could, and I'll TRY to accompany you!'

We both giggled. Grethe knew the accompaniment was fast and difficult, but she trusted me to play it. I liked the uncomplicated relationship between us. I liked the way my students treated me – always friendly, but never disrespectful.

'Great. But there's one more thing I want to ask, Miss Russell. Jan Erik would love to sing too. Can I tell him to come and talk with you?'

'I can't possible even SPEAK to him unless he promises to find something with a very easy piano accompaniment.' I kept a straight face, but neither of us could help bursting with laughter again.

Jan Erik sought me out soon after. He also wanted to sing a couple of solos at the English Evening. I trawled through the music I had brought back from London at Christmas and found two English folk songs I thought would be suitable: Thomas Arne's 'The Lass with the Delicate Air' and Charles Horn's 'Cherry Ripe'. So, the three of us - Jan Erik, Grethe and myself - would be performing at an English Evening during a period of almost total darkness, in sub-zero temperatures, more than 1,600 miles from the origin of the music's inspiration. I loved it!

***

In early January I received a polite note from an elderly gentleman signing himself 'Vigleik Tosk'. He played the violin, and he had heard that music was to be included in an upcoming event, called an English Evening. I remember wondering how he knew that I was the person to contact. I'd never met him, or even heard his name before. There were few who even knew our plans. We had not begun to advertise it. The way news travelled in this small, tight-knit community never failed to amaze me. We agreed a place and time to meet. He arrived at the Flysts exactly when he said he would.

Vigleik Tosk was a diminutive Rumplestiltskin of a man: small and wiry with long, strong, artistically musical fingers. 'I wonder what kind of sounds he manages to produce with those?' I thought to myself when I saw how he used his fingers to gesticulate as he talked. He was unbelievably well-mannered. In fact, had he been differently dressed, I might well have believed he had somehow morphed straight from the lavish and culturally exquisite court of Louis XIV of France!

'May I play to you?' he asked.

The whole Flyst family plus me and Vigleik Tosk were sitting round the piano in Bente and Jon's living room. Although none of the Flysts themselves played, they frequently asked me to do so of an evening. I had always accepted their invitations because it helped me to practise, and felt good to play for others, especially if they enjoyed it. They were thrilled at the prospect of being further entertained. I agreed to accompany the intriguing Herr Tosk whom they also had never met.

'Yes, please do,' I said. 'Do you want to play a bit on your own, unaccompanied, or would you like me to play for you straight away?'

'Well, my dear,' - he always called me *my dear* from the very start of our acquaintance - 'allow me please to play a few bars as a kind of audition, if you will. I don't want to trouble you to play at all if you think there would be too great a disparity between us.' Vigleik was humble, charming - and played like a dream.

When he had finished, I said, 'Well, it's clear to me that if you don't play the whole of Vadsø will be hugely deprived! So, what had you in mind to perform?'

I cannot now recall what we agreed. But I remember that, encouraged by Jon and Bente, we rehearsed and polished the pieces on which we'd decided. I also remember thinking we then had a complete programme. It was varied and interesting, involving of a range of contributors with something for everyone to enjoy, whatever their standard of spoken English or what they knew about England. It never failed to amaze me how sterling these people were. All around there was a wealth of hidden talent and skill.

To bring it all together and make sure everything ran like clockwork, my two adult English classes agreed to work collaboratively. They met as usual for our classes. Otherwise, they worked together to plan and sort whatever needed doing.

At one such meeting, Fru Andersen, a lovely elderly person, asked if the evening could be rounded off with what she called 'old time dancing'? She had been introduced to it while she and her husband spent a year in England for his work. Herr and Fru Andersen loved a programme in those days called *The Black and White Minstrel Show* – rightly unacceptable as a format a few years later - and *Come Dancing*. They had been thrilled to have had a colour TV in the furnished house they had rented and had learned to love the music of the former and the grace and elegance of the latter. Nowadays, *Strictly Come Dancing* is the modern equivalent and appeals to a much wider audience. Fru and Herr Andersen had been inspired to learn how to waltz, quickstep and foxtrot as well as the format of country dances, like *The Dashing White Sergeant, The Gay Gordons* and various *Scottish Reels*. They went regularly to tea dances at community centres in England and thought a chance to spread the fun of their experience too good an opportunity to miss.

There was so much to do that many of us, including me, seemed to forget about the dark and cold. Mette repeatedly said that she had not expected her new job to be so much fun. She would often drop in, and we would invariably make a pot of tea and chat through the arrangements we still needed to settle. The Evening was widely advertised. Everyone in the town knew about it.

The event was a great success. The Nok4 tickets - probably about four shillings then and equivalent to £2 now - included cups of properly brewed tea and slices of variously flavoured Victoria sponge cakes, rather than the usual Norwegian fare of coffee and *smørbrød* - Norwegian open sandwiches, a feast in themselves – or *bløttkakker* – very, very creamy sponge cake. Homemade English sponge cakes were all sold out, and the whole atmosphere of the evening was hugely enjoyable. Øystein's journalist friend was a brilliant communicator. His talk was achingly funny: he should have been on the stage. Everyone enjoyed the dancing, and the write up in the newspaper was glowing.

Not long after the event, daylight began to appear although the days were still short. People returned to walking upright, looking straight ahead, instead of down to see where they were putting their feet. I could have sworn that every single person had a permanent smile stitched on his or her face. Relief and joy that darkness was once again yielding to the light was almost palpable.

Chapter Twenty-Three

Hammerfest

It was Mette who suggested I should go to see Denis in Hammerfest. She saw I was drained after the English Evening. I had loved doing it, but I did not want weariness to affect my teaching. Also, I had not realised how much the then mostly dark days – with just minutes of daylight - would sap my energy. I was warned I might find it taxing and was surprised just how true that proved to be. I remember being curious to experience what it was like without natural light for weeks on end, deciding at the same time that I would not let it bother me. Arrogantly, I had believed that what I had been told about the difficulties of the dark time would somehow not apply to me! Now, at the time of writing, I know and understand what lack of sunlight means. The change in melatonin levels and the lack of vitamin C alone can cause both physical problems and serious depression. How naïve I was then to dismiss such talk as ill-informed and feeble minded! On top of that, the extra work of the English Evening meant that a change of scene was a most appealing prospect.

A nationwide 'ski-break' was imminent. At that time, schools closed for at least three days in late February for people to enjoy daily, family ski trips or time at their family's ski cabin. Even in those days, and certainly in southern Norway, many Norwegians had access to their own, their firms, or something akin to Youth Hostels' winter cabins to retreat to for days of skiing, relaxation and fresh air. In the South, families looked forward to the break and took it seriously, planning time away so that, en famille, they could ski for miles cross-country, enjoying all the benefits of clear, pure air and glistening, pristine snow. The sun's glare, even though the temperature could be well below zero, provided real warmth – actual heat even. I knew this because I had been fortunate enough to join such a trip when I worked in the South. Lengthy, daily, family ski-trips in those days before climate change, when an abundance of snow could be reckoned on, were an important part of Norway's overall social and communal fabric – healthy as well as enjoyable. I could not believe how wonderful the experience of every trip was. I never felt cold. I just loved the fabulous landscapes and enjoyed breathing such incredibly pure, clean air. An experience I shall never forget – especially in today's polluted atmosphere.

Life was different in the Arctic, however. Not just because the days were much shorter, but because skiing in almost total darkness was not as enjoyable. It was certainly not as safe, especially for those of us who had not skied since we could walk. Also, there was not the same access to cabins – even those provided by the *kommune,* echoing the Youth Hostelling culture of other European countries - because the vast expanse of Finnmark tundra, way above the tree line, did not lend itself to as many desirable cabin venues as the southern terrain. Nevertheless, I was looking forward to the upcoming, long weekend break. I knew there would be opportunities for short, daily ski trips in limited daylight and that I would be able to borrow skis if I needed to – since I had left my own in the South – even though it would be several more weeks before the roads were sufficiently clear of snow to make getting out and about an attractive opportunity to enjoy a long expedition.

Mette and I were chatting about skiing in the dark one evening, welcoming the prospect of the long, free weekend ahead.

'There are other English teachers in the Arctic Circle, aren't there?' she had asked.

'Yes', I said. 'Two - in Harstad and Hammerfest.'

She thought for a minute and then said, 'Well, why don't you go and see your colleague in Hammerfest for a couple of days? There would be time to get there and back on the *Hurtigruten*. It would give you a break and you could mull over together what it's like to be a *laerer* in this part of the world. I'm sure you'd have much to talk about.'

I hadn't given thought to travelling after my adventurous return after Christmas. Since I had not been allowed over the border into Russia, I had not been tempted to sally forth anywhere else either. It would have been difficult at this time of year anyway since the only real and reliable means of transport was the *Hurtigruten*, and that was not a particularly attractive prospect to me. But I warmed to Mette's suggestion. The *Hurtigruten* was a reliable surrogate bus or train. A short trip felt a different proposition from my experience in early January!

I knew my colleague in Hammerfest from our *Friundervisning* gathering in Oslo to prepare us all for the year ahead. Those whose first year it was could ask about living in Norway. And those of us who were back for a second year were briefed about our new assignments and used as resource material for our new colleagues, able to answer questions about teaching in Norwegian schools and living in Norwegian communities.

I remembered Denis well. He was an outstanding linguist with a warm and friendly personality. He had worked with the British Council teaching English in another country the year before, following his Oxbridge degree in Modern Languages. He had an excellent ear for pronunciation and nuance and an innate capacity to make language jokes in both English and any other language he knew. He could get his tongue around the most complex and difficult of alien words and sounds with an infectious sense of humour. He was widely read, highly intelligent and good fun. We had chatted once or twice, and I knew he would not mind me asking if I could pay him a visit.

As *Friundervisning* teachers, we had been encouraged to go and stay with each other to get to know the country. Colin, our colleague in Harstad, came to stay with me in Vadsø for a few days at the end of May during the midnight sun period. Harald, a colleague who taught Maths in the gymnasium, offered to put him up and be his tour guide. That was a huge relief to me since I found it difficult to get regular sleep when it was light all the time and often felt weary from the lack of it.

Denis would know how attractive Hammerfest was for all kinds of visitors to explore even in those days. It already had a reputation as the most northerly town in the world, worthy of investigation in its own right for that reason alone. It had begun to attract the attention of the more tenacious and adventurous of tourists, even in the mid 1960s.

Nowadays, Hammerfest is famed for its production of natural gas on the tiny island of Melkøya, connected to Hammerfest's mainland since 2003, thanks to the work of some of Norway's expert tunnel engineers. Even though the small island is an industrial plant, it is an impressive sight to behold. Its cleanly constructed tanks and pipelines make it look like a shapely, clinical moonscape. From it, a pipeline of some 8,800 kilometres – approximately 5,468 miles – takes the gas, which Norwegians themselves do not consume, to other parts of Europe, including the UK. Today, visitors travelling on one of the modern, luxurious *Hurtigruten* cruise ships can not only spend an hour or so in Hammerfest itself, but attend an up-to-date lecture on board about the history of the oil development and the processes that enable us in the UK to receive and benefit from Melkøya's gas production.

The Meridian Column at Fuglenes - Hammerfest's nineteenth century recognition of its furthest north, European position - acknowledges the town's status as the most northerly town in the world even though neighbouring Honningsvåg, literally, Honey Bay, lying to its east, lies even slightly further north. Until recently there were fewer than 5,000 people living in Honningsvåg, so it did not have the qualifying number of residents to call itself a town. Today, however, it has many more residents and is increasingly referred to as a town. At the time of writing, I remain unsure which of the two venues is deemed the 'correct' home for the Meridian Column by those who have the authority to decide. Nevertheless, it currently remains at Fuglenes, where it has been for nearly 200 years.

Long before global warming – well over 200 years ago - Hammerfest was also famed for its ice-free harbour. This still is, and certainly was an unusual asset for any Arctic harbour. Even so, it did not escape several, severe Arctic storms in the late nineteenth century when the damage to it and its immediate environs was so severe that even Queen Victoria was moved to donate towards the harbour's reconstruction. Hammerfest's other claim to fame is that it was the first European town to install electricity. The good burghers of the town bought a generator from no less a person than Thomas Edison in 1891 and invested in street lighting that same year – the first northern European city to do so.

However, Hammerfest suffered greatly during the Second World War. Before it was razed to the ground by the departing Germans, it had been a particularly important base from which they could track Russian ship movements which might threaten their own shipping - especially their U-boats well protected in the deep fjord waters of the Arctic. The feared, largest battleship of the German fleet, the Bismarck, was occasionally rested deep inside many of the waters around Hammerfest. The Germans could also be alert to any strategic Russian and Finnish troop movements. Today, Hammerfest is an entirely sophisticated, modern town, much sought after for its bird and animal life and respected too for its Sami population, in addition to the interesting elements of its historical past.

So, I dropped Denis a note to ask. He responded promptly and seemed delighted by my suggestion.

My imminent adventure meant I would have to take the *Hurtigruten* once again and sail round the North Cape in mid-winter. February and March were months when, in those days, the Arctic seas were known to be particularly rough. There were huge rolling billows instead of waves, and gale force winds would buffet the ship both up and down as well as side to side. Getting to Hammerfest was not a pleasure trip in those days, well-before ships were fitted with steadying mechanisms. But, even with my recent January experience in mind, I knew it would be a special experience with much, much calmer waters once round the North Cape. I would have the chance to take some photos of the coastline which I knew would be stunning covered with snow. I was not to be disappointed. The voyage from Vadsø to the North Cape itself was windy and choppy, but once round it, conditions were calmer and magically beautiful in the winter sun, even though still freezing-cold at many degrees below zero.

We arrived at Hammerfest in the short spell of early morning daylight – a bonus. The town was nestled against a backdrop of clear, soft, blue skies and gleaming white tundra. Smoke from the Findus factory was rising straight up in what seemed like a wispy, pencil drawing in front of its dramatic backdrop of white-capped cliffs, the consequence of low temperature and absence of wind. It was too early for many to be up and about. The whole sight was much more welcoming compared to my arrival in Vadsø the previous August, but the quality of silence was the same. The boat's engines were turned off for the last few yards before we docked making our entry into the harbour a surreal experience in frozen and silent beauty. I have never forgotten it.

The day was sunny and clear. Albeit briefly, it produced a special quality of ice-cold light as the sun rose slightly higher. It had no warmth to shed but it made the snow glisten and dance. I loved that, even as I knew I had to take care on the slippery, pavement-less quayside, and while I could also still feel the ship's movement, swaying up and down beneath me. But without mishap, I managed to walk to the small hotel close to the harbour where I was booked in for a couple of nights.

I was shown to my room, typical of that time: basic, but warm and welcoming, smelling wonderfully of freshly cut, seasoned wood. My quarters also boasted a shower alongside the washbasin and loo. Best of all, the view of the harbour was clear and uninterrupted.

'Could you give me a ring at noon, please?' I asked the female porter who had shown me to my room. 'I shall probably sleep till then and I'm afraid I didn't bring my alarm clock.'

'Of course. I'll tell reception.' She smiled and closed the door quietly behind her.

I began to disrobe. It always took an age to do this whenever one went into any sort of building for any length of time after being out in such a freezingly cold climate. It was the same for everyone throughout the whole country. We always had to remove layers of waterproofs and woollens that had to be carefully folded and either hung up or put over the backs of chairs. Heavy boots and thick socks, sometimes several layers, had to be removed too to change into lighter, indoor footwear. When invited out for the evening or to a party, at least 10 to 15 minutes always had to be set aside to disrobe and change into comfortable, suitable indoor clothes. Only then was it possible to be sufficiently relaxed to socialise in what was always the toastiest warmth once inside any Scandinavian building. No wonder every modern house had a large space or room built and set aside for changing gear from outer to inner – and back again!

I needed to lie down: sleep even, if possible. But before I relaxed completely, I watched the *Hurtigruten* prepare to depart. I heard a good deal of clanging and banging even through the triple glazed windows. The air was so cold that sound travelled. Eventually, it weighed anchor. I watched as the ropes were untied and unwound from the jetty bollards, as the boat heaved itself from its moorings and glided through the protection of the sheltered harbour, out on to the vast expanse of open sea, where it was the only boat in view. Now, the sea was calmer than it had been on the other, eastern side of the North Cape. I watched its smooth exit from the sheltered calm of the harbour, and out beyond. Free from that protection, the ship seemed to dance as it was tossed from side to side, disappearing into the distance, getting smaller and smaller until it turned into a mere dot - and in a moment it was gone.

I lay down on the bed and let my whole body sink into its welcoming comfort. Slowly, I began to relax. I let my mind drift. I began to recall my journey north, along the coast the previous August – the rugged beauty of the coastline at that time in late summer, with so many defiant homesteads and small farms that swept down to meet the water's edge. The *Hurtigruten* had seemed to come upon them suddenly, intruding in what must have been the glorious beauty of a precious view from many a kitchen window in the tucked-in homes along the shores. I recalled the moored, bobbing motorboats, jetties large and small, and the backdrop of protective mountains and hills, now presumably entirely snow covered. Then my thoughts turned to Per Johan and his epic *Finnmarkvidda* ski crossings, the fun of the weekly choir practices and the friendly banter that had become such a feature of it.

Suddenly, out of nowhere, a sharp stab of pain hit me slap bang in the pit of my stomach. It took me by total surprise. But I gradually realised that it was an early reminder that in just a few months' time, or rather weeks, until the middle of June, I would be leaving. The shock unnerved me for several minutes. I did not want to think about being deprived of such a special and beautiful environment or leave the experience of working in a climate full of such wonderful people. But I must have drifted off to sleep at last, because the next thing I knew, my phone was ringing.

'*Frøken*! It's twelve o'clock. You asked for a call.'

Denis had said he would pick me up from my hotel and we would find somewhere to have lunch. I needed an hour to be ready – to feel fully rested, awake and alert. As I had expected, he arrived exactly at the time he had said he would.

We might have got to know each other if we had travelled north the previous August on the *Hurtigruten* together, but Denis had wanted to spend time in Oslo with some friends who lived there. Then I think he flew to the recently built airport in Alta and on to Hammerfest by bus. But we had at least met and knew something of one another's destination and prospects. His flair for languages meant that he was already streets ahead of me in his command of Norwegian. Although I had been immersed in it for more than 18 months and he for only six, he was virtually fluent, especially in pronouncing the special lilt of the North Norwegian way of speaking. And his grasp of nuance was amazing – and often very, very funny. He revealed many utterly hilarious situations and predicaments he had found himself in whilst teaching abroad in the last 18 months. He could have been a brilliantly successful comedian!

We decided to stay in my hotel for lunch. It had its own small restaurant that was warm and quiet. We fell to talking almost at once. We agreed there were special challenges – adjusting to the cold and the sense of confinement: not being able to get away for a weekend. that sort of thing. I had been able to do that on a regular basis the year before in the South. I made weekend visits to the opera or the cinema in Oslo on the train, and monthly trips to see a colleague in neighbouring Sandefjord who had become a good friend. We agreed that the people we worked amongst were fantastic: stoical, sane and well-adjusted. They may not have been widely travelled but they were certainly well read, reasonable and kind.

Denis and I shared personal stuff about how difficult some of the demands and rigours of daily life really were in the Arctic Circle at that time. Ordinary things like how to prepare to get out and about, being sure to wear the right kind of clothing as well as remembering to allow oneself time to get ready to wear it, and all the time that took to be factored into daily life. Denis particularly minded about the absence of fruit. He had come to rely on his freshly squeezed orange juice to start the day and bemoaned the overall lack of vitamin C – but even his complaints were light-hearted and humorous. I also minded about the lack of vitamin C, although lately, I had been able to buy three or four oranges most Saturdays - the only day they seemed to have become available - on my way home from school. I felt it was a worthwhile, well deserved, weekend treat in spite of their exorbitant price. After all, there were not exactly a huge range of treats to spend money on in Vadsø.

Eventually, we fell to talking about the nature of language teaching itself. It was clear to me that Denis's students, young and old, were much more sophisticated than mine. Hammerfest's population was about twice the size of Vadsø's, closer to 4,000 people. In Hammerfest there were also rapidly expanding industries – many to do with fish processing, but also chemicals. There were many more professional people and burgeoning entrepreneurs in Hammerfest than in Vadsø – engineers, lawyers and businessmen were developing prospects and putting down roots. The overall ambiance was different, even though Vadsø hosted a cadre of variously skilled, but equally professional, civil servants.

Visiting Hammerfest for a couple of days helped me to understand exactly why it had been important to the Germans as a strategic Northern Base from 1941. Visiting it also helped me to absorb far more about the importance of the Northern fjords. During the recent *Hurtigruten* trip with my two friends - en route from Honningsvåg to Tromsø to be there in time for the Sunday service - I remember Ann saying out of the blue just how impossible it would have been for the Allies to have located any German U-Boats. Apart from the astonishing beauty of the fjords we sailed through, their widths were immense and their depths incalculable. How the Allies would ever have been able to find a U-boat hidden in such a place is hard to grasp. No wonder top naval sleuths had to guess where the Bismarck had been hiding, using their best, strategic calculations. This was all new information for me and helped me to understand how important Hammerfest was. Sadly however, that did not spare it from retreating German annihilation. The only building left standing in 1945 was a tiny, little used, chapel. However, in the 20 or so years following, by the time I visited Denis, Hammerfest had entirely rebuilt itself and was still growing apace. The streetlights, already in use well before the war, had been restored and extended. Visiting it on the *Hurtigruten* in 2019 with Margaret and Ann was like approaching a Swiss town nestling against the Alps from one of their beautiful lakes. It is clean, orderly, prosperous and well cared for – safely nestling as it does, against and enveloped by, the protective *vidda*.

Its overall more sophisticated and advanced amenities by comparison to Vadsø impressed me. Living there in the weeks without natural light but relying on street-lights would have been quite unlike the experience of total darkness of Vadsø. Even all those years ago, there was a thriving Findus fish factory, a growing petrochemical industry, and a flourishing fishing industry. Many of these projects relied on investment from the Norwegian government, and some from other worldwide investors too. Even all those years ago, there were signs of small businesses growing up among competent and innovative individuals and groups of fishermen beginning to work together. Hence, Denis's adult classes included a plethora of young and ambitious men and women who needed to speak English really well in order to get in-coming business orders and make transactions abroad. Being able to speak English as well as just knowing it, was absolutely THE THING to be able to do in a place such as this.

Denis was just the right person for the task. His teaching was obviously creative and good fun, in addition to the fact that he knew such a lot and could relate to all sorts of ideas and experiences. He loved finding out vocabulary for the most unusual parts of machinery and operating procedures. He also picked up Norwegian expressions and idioms quickly and had made many friends. He seemed to be invited out into peoples' homes for meals all the time. In conventional set-ups wherever he was offered hospitality, wives and children in the household could also learn some English. His presence was hugely appreciated and suited him down to the ground. For him, this was an absolutely ideal place to be - doing what he clearly relished, and it was all extraordinarily well suited to his skills.

Over a cup of coffee, we began to talk about some of the specifics of our roles. We agreed that the *Friundervisning* organisation itself, so far away in Oslo and functioning as it did in such a different milieu from that which we both experienced here in the far North, was annoying at times. It could also be frustrating to be endlessly dominated by the all-encompassing *pensum* – the national school curriculum. I understood this more particularly. I had many more school classes to teach than Denis. He compared it to a similar organisation in Finland, a scheme also endorsed and supported by the British Council where he had lived and worked the previous year, and where he had been allowed to be much more of a free agent – which he had appreciated. He began to doodle on a scrap of graph paper he had to hand as we chatted.

'You don't teach Maths as well as everything else, do you?' I would not have been in the least surprised if he had said yes: but he didn't.

'Goodness no! I just picked up this wad of graph paper from a waste-paper basket somewhere in school. I couldn't have them throw it away, could I? Even though making paper to the Norwegians is like picking tea in Ceylon! I thought it was a waste to throw it away. I was sure it would come in handy somehow.'

'Indeed! It seems to be doing precisely that. What are you drawing exactly, then?' I was intrigued.

'As we were talking, I just had this idea about the best way to describe an English language teacher. Did you have language assistants when you were at school - who came to help you speak French, Italian or German? Didn't you find them a special kind, or breed, of person? Very earnest, I'd say they were. And in my experience, they always seemed so anxious to please. Well! I don't see myself like that at all. And right now, I just felt inspired to produce this little piece of nonsense. It just, sort of popped into my head. What d'you think?'

I took the sheet of graph paper Denis had been working on and immediately began to smile. This is what he had written: 'The *Sprawklairer* bird is a dying species. It exists in two distinct sub-species, the indigenous type and the migratory form known as the *reisende lektor*.

At this point, I laughed out loud. 'How clever!' I said. *Språk*, is the Norwegian word for 'language', and *laerer*, for 'teacher'. Juxtaposed, the pronunciation was exactly the same, as the name Denis had given to the dying species of bird that would be enunciated when spoken out loud. *Reisende* means 'peripatetic' and *lektor* was the word used for a qualified teacher who taught any subject in a secondary school or at a higher level still.

Denis's description continued: 'The species was first discovered and refined in London by selective breeding methods by a well-known ornithologist and vermin-specialist from Norway,' he continued. Here, he was referring to the wonderful Norwegian lady who had recruited her team of English Language Tutors at The British Council in London – which included both Denis and me - for dispersal all over Norway. She interviewed us all personally and agreed with the government's policy that learning English was a key element in the necessary programme of developing and continuing renewal of the country's economy. Knowing and speaking fluent English was essential if Norwegians were to step out and resume their rightful place of influence in the world, and if they were going to buy and sell on the world market – both goods and services. She was exactly the sort of educated patriot who would have been a real thorn in the Nazis' side.

I went on reading. 'She had been attempting to make the species settle in many parts of her country and is a specialist in her field: she has even considered the possibility of founding breeding colonies on volcanic atolls in the Arctic Ocean. The results of her research have produced some remarkable varieties after experimentation. One of these is the *Sprawklairer*, a sub-species of the *reisende lektor*!'

Under this scribbling, Denis then drew a sketch of a couple of scrawny, bewildered looking and irritated birds with long beaks and very little plumage, sitting on a nest. Underneath the picture he had written: 'a family of *Sprawklairers*, sitting on their *pensum*'. This was a reference to the nationally controlled syllabus, which all students were supposed to be studying at the same time. The note continued. 'Due to the unfavourable natural conditions prevalent in their habitat they have developed a kind of special solidarity for defence against their natural enemy the wild and ferocious *Free Under Visning*.'

It was a creative, spontaneous piece of scribble of pure genius. We both laughed loud and long at the idea of ourselves, portrayed by the two birds sitting on their *pensum*. The concept itself was brilliant, but it was the look on the birds' faces that absolutely made the whole thing. It was inconceivable that birds, even in Walt Disney films, could appear to look so perplexed. But here were these two disgruntled creatures looking indignant, disorientated and disbelieving at each other!

All too soon, the day passed. I felt exhausted by the chat, my journey and a disrupted sleep pattern. But I was also beginning to feel renewed and restored after so much laughter and so many shared experiences and expressions of solidarity. Eventually I made my excuses and returned to my hotel. We had agreed that the next day we would wander round the town. Denis said he would take me to see his school and show me where he taught his adult classes in the town's community centre. After one more meal together, I would leave to board the *Hurtigruten* back to Vadsø.

I wish I could remember more of my visit and recall all of the conversations we had. Once I left Norway, I lost touch with Denis, but was reconnected with him recently in the most extraordinary way. I have a daily message box which automatically fills itself up with all kinds of Christian news, national and international. Recently, I was notified about the retirement of the Chaplain to the Chapel Royal at Hampton Court, by the name of Denis Mulliner. An unusual surname, not that common I thought. My follow up detective work led me to the Chapel Royal online where, sure enough, I learnt he had been the Chaplain for many years, from which role he was now retiring. There were many charming photos of that place of worship and its community and included one of Denis with Her Majesty the Queen since she delivered her Christmas Message at that Royal Peculiar in 2010, and Denis was looking after her while she was there to record it. I engaged briefly in a couple of emails with him, to confirm that he was indeed the colleague I remembered and explained that I wanted to include him in my book about my own Arctic adventure. He will have many, special incidents to reflect on with his family, as well as the respect of many colleagues. I hope his retirement is long and happy.

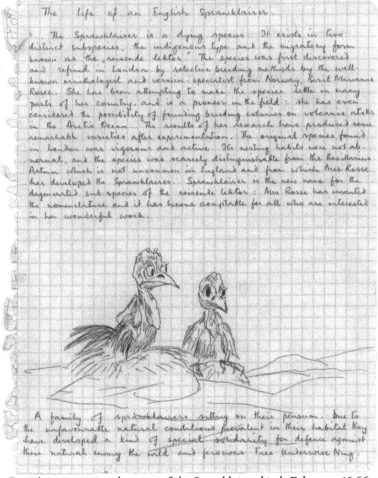

Denis's imaginative drawing of the Spawklairer bird, February 1966.

Chapter Twenty-Four

A Good Read

It was at the beginning of my first year in the South that I discovered what avid readers Norwegians are. For the first few weeks of my year there, before my timetable was neither confirmed nor operational, the only person I knew was my local boss. He suggested I used the unstructured time to explore the towns where I was to teach. I could find out where and when I could catch a bus from venue to venue. Thus, I could work out where to shop and learn when shops would be open - limited in those days to just a few hours every day - as well as the location of the factories, operational plants, school and community centres where I would be teaching. This was helpful, especially as I soon realised that all the buses ran strictly on time.

In the process of getting my bearings, I discovered a sizeable town library. I was pleasantly surprised to find how well stocked it was, including many books in English. Judging by their appearance they looked and felt as if they had been frequently borrowed too. There was an array of Agatha Christie and Ngaio Marsh crime novels, so I borrowed plenty of light reading 'who -dunnits' to keep me going during my first weeks when I had not yet met my classes or begun to make friends. The library building itself also impressed me. It was light and warm with plenty of places to sit, relax and read. There were quiet, secluded alcoves with chairs and tables to sit at and work. The library was well used and always busy whatever time of day I called in.

My local boss was a typical Norwegian patriot. He spoke brilliant English which absolutely riveted his two small boys, and impressed his wife, who knew he was fluent, but had no idea that he could sustain endless and specific conversations with a native. During my first weekend, he drove me out and about, together with his wife and sons, to pick berries in the local woods and enjoy a smørbrød picnic by a lake. Then he drove us to see as many interesting places as possible, prompted I felt sure by suggestions from his wife. He told me several times while we were getting from place to place that his sons were mesmerised by his knowledge of English – as well as being in the company of an English 'Miss'. His Christian name was Lars, and he loved all things English.

It was Lars who had found me somewhere to live. He had chosen rooms with an elderly couple, market gardeners who lived in the middle of nowhere between two of the main towns where I was to teach. This was a thoughtful solution in terms of my being able to get from one place to another, especially as the family were obviously delighted to be hosting an English person to lodge in their midst. However, his choice meant I was isolated from most of the facilities I needed, such as the library, shops, the bath house and even the church. Most importantly of all, it was impossible to get to know anyone. So, it was my regular bus trips to the library in those early days that coincidentally helped me to find somewhere else to live in the nearest town centre. I discovered a suitable bed-sit, at the top of a hill with a great view of the whole town. It was adequately furnished, and a warm and cosy place to which I could invite people for a cup of English-style tea or just a comfortable chat. It had a small galley kitchenette, a shower room with a washing machine as well as a large bed-sitting room. I could walk from my new home to several teaching venues in that particular town too.

My bed-sit belonged to the man in town who owned the 'radio and all-things-electrical' shop. Sadly, I do not remember his name, but I recall how kind and helpful he was. I had been told about him by someone in the choir that I had joined because Lars had asked me what I liked to do in my free time. He was thrilled that I said how much I enjoyed making music and singing because the main town where I was to teach had a nationally recognised choir with a well-known and widely respected choir master, to whom Lars introduced me. And it was subsequently someone in the choir who told me about the man with the 'radio and all-things-electrical' shop. I eagerly sought him out.

He was an elderly, kind and approachable individual whose name I can no longer recall. He spoke no English, and I knew no Norwegian at that time, but we managed to communicate somehow. The first time I went to pay him my monthly rent – which he wanted in cash, put directly into his hands - I asked if it was also possible to rent a radio – or a wireless as it was called in those days - for the whole year from him. I had been taught how to ask that by someone I met in the choir who has been a close friend ever since - for the last 56 years, in fact, and we are godmothers to each other's children. At first, the owner of the 'all-things-electrical' shop was surprised that I would want to rent a radio, but he readily agreed to accommodate me. I do not remember exactly how much I had to pay each month, but I definitely remember it was a ridiculously small sum even then: what would nowadays be about 50p. It was more than worth it, however, since it enabled me to listen at certain times of the day to what was called the 'BBC Home Service' in those days – a station that eventually morphed into Radio 4. My pad was at the top of a hill so I could pick up several BBC stations easily and clearly. At least it helped me to be up to date with the world's news, and I could listen to concerts from London on the Third Programme – now Radio 3 - in my evenings when I was not teaching. That was lovely at the end of a day when I was tired, as I tried to unwind, organise a meal for myself and probably prepare a load of work for the next day. I also clearly remember listening to most of Winston Churchill's funeral service as it was broadcast live from St. Paul's Cathedral. There was no time to listen to much else, and no TV in Norway in those days although there was a good deal of excited chatter that it might be coming to Oslo and its closest environs within a year or so.

Looking back as I write, I cannot help wondering what this kindly, gentle and polite Norwegian gentleman must have thought, or more particularly, felt, about my request to rent a radio. It was not that long after the war after all, when owning a radio could lead to one's immediate death – being shot on the spot, no questions asked. I have already mentioned hiding the Bismarck in Norwegian northern fjords in the previous chapter. In the great black and white film which stars Kenneth Moore as the senior naval officer to track and sink the Bismarck to prevent it from taking out any more convoys with supplies of essential food and equipment from the United States to the British Isles, a member of the Norwegian Resistance movement is contacted right at the beginning of the film. The top military brass in London need to identify a vessel known to be lurking in some deep, northern *fjord*, because they believed it had to be the 'Bismarck' waiting on further orders from Berlin. This was known to be a highly dangerous thing to do because radio emissions were quick and easy to detect. Sure enough, this brave, Norwegian patriot was found and shot within minutes, without hesitation. Many other wireless operators suffered the same fate. I wonder now whether the fact that my chivalrous landlord had only the one wireless available for rent echoed for him any reservations or recollections of the previous dangers of owning one.

At first, I found the absence of media access a sad and dreary state of affairs. In England, BBC TV was already broadcasting BBC2 at that time and ITV had been functioning for at least five years. But I quickly came to see that there was little sense of lack for any Norwegian since they were all the most avid of readers. And I also soon discovered from my adult classes just how widely read and well informed they were about many, many things – world affairs and international politics in particular, as well as specific details about British politics. Their overall knowledge astounded me, and frequently put me to shame. They were often keen to discuss what they had read from books and daily newspapers.

As I write now, many public libraries in the UK are under constant threat of closure, not least because of dwindling footfall, as well as the gradual and sad loss of funding. Increasingly, they are seen by the local authorities, who pay for them, as an expensive, under-used luxury rather than an immediate, informative resource. Many local and national politicians in the UK who have to balance both local and country-wide finances see libraries as unaffordable and unnecessary extras.

Today, the use of libraries in Norway could not be more different. They have always been well used and appreciated all over the country. It is unsurprising, therefore, that a specific number of magnificent, architecturally striking, public libraries have been built in recent years. The annual, official survey for 2019 shows that at least 14 per cent of all Norwegians read more than 21 books a year. Only four per cent of Norwegians read no books at all. In 1985, the Norwegian government passed into law the stipulation that all counties in Norway MUST have a public library. And even though access to some libraries may be difficult – impossible for some readers even, for parts of the year, such as the remotest of islands around the whole of Norway's coast, as well as many Northern, Arctic towns and villages – such places are regularly reached via vans and ferries. Their reliable timetable keeps their readers up to date with a constant supply of books as well as important magazines and newspapers, managing to reach even the most inaccessible of places.

If you google 'Norwegian Libraries', the first response details six new libraries which also serve as vital community centres. They have been built so as to answer every possible local and cultural need, as well as attracting international attention and prizes for their design and construction. They are beautifully sited too. Since there is so much space in Norway, many recently built public buildings have been built where they are both accessible and yet also have the most magnificent of views, often of local *fjords* or lakes, to which they also may have easy access for boating, sailing and swimming following a trip to change a book or find information or share lunch with a friend or attend a live concert.

When I lived in Vadsø, I was genuinely surprised that in spite of its remoteness, it too had a library. It was tiny. Nevertheless it stood in the centre of the town. In spite of its size, it managed to serve as one of the town's main social hubs. It was only open for a few hours every weekday, and if my memory serves me right, the librarian performed her duties as a labour of love, receiving only the occasional gratuity because the *kommune* had no money with which to pay her a proper salary. (Or perhaps she may have refused to accept their payment.

I do not recall which.) Those who ran the town had to use what little money they had to keep everything going and everyone safe in the most difficult of climates and remotest of venues. But albeit the library operated on a shoestring, the librarian was always ready with advice about what individuals might like to read next. She spent time and effort acquiring books from libraries in Oslo, even though she was the one and only library employee.

Every now and then the librarian would order a film, rented from a source in Oslo. This is yet another process I cannot recall, but I definitely remember that folk were able to watch films courtesy of the one and only person in town who could work a projector. He made himself available for a couple of nights every six or seven weeks, whenever a film from the South was available. There was a small hall with staggered seating where we watched these films. I distinctly remember the James Bond film that arrived to Per Johan's great delight, at the time when we were reading the exact same book.

Before my recent return to Vadsø, I had made arrangements over the phone to visit the new, secondary school. It was in the final stages of being built, but all classes were now functioning normally. The building where I taught was still there in the town but was nothing like big enough to cope with the increased school population, which included teenagers of refugee families from Syria seeking new life in Arctic Norway, I wanted to book ahead and chat with students and find out what life was like for them and what they thought about living so far north. But my well-laid plans fell apart because the school had forgotten that the time that we had agreed over the phone when I could go and do my face-to-face research turned out to be an important exam week. Hence, I decided I would use that time to find out what had happened to the library in the time since I lived there.

To begin with I could not find it. **I** could not believe that the town no longer had a library, but it was nowhere to be seen near the town centre. Eventually, I came upon it almost by accident, when I was wandering round what had now become what could genuinely be called the town's outskirts. There were enough new roads and buildings to give its additional, expanding area such a name. The sight of the library building, a hundred yards in front of me stopped me in my tracks. Ahead, I could see a large, attractive, one-storey, wooden building which had some extremely healthy-looking bushes in front of it. This astonished me, since any sort of vegetation rarely thrived in this wind-swept, Arctic town unprotected from the elements. The newly made road leading right up to it meant it looked like a convalescent home, or a small-town American hotel – except that it seemed far too big for either of those. Like nearly all of Norway's new civic buildings, it was sited close to water, with great views across the Verangerfjord. It was such an impressive and unusual sight for Vadsø that for some minutes, I could hardly take it in. It took me a while to realise that I was in fact looking at the town's new library. It was a veritable jewel in Vadsø's crown.

I made my way inside where it was even more impressive. It may not be in the running for any architectural prize such as the magnificent Vennesla Library in Agder, or the Stormen library in Tromsø and it may not emulate any of the splendid centres of culture like some of the libraries in Oslo, but as a place to sit, relax and read, it is a truly wonderful facility in such a remote place.

I wandered round it for a couple of hours. I wanted to know what kinds of books stocked its shelves and how everything was organised. First of all, I explored a delightful, area for children, equipped with tiny chairs, and any number of soft toys to attract and play with. On display were many special and appealing, colourful books for little ones to enjoy with comfortable seats for accompanying adults.

For grown-ups, there was a massive choice of reading material from the most recent political biographies, through various fact and fiction collections, to whole shelves devoted to learning English, several other foreign tongues as well, with the corresponding tapes and CDs. An abundant stock of newspapers from around the world were spread around. There were any number of DVDs, films and 'How to' pamphlets and tapes. There were lots of books in English, as well as Russian, Finnish, German and Arabic.

In total, the library houses some 85,937 books. This total includes 36,198 books in other languages. In addition to the four already mentioned, there were books in French, Swedish, Danish, Icelandic, Kveeni – which is the language of the Finnish Sami people - Farsi – Spanish, Somali and Tigrinja – spoken by Eritreans, and northern Sami, generally the language of Sami speakers in Finland. I also learned that the library holds parish records as well as all the census reports between 1801 and 1910. In addition, it keeps Probate records, Court records, Land records and Farm books. In fact, this superb new library houses pretty much all the information about life in Vadsø for the last 250 years.

It was a school day, so there were only a few of us in the library late morning. It felt like a luxurious 'knowledge cathedral'. Compared to the British Library in London, where I often used to work in recent years, it was quieter and much more comfortable and user-friendly. It would be joyous to work there I felt sure. For a town of not quite 7,000 people it was a wonderfully, almost exotic, resource

I thought. What a great place to be able to browse, to write, to sit and think or complete one's daily homework! I wished I had had time to stay there reading and browsing for the whole day. But I knew I needed to move on and get back to my hotel. Ann and Margaret would be excitedly waiting for my report.

On my way out, clearly displayed near the front desk, I found an array of postcards for sale, including some old, sepia photographs from the turn of the last century showing tall sailing ships in the harbour. There was no sign of a church at the centre of the town in these earlier photographs. There were far fewer houses overall even than there were when I lived there 55 years ago. There were postcards of some local Sami people too: a family in a typical wooden-cabin Sami home, a couple of Sami waiting for a bus in what looked like a snowstorm, and Sami in full costumes in deep snow tending a reindeer herd somewhere on the *vidda*. I took my collection to pay at the reception desk and had a chat with the librarian who was rightly proud of his emporium. I explained how different it was from the one I remembered – from a time long before he was even born. He was polite enough to seem impressed and amazed. I asked who had paid for the building. He explained that it had cost NOK50m overall – somewhere in the region of £4,5m - to build and was finished in 2003. Finnmark County paid for it initially but Vadsø pays rent for the building and will continue to do so until 2028 when it will become a co-owner of the library together with the county of Finnmark.

Currently, I live just outside a small market town in the South West of England with a similar number of inhabitants as Vadsø. We are fortunate to have a library at all. Many similar towns and villages in this part of the world do not. Our library is well used by people of all ages. But it is not in anything like the same league as the library in Vadsø in terms of cosmopolitan resources, comprehensive book choices in several languages or technical devices. I find the contrast fascinating – at the same time as I know just how fortunate I am to live in a small village in England where there is even a library at all.

Chapter Twenty-Five

Gone Fishing

I returned from Hammerfest in days that were short but bright. The season of total darkness ends with the first glimmers of daybreak and twilight on January 17th in Vadsø. So, when I sailed home from Hammerfest in the latter part of February, there were already a couple of hours of morning and evening light in response to the turning of the earth's curve. But it was still fiendishly cold. Even on the sunniest of days, it was essential to wear several layers including thick, warm woolly under garments, especially outside. And it snowed every day without fail. Sometimes there were heavy falls overnight, so there were always well-swept, heaped up, glistening, piles in the morning. The first job of every household was to sweep away what fell overnight, otherwise it was impossible even to open the front door, let alone leave the house. As yet, there was no sign of a thaw even though the sun shone brightly. Today, climate change has caused winters there, as here, to be considerably milder. Nowadays, snowfalls are neither as prolonged nor as deep as they used to be. Indeed, in recent years in some parts of Norway, albeit further south, there has been no snow at all.

During this return trip - with time to myself - I became aware that I was now more than halfway through my stay. Stabs of real sadness kept prodding me inside, even as I soaked up the breath-taking sight of clear blue skies and a deep blue sea set against the gloriously pristine, and sparklingly white landscapes of coastline – sharp, rugged rocks and cliffs right down to the water's edge. There were no communities or moored boats for mile after mile, but hundreds of sea-birds and playful seals to entertain us as we watched from our portholes.

Eventually, the *Hurtigruten* turned sharply into Vadsø's harbour. My despondent musings were interrupted by an astonishing sight. Crammed into half the harbour was a mass of tightly-anchored fishing boats, close-linked to each other and several boats deep all along the quayside. Dozens of fishermen were bustling about, heaving thick ropes or carrying baskets of shiny, wriggling herrings and small sardines from boat to boat until they reached the quayside where there were men ready to receive them. It was exciting to see - busy, noisy and joyful, judging by all the whistling and laughter emanating from it. It was unusual to see so many men at work together in this remote town, and to hear them calling to each other in their protective fishing gear. The whole scene lifted my spirits at a stroke. There were even a few Sami in their *gakti*, adding sharp splashes of colour to the scene.

'The fishing fleet is in, Miss. I'm guessing that's what's surprised you, is it?' One of the sailors waiting to throw a docking rope on to the shore saw how taken aback I seemed.

'Yes, it absolutely is. Where on earth have all these boats come from? There are so many. They can't all be from Vadsø, can they?'

'Well, no, only some are from Vadsø. The bulk have come from all over the Arctic. They gather here once everyone knows fish have arrived to spawn. The Gulf Stream keeps the waters above freezing when it flows up from the South to the Polar seas. It brings shoals of herring and sardines here every year because it's a warmer place to spawn. The fishermen scoop up as many as they can. There are loads and loads of herring – making the whole process a "piece of cake". Isn't that the English expression you use in such circumstances? And then the fish are either loaded on to much bigger boats, which aren't here yet, or taken by individuals to nearby processing factories – like the one in Hammerfest, where we've just been!' He grinned.

'Indeed, it is!' I said, answering his question about the expression he'd used. 'Wherever did you learn that?'

He knew I was English even though he spoke Norwegian to me. I thought he must be yet another Norwegian sailor who had worked on ships all over the world since he also knew several other English expressions that he must have learned from sailors. Many Norwegian sailors picked up a range of colloquial words and phrases in those days. I was constantly struck by the fluent speech of sailors who had worked alongside English-speaking colleagues – especially if they had spent long spells of time away from home as their floating factory ploughed on from port to port. Sailors chatted the evenings away, eating supper with English mates, playing cards perhaps, or other games – acquiring the pronunciation and rise and fall of English phrases and sentences with such exact intonation they could easily be taken for native English speakers. Whereas I had also noticed that many well-educated, sophisticated Norwegians who had studied English at length, knew a fantastic number of words and phrases, but invariably spoke with an accent that gave them away as 'foreign'. Sailing for long periods at a time with a crew of largely English speakers was an excellent way to learn the language.

'I've sailed all over the world, Miss,' he said. 'An English mate of mine on the same ship taught me all sorts of expressions – just for fun, you might say. And although I don't remember all of them, that's one I definitely do!' He paused and smiled. 'He knew I happened to like cake quite a lot! So, he thought it would amuse me to know the expression!'

He smiled a lot, whistling loudly as he busied himself throwing the rope to his counterpart on shore waiting to tie it to a bollard. I was surprised how much room there actually was for us to dock as the skilfully-guided approach towards it was so accurately manoeuvred.

When he was certain the ropes were secure, the sailor carefully lowered the gang plank. He worked automatically, but carefully and thoroughly at every single task he needed to carry out, throwing out further titbits of interesting information about anything he thought I might like to know as he worked at loading and unloading small pieces of cargo, heaved ropes and inspected safety mechanisms. In those days, intermingling between passengers and crew was easy. Nowadays, ships are bigger and different. Strict safety regulations prevent much contact between crew and passengers and close interaction with the crew is difficult. Eventually, I disembarked, smiling back to the various grins, and waves from himself and his colleagues.

Although it was terribly cold, I lingered for a few minutes. I wondered if it was true that seafaring was in the blood and was handed down from one generation to another so that it was indeed a 'piece of cake' to hop from boat to boat, fish in deep waters in the winter ocean swell, and guide large passenger boats safely into harbours of all shapes and sizes. In any case, however, this was the far North East of Norway. Although many Viking longboats were made inland in the centre of the country all those years ago and were then navigated along rivers before finally emerging into open sea, most Vikings came from the South West. So, the Finnmark sailors may not necessarily have Viking ancestry in their blood or their genes. Even so, every bit of activity I could see all around the harbour, seemed easy and straight forward. Yet I knew that one small slip or false step could seriously hurt someone, not least because of the immediate impact of falling into the freezing water. The shock of that alone could lead to a heart attack. And, once on shore, I saw that more than a quarter of the harbour's sea was actually frozen solid underneath a thick layer of ice!

After a few minutes, feeling the need to move rather than freeze, I made my way home to Jon and Bente's. They were looking out for me. I could see them waving from their kitchen window. As soon as I got to the front door, I was greeted by the wonderful smell of coffee - and Bente's warm smile.

'We've been waiting for you,' she said. 'I've made a pot of coffee - or there's properly made tea, if you'd prefer! Why don't you just drop everything, take off your things and come and tell us all about your trip. We're longing to hear how you've got on.'

The smell of coffee was irresistible, so I dropped my bag and started to disrobe in the hall. I surveyed their *stue,* thankful for its warm glow of burning logs from the *peis* and the coffee table in front of it loaded with coffee and *smørbrød.*

'You managed to get off the *Hurtigruten* all right then,' Jon teased. 'No rope ladders to climb down this time?' He grinned.

'Thankfully, yes. But I was astonished to see all the fishing boats in the harbour. Did you know they would be here? I suppose it's an annual event.'

'We don't know exactly when the herring fleet will come,' Jon said. 'Personally, I know very little about fishing. But ever since we've been here, the fishermen have come every year once the herring have arrived. Once they're here, the fishermen go out to sea every day for several weeks. They work like mad, non-stop. They harvest as many herring or sardines as they possibly can. They have to, since most of them have to live off the money they make in these few weeks the rest of the year.'

Jon carried the tray of cups from the kitchen into the *stue* so that we could sit as close to the *peis* as possible. He knew I would be really cold in spite of my brisk climb back from the harbour. There is a special chill that really IS to one's very bones, in spite of vigorous exercise, when the temperature is 15 – 20 degrees below zero. Jon set the tray down on the coffee table and lit the solitary candle beside it – par for the course for coffee drinking round the *peis* at any time. And although it was early afternoon, it would be dark soon. Jon continued, 'They may also do the odd bit of salmon fishing later in the year, once the rivers thaw around late April-May time, but this harvest will be their main source of income and will have to keep them and their families afloat until the chance of another harvest haul.

'*Nordlaendinger* have been self-reliant for centuries. People who've lived here and go back several generations have to be jacks of all trades – farmers, fishermen, woodworkers or joiners. They're brought up to be skilled in all these tasks, AND they help each other out otherwise no one would be able to do what was necessary for families to be safe and comfortable at home, and also thrive, d'you see?'

I found it difficult to take in. Could a family really live off cash from just a few weeks of fishing? But then I remembered that my friends in the South – which had a much more prosperous economy overall - filled their freezers every year with fish they caught themselves in local waters from weekend expeditions in their small, motor-boat.

'How come I've never seen any of these boats before? There are rarely any fishing boats at anchor in the harbour, apart from the odd one or two every now and then, and only for a day or so,' I asked.

'Ah! Well! Fishermen come from all around the coast, you see. And from as far south as the Lofoten Islands. They keep their boats securely laid up when not in use through the winter months. They're part of the family's capital income, d'you see. If you were to walk for a few miles in each direction along the cliffs, you'd also see the odd boat hauled up on to the shore here and there. Sometimes, they're pulled well up, and are kept under canvas for protection from frost and ice: some even in boathouses. And, of course, fishermen come from places round about because the waters round us here are safer and more sheltered than in many other places, as well as free from underwater rocks and strong currents, you see. There's safety in numbers too if the sea gets rough or there are sudden squalls or gales, there will always be someone within hailing distance to help.'

Jon was so engrossed in telling me all about the fishing fleet that he said 'd'you see?' at the end of virtually every sentence as Norwegians invariably do when they are excited about what they're saying and want to make sure their hearers are still listening properly.

I wanted to see what had happened to the fishing industry in Vadsø – and indeed in Finnmark as a whole – on my brief trip back in 2019 with Ann and Margaret. Sadly, it seemed that my fears that it had not only changed but disappeared altogether were well founded, and not only as the result of climate change. Climate change – which has encouraged the herring to spawn further south once the warmer waters of the Gulf Stream were no longer essential as the planet has warmed - is only partially responsible for its decline.

Historically, Finnmark had always been the most fish dependant county in Norway. Fishermen farmers were not just Sami who lived near the coast, but also many Norwegian small-holders who grew what crops they could in the short summer months, kept a cow for milk and hens for eggs, relying on their annual harvest of the sea to keep the family fed and warm for the whole year. After the war, the Norwegian government poured money into Finnmark to make it safe and habitable again for the huge majority of Finnmarkians who returned, even after their homes and livelihoods had been burned or ruined by the retreating Germans in 1944-45. Most Finnmarkians had also refused to accept the Norwegian government's offer of help to relocate further south if they chose to resettle there after 1945.

In the years following the war, the government in Oslo wanted Finnmark to become less isolated and a more cosmopolitan, modern society. It saw an opportunity to rationalise and develop the fishing industry there, along new paths of economic practice and development. In the 1960s, fishing was still a key contributor to Norway's balance of payments especially as the government tried to recreate a strong, post-war economy.

Oslo wanted to expand the Arctic fishing industry. Plans for greater mechanisation and closer business ties between Oslo and Finnmark included offers of fishing licenses, quotas and guaranteed rights to help progress a substantial, thriving industry in Finnmark. The government also wanted to provide sophisticated fishing vessels with processes on board to clean, fillet and market fish almost straight from the sea into packaging plants. Advantageous financial deals to adjust to a different way of life were offered to many Finnmark fishermen too. But it would have meant working differently from what they were used to, and it would gradually have changed their way of life. Many fishermen did not want that.

Furthermore, offers of grants and loans were made available to Finnmark fishermen to help establish and develop freezing and filet-processing plants along the coast. Proposals that would make it viable to acquire ships suitably equipped with mechanical processes to prepare fish for sale largely fell on deaf ears, however. The government wanted many more thriving operations like the Findus factory at Hammerfest which took fish from fishermen, processed prepared and packaged it ready for market. However, the culture and traditions of those who lived in Finnmark meant that such economic proposals and offers of help were not as welcome as the Oslo government had hoped. Many Finnmarkians found the simple way of life close to nature, with adequate provision for daily needs rather suited them.

But although a gradually warmer climate has reduced the numbers of fish seeking Arctic waters and local people were not inclined to be lured en masse into mechanisation, other factors have also contributed to the decline of the fishing industry. Many Sami have moved away so that reindeer herding can prosper from a more certain reliance on fallen snow, more likely to be found deeper into the more central areas of the Finnmark *Vidda*. Climate change has encouraged hungry seals to hunt for more fish including herring. Increases in the numbers of people living in Finnmark and the kind of employment they were happy to seek have also played their part in an industry in decline.

In recent years, the population has substantially increased in both Hammerfest and Vadsø – the main centres of fishing in Finnmark. Education has also changed and developed over time, and thus, so has the pursuit of all kinds of employment. After the discovery of oil in the North Sea, as well as the developing gas industry in Hammerfest, increasing numbers of people in Norway's work force have chosen to move away from fishing and towards other industries. Salaries are higher in these new industries, especially in any offshoots from oil and gas in Finnmark as in the rest of Norway. So, the Arctic fishing industry continues to contract. In addition, in recent years it has been substantially overtaken by the market for Russian cod. The Baltic fishing industry continues to grow thanks to the Russian government's provision of larger fishing vessels at the same time as herring is declining in numbers in Norwegian waters.

Looking back now, I am sure that Øystein was keen to help develop Finnmark in every way he possibly could, be it in education, politics or fishing. At one point during my stay, I was asked by one of his colleagues to translate Finnmark's fishing laws into English. I wish I had talked with him about fishing to learn what he thought, especially as my current research about its processes and practices in Finnmark has revealed so much I had no idea about at the time. I also wish I had thought to talk at length with some of the fishermen who harvested the sea during those mid-February days about their way of life. Sadly, at the time I never thought to do that.

***

Inevitably, Øystein called in to hear about my trip to Hammerfest a day or so after my return. He particularly wanted to know how our nearest Finnmark town was doing in all things *Friundervisning*-wise, especially knowing how different the culture and life-style there was from that of Vadsø. It still is. Hammerfest remains a more industrial and sophisticated environment than Vadsø. Øystein had suspected there would be more adult English classes there than in Vadsø and knew the clientele would be different including both genders, all ages, professional people as well as housewives and pensioners. Even though he no longer had responsibilities, he was still keen to support the overall *Friunder-visning* vision which he saw as an important contributor towards developing the Finnmark economy. I respected his interest in people and his forward thinking, as well as what he knew about many social and political issues. I tried to tell him as much as I could about Denis's work.

As I write, I suspect there must have been many conversations in Oslo about whether or not to send language teachers to Finnmark because of its remoteness, its harsh climate and its lack of basic facilities, including the terrible shortage of decent places to live. On the other hand, the region needed to be included in all the national development programmes the various government departments were supporting at the time. Anything that Øystein could contribute to that conversation I knew would be greatly valued.

'Changing the subject,' I said eventually, 'there's something I want to ask your advice about. You know Marcus Svenungson? The man who teaches juniors – a tall, big, always laughing chap, with a huge, warm heart?'

'I do! Why? What's he done?'

'Nothing – yet. It's what he WANTS to do that I need to ask you about. He's suggested that I should take a trip with three or four of our colleagues, way out into the depths of the *Finnmarksvidda* to his family's cabin on his snow scooter. I'd love to do it. I think it would be an amazing experience, and I know I'm fortunate to have the opportunity. But my colleagues are dragging their feet about it. They say it will be far too cold and hardly worth it since there will be nothing to see, and it may be dark for part of the time. But they say they would go to keep me company, if I really want to do it. Do you know why they might not be too keen to go? Am I making an issue here where there isn't one?'

Øystein thought for a moment and then said, 'It's true. It will be unbelievably cold. Maybe that's why they're dragging their feet? No matter how many woollies and furs and reindeer skins and thick underwear and socks and gloves you wear it will be vastly colder than you've ever imagined possible! I can see that you want to do it: clearly, it would be a wonderful and unusual experience.' He paused for thought, and then said, 'I think you definitely should do it! You'll regret it later if you don't. But be warned. It WILL take you hours – maybe days - to warm up afterwards.' He grinned as he spoke. He seemed almost pleased that I might have to suffer for daring to accept such a challenge – but I knew that could not be.

I agreed to take up Marcus's offer, and so my colleagues agreed to join me. Øystein was right. It WAS very, very cold indeed: excruciatingly so. But also, a stunningly beautiful experience that I was so glad I had accepted. We were a party of five on two Canadian snow scooters. There were no seats. We had to sit with legs akimbo in the middle of the sledge so that we could not risk falling off. We were driven along at high speed, which meant that a biting breeze accompanied us as we sped forth to reach the Svenungsens' cabin.

The sight of mile upon mile of virgin snow set against the sky of clearest blue was an awesome and silent beauty; and there was so very much of it. And the quiet was so loud! The landscape was vast in all directions. No words can describe what I saw and experienced. It was as if we were alone, on top of the world, where no one had ever been, making tracks through deep, pristine snow. I really understood what it meant to be lost for words. I knew I would never be able to tell anyone how it really felt, what the experience was really like to be in such a place feeling like a tiny speck amid such immensity. I was so glad I went though I have never been so cold in my entire life.

The Svenungson's cabin was literally miles from anywhere. I understood that its location was chosen so that it was possible to ski to it from Vadsø in under four hours, light the stove in the cabin, cook or heat up a well-cooked stew, or fish pie or something adequately reviving, as well as thaw out completely. Then, the party would set off for the return journey to Vadsø, having let the stove out and locked up the cabin to keep it secure until the next visit. I gathered reindeer passed by it sometimes, and left holes where they had pawed the ground to try to find the moss that they found so nutritious and delicious. In the so-called 'spring', the snow often thawed sufficiently for the ground to be exposed. But that was rare, apparently. During the few weeks that offered even a touch of summer warmth, the family would hike to the cabin to stay overnight so that they could pick the rare and delicious cloudberries from plants growing at ground level right across the *vidda* – a dessert delicacy, often served with cream to visitors after a first course of local reindeer meat or fresh-water salmon.

Øystein had been exactly right about the cold. It took me the best part of three days to warm up again afterwards in spite of all the special furs and woollies I had been lent for the trip. I wondered if my blood would ever defreeze and flow properly round my body once again. I knew I would remember the experience for the rest of my life.

Last year, Ann, Margaret and I took the bus from Vadsø to Honningsvåg across the very same *vidda*. This time on a modern, well-kept road in a warm bus,

215

at a time when climate change had fundamentally altered the whole landscape. There was snow all around, for sure. But there were also massive swathes of Finnmark tundra where the reindeer moss was exposed in vast stretches. Currently, reindeer have to adapt to access their food. They rely on being able to smell, rather than see the moss through layers of snow. But even in these days of warming climate, it is still possible for reindeer to find the coverings of snow they need, in the 8,500 square miles of tundra that is the Finnmark *Vidda*.

Our bus tour was amazing. The trip took 10 hours, with just two stops to change buses at Varangerbotn and Lakselv, as well as ordinary stops along the hundreds of miles of main road to pick up or set down passengers who had the enormous good fortune to live somewhere nearby in that beautiful part of the world. Either side of the bus, there were long stretches of tundra with occasional herds of grazing reindeer both close to the road and some distance from it, always intensely involved in scouring beneath the snow to smell out what is to them, such delicious food. Occasionally, an Arctic hare would bound past at speed. Our view was framed the whole time by rugged, snow-capped, rocky-mountains in the distance. We were fortunate travellers indeed. Wherever we looked we could not help but feel overwhelmed by the sheer grandeur of the natural world. Our journey shot past. We may have dozed or conversed for short periods, but for most of the time we sat completely stunned by what unfolded around us.

It was early in the season by normal tourist standards and the Norwegian school holidays were yet to begin, even though it was well into the Midnight Sun period in early May. We had booked to glamp in Honningsvåg at a typical camp site which offered both tents and huts. Our hut was well heated and cosy with comfortable beds and beautifully folded and ironed sheets and soft, enveloping duvets. So early in the season, we were the only campers and had the whole site to ourselves. We watched a reindeer herd drink at a freshwater pool, slap bang in the middle of the compound. Eventually, once we had finished sharing how spectacular we thought our bus-drive had been and had agreed who was the most reliable of the three of us to be sure to wake us up in good time in the morning, we sank into our beds and slept for a few hours before our taxi arrived to take us to catch the early morning *hurtigruten* to Tromsø.

I don't know exactly where in Honningsvåg Per Johan lived. But I wondered while we were there, if he was living there still. He would surely be a grandfather by now. If he was still living anywhere near that town, he would now have many, many more neighbours than he did 60 years ago. Today, there are enough people living there for Honningsvåg to qualify as a proper town. Per Johan will have seen remarkable changes in his life-time. Climate change might have gradually hampered his journey on skis across the *vidda:* even made it impossible perhaps today. But now, he would be able to drive his car from his home to the school in Vadsø, thanks to the tunnel under the sea that links the *Finnmarkvidda* to the island of Magerøya where Honningsvåg is sited. The drive would take him just five hours rather than the three days it took him to ski 60 years ago.

***

We three Arctic Musketeers had discovered the *Hurtigruten*'s timings exactly fitted our travel needs. The next morning, we boarded one of the fleet's liners at 5 45am before any of the cruise guests were up and about. We found comfortable loungers in the most central part of the viewing deck and made camp. Breakfast was not yet being served, but we were able to drink coffee for an hour or so and enjoy the stunning scenery in the early morning mist. It was a remarkable experience. The Finnmark fjords are quite different from those in the South West that always draw holiday crowds to gaze in awe at the majestic cliffs surrounding the waterways. It is the only place on earth I have ever paused to wonder if it was actually visited by the Psalmist whose thoughts in Psalm 121 were paraphrased by the hymn writer thus: 'I to the hills will lift mine eyes, from whence doth come mine aid.' The Finnmark fjords may not have such steep cliff-face surroundings but the majestic beauty of their width and the stunning landscapes of the slopes that fall down to them is breath-taking.

We were due in Tromsø at midnight. As we sailed into Tromsø underneath its spectacular bridge, many of our fellow passengers who were on an organised cruise were also lining up to disembark. They were due to attend one of the town's midnight, orchestral concerts in the so-called Arctic Cathedral where we were to worship the following day. The acoustics were apparently magnificent. We were content, however, not to be joining them, since the whole experience of our bus and boat ride across one side of Finnmark to the other gave all three of us a deep and indescribable delight. There are not words to convey the glory of it all, the majesty, the power and the peace. It was all pure gift. And the timing of it, to fit exactly with our travel needs was also, frankly, miraculous.

So many emotions surfaced for me on those two days especially. They brought back precious memories of working with people who were strong, humble and gracious. Even as I write the over-used, but real expression of the lump in the throat and the pricking behind the eyes are taking me back to the life-changing experience of living in southern, and then northern, Norway for two years just as I was starting out on life. I could not have been more blessed or enriched by the wonderful experiences I was given. I am also massively grateful to have been able to re-live much that I had forgotten. Writing this has helped me recall and revive many inspiring feelings that I experienced so poignantly in the past.

Chapter Twenty-Six

The Joys of Spring

I have no accurate knowledge of climate change temperature or weather conditions in Norway. But May is still a special month when nature's developments are dramatic. Today the changing seasons are less extreme but still marked. Spring arrives in May with a miraculous explosion of greenery and blossom in just a few lengthening days that enhance key national celebrations. When I lived there, it was as if the whole nation was renewed in just four weeks.

I remember how different the days of May were in Vadsø leading to the start of the Midnight Sun period, when there is daylight the whole time from May 17th to July 27th. In the previous year in the South, May's lengthening days led up to the summer solstice when there were only three or four hours of darkness before dawn the following day. For 10 weeks in Vadsø, the sun just moves from left to right in the Arctic sky in continual daylight. In the South, days gradually shorten after their midsummer highlight. In the whole country, summer draws to a close in early August when the school year begins, and holiday-time ends.

The Arctic days of continual daylight lifted my spirits. My recent return visit with Margaret and Ann was also in late May. Some of our days were chilly and cold. It even tried to snow intermittently but melted at once. However, most of the time, the 24 hours of daylight were bright and beautiful. I had not noticed any use of heavy curtain material when I lived there years ago. But the drapes in our hotel bedrooms made sure no hint of light could get through to wake us in the middle of the night. Hence, we slept well and were never tired in the morning.

As well as bringing new sunshine, light and warmth May also hosts three National days in Norway. May 1st - Labour Day - starts the month and is celebrated throughout the country. Norway respects every avenue of work required from every individual. National attitudes and an agreed ethos drive the commitment to everyone being able to earn a decent wage or salary. Differentials between pay grades are minimal. Those who command large salaries are expected to fulfil great responsibilities. Those earning smaller salaries enjoy differentials that are narrower than in many other European countries and are fairly negotiated and agreed. At all levels, people are well paid.

On May 8th, the nation recognises the ending of the Second World War, remembering the date when the Nazis surrendered to the Norwegian government in Oslo in 1945. It is quietly acknowledged nowadays rather than nationally celebrated. The vitally important day that everyone looks forward to soon follows as an important celebration of national pride and togetherness, on May 17th - or *Syttende Mai*.

I had learnt exactly how significant a day this is in my previous year in the South. I had been invited by the Rektor of the Gymnas where I taught to join the rest of the staff in the civic procession around the town, walking behind an excellent town band. I did not realise exactly how honouring this invitation was, however, until I arrived at the start. I was used to smart, military uniforms on civic and national occasions in the UK. So, the splendid array of national costumes – *bunads* - took me by surprise. They looked wonderful, setting a different tone from that of the military uniforms I was used to. I had only recently come to understand how significant and important the Norwegian *bunad* is, both in family and national life since I had been told I would be provided with one to go and sing in Iceland with the well-known choir of the town where I lived. The sight of so many people in their various national costumes - as well as everyone else dressed in their Sunday best - meant I was glad I had had the foresight to wear something formal and smart. The whole town turned out to watch the parade waving flags and cheering, finally singing the national anthem together. The whole experience was emotionally powerful.

I knew about the various *russ* pranks allowed – even encouraged – to be perpetrated on the staff who had taught those in their last year of school. I could see objects dangling from roofs and windows, and banners with words that I regret I did not understand because I had no idea what many of the specific relationships between staff and pupils were. Nevertheless, I could not help being excited and impressed by the extraordinary mixture of dignity, celebration and fun that was both solemn and joyous. After the parade, everyone went home to their families – extended on that day by every possible relative able to make it to the same place – to celebrate with mountains of special food, music, games and fun for the rest of the day.

My experience of celebrating May 17th in Vadsø, however, was different. There were fewer people of course, and it was much colder. The day began with an almost freezing drizzle. However, the degree of celebratory enthusiasm was just as genuine, albeit louder and less constrained than it had been the year before in the South. The ingenuity of the Vadsø *russ* astonished me too.

Alf, of course, had been voted *russ* chairman. There could not have been a better choice. Everything was good humoured and harmless: and the originality and inventive ideas were inspired. I marvelled at what these leavers had managed to do. I had no idea how they had been able to get around to accomplish everything - hangings from chimney pots, banners across the street, boots dangling from the church bell tower - every prank at the expense of one teacher or another.

'My word!' I said. 'Who would have thought there would be so many people here today? Where HAVE all these people come from?'

I could see crowds gathering already as Jon and Bente, Anna and Anders and myself left our house.

'No one wants to miss anything,' Bente said. People have come from everywhere this morning. There won't be a single person in the whole of Finnmark who doesn't go to their nearest town today.'

I was also surprised how many people were wearing *bunads* and how varied they were. They were always worn on special occasions, such as weddings, christenings, confirmations and any other important family events. In fact, they were THE go-to outfit for all important and formal occasions – equivalent to English 'morning dress'. In Vadsø, so many people came from other parts of Norway, there was a diverse display of *bunad* design: a plethora of styles and colours. There was a plentiful display of jewellry too. Many national costumes were adorned with gold or silver jewellery - for men and women - which would have been handed down from one generation to another or given on special occasions to the wearer of the bunad as an investment. Jewellry was always treated with great care, stored in tissue paper, carefully stowed at the back of wardrobes or if possible and preferably, in a safe at the town bank. In Finnmark especially, it must have been particularly beneficial to wear national dress on May 17th since the thick, heavy, woollen cloth helped protect against the damp and cold. No one would ever wear a coat over a bunad. It simply was not done to cover up the splendour of a national costume.

We found an excellent place to stand and watch where we could admire the main street, tastefully bedecked with the Norwegian colours of red, white and blue. There were Norwegian flags everywhere. The *russ* pranksters' team had managed to move various bits of property, which they knew belonged to individual teachers, and drape them over front doors and windows or wherever they could reach to be visible: clothing, personal possessions, balloons, banners, flags, tin cans – a whole range of things.

'We never did anything as daring as this in our day when WE left school,' Bente commented. 'This lot have been wonderfully imaginative. But then rural, mid-Norway where we come from is a much more restrained and muted kind of society than here. What can you expect from a load of farming stock?' As usual, Bente followed up her words of wisdom by bursting into hearty laughter. She always did that when she had said something important or profound. Jon laughed too: he couldn't help himself. He always laughed whenever Bente did.

Then I saw the most remarkable prank of all. The final *piece de resistance* was that somehow, the *russ* committee had managed to put Rektor Anderson's car at the top of the Town Hall steps. I thought it looked incredibly precarious before I spotted the tyre blocks securing the wheels. 'What a relief!' I thought to myself.

'How on earth will the Rektor get his car down again?' I asked

'Oh! Don't worry!' 'Getting a crowd of folk to lift it down again will be as much part of the fun as it was putting it there in the first place,' Jon said.

Everything about that May17th was extraordinary. So many people greeted each other with warm smiles, and shook my hand too, as they said *Gratulerer med dagen*. Literally, 'congratulations on today!' I loved that people said *Gratulerer med dagen* to me, even though they did not necessarily know who I was. It made me feel included and it was as if everyone took it for granted that I belonged.

***

Whatever delights May inevitably brought however, I knew I needed to face up to the fact that my remaining days in Norway were running out. Such awareness filled me with a particular sense of unease because there would be so many things I would miss as well, of course, as individual people. I knew that something of these people's unique spirit had changed me.

However, in spite of these waves of dejection, I loved that the days were getting lighter and longer. I would sometimes even experience a curious mixture of joy and regret – both at the same time. This was for real. Perhaps there was some sort of weird alchemy living in such a remote place where light and dark and hot and cold were so extreme.

Who knew what paths lay ahead for these young people I had taught? Who knew what my future held or how it would unfold? And then I recalled that I had had similar feelings when I had first arrived in Vadsø all those months ago when I had had no idea what lay ahead. I recalled how desolate I had felt when I saw the boat on which I had spent so many days sail away from the harbour, leaving me in a strange place, far away from any connection I had and where I knew absolutely no one. I had not expected to feel so profoundly different just a few months later, or that, when it came to it, I would really mind my time coming to an end. Now, I not only had to leave Vadsø, I also had to leave the country. How could I have known how much I would get to love it and its people so well and admire them all so much?

At the same time as I was experiencing such thoughts, the heavy snowfalls, and light flurries of snow or sleet, and the general experience of harsh and difficult weather were gradually tailing off. The bitingly cold gales with their stinging, horizontal rain finally disappeared altogether, giving way to drier days and gentler winds. Iced rivers began to thaw. Slowly, the temperature began to rise.

These changes seemed to affect the atmosphere. I could sense an even greater warmth in how people related to each other as spring advanced. Everyone seemed to be smiling more broadly. It was possible now to look up instead of down so we could smile at one another once again instead of devoting our entire attention to taking care of where we walked. More than that, now no one had to defend themselves against aggressive cold and wind for a while. So, it was not surprising, I thought, that it seemed as if people almost began to skip along. Even I no longer needed a *spark* to get around.

It also seemed as if my days were becoming busier and fuller than ever. My evening tea parties were flourishing. It was as if my students realised that if things were going to be said and done, they would have to be done soon. Every day seemed precious, and every hour needed to be made to count. I sensed there was a fresh sense of reality and engagement in these evening gatherings which continued to be well attended.

'When's the next one? Are you having any more? You haven't stopped having them, have you?' students would ask. And once the usual rituals of passing round tea and cake were in full swing, they would say, 'You aren't really going to leave in a few weeks' time, are you, Miss Russell? What will we do in the evenings once you've gone? Who will teach us proper English?' Questions such as this also continually cropped up in class whenever an opportunity presented itself.

There was also a definite change of mood at the evening tea parties. The topics of conversation became much more serious and questioning. The most frequently addressed issue that regularly cropped up - because it dominated international news at the time - was where exactly the talks between the British Prime Minister, Harold Wilson, and Sir Ian Smith, the Prime Minister of Rhodesia - as it was called then, Zimbabwe as it is known now - were to be held, and why were they to be on a British ship – The Tiger – at sea and not in a proper discussion room in either Britain or Rhodesia. There was also talk about the suitability of naming a country after an individual – Cecil Rhodes – who was white and did not actually live there. I am sure that if I had been living there at the time when the newspapers had moved on to feature the state of affairs in South Africa and its apartheid system, I would have been seriously questioned about that too.

Months previously, Grethe had already asked one evening, 'In any case, WHY aren't the black people there allowed to vote already, especially as it is actually THEIR country?' Most students were at a loss to grasp how anyone could think that the right to vote was not inalienable.

Many of my students were also familiar with Martin Luther King's 'I have a dream' speech, made in 1963. That also inspired them, although they understood that its context was different from Rhodesia's. They knew that it concerned issues of race with overtones of ownership and control from longstanding roots of slavery, and that it was also about access to education, housing, welfare and jobs.

Time and again, the same topic emerged for updates, and confirmation of the fact that it really was true that people were not allowed to vote because of the colour of their skin.

'I can understand the situation in Rhodesia makes no sense to you,' I said several times in every discussion, and on many, many occasions. I had to explain -----'It isn't possible to defend the situation there being allowed to continue. You're right. It MUST change. But white Rhodesians are afraid of what will happen when things are different. – which they will be if it is the case that it is no longer just the whites who have the right to vote and a say in how they are governed: even to stay in overall control. There will also be terrible anxiety about what scores may need to be settled and how. It sounds, and probably is, horribly patronising and controlling. It remains a real issue, nevertheless. There is genuine concern about the possibility of lawlessness and extreme violence as the struggle for democracy rolls on.'

I recognised how hard it was for these young people, who lived in a society that emphasised fairness and rights, and who only knew a particularly precious and all-pervading sense of personal and national liberty, to grasp that other ways of life could be defended or explained at all. To understand the power and danger of fear, however, was something they were able to respect. They had been told enough stories about the War from their parents and grandparents to know that to be true. They had some inkling how minorities like the Sami had felt in the past as a minority. Indeed, as I write now, I can say that long after I left Norway, deep and important issues about the Sami people, their land, their rights and their way of life emerged in several troubled years of struggle before the Sami were finally and properly acknowledged as a people with their own life-style, that would be properly protected in the future.

Evenings spent just playing charades and consequences and having fun now seemed to have been light years ago. It intrigued me to think how much the thought of time running out could sharpen the ways in which one person wanted to relate to another, and at what kind of level. Conversations were also always punctuated with the same question put in any number of different ways. 'You aren't really leaving us, are you?'

I tried many times to explain exactly what the *Friundervisning* scheme was all about - that it was not possible to stay because I would have done my two years. I also said how hard I would find it to leave. It was going to be a terrible wrench. I had made good friends and I had come to love the Scandinavian way of life with its freedoms and its magnificently rugged landscapes that somehow underpinned the strength of the people. I had even come to befriend the harsh climate and the aggressively unfriendly, powerful and dramatic seas. All I could think to say, remembering the somewhat pious comments of a padre who had accompanied myself, and other school colleagues with boys from Marlborough College to Oberammergau, when he spoke at a service at the end of the trip. He explained, 'All life is about meeting and parting, isn't it?' I had thought it a pompous thing to say at the time, not grasping what he meant. But today as I write, I understand the truth of it. That all life is about connecting and separating. What I did not know then and maybe still have not learnt, is how to part well. After all, what we long for in life, maybe even without knowing it, is connection.

'Aren't you pleased to know there will be someone in England you know well, who you can contact and visit when you eventually make the trip – as you all surely will, one day?' This was the best I could come up with.

At other times, I would say, 'Well, if I give you my address, you can always write to me, can't you? That would be a way to keep in touch, and it would help you to keep on track with your English too. Now, we really must get on with some work, or we won't get through the syllabus as we're supposed to. Can we do that now, please?'

Mette also expressed sadness that I would soon have to go.

'I don't know what's going to happen once you've gone,' she said somewhat ruefully to me one day. 'I don't know whether Oslo is going to send another English person here. They seem non-committal when we speak on the phone. I wonder if they haven't come to think that Finnmark is too remote a place to send any young person from England again. The lack of accommodation is a major problem, I think. So, I'm probably going to have to find someone else next year to teach the *Friundervisning* English Language classes and inspire some events: someone who already lives here.' She laughed in a kind of superficial way.

'Do you mean you yourself?' I asked. 'You'd do a great job, Mette. And you'd enjoy it too, wouldn't you? You'd be great, honestly you would: you're such a brilliant communicator.'

Øystein also said he would be sorry to see me go, but I knew he and I would stay in touch – if for no other reason than that he would be pleased to have someone English with whom he could communicate regularly to keep a channel of information open. He would be leaving Vadsø himself in a year or so anyway. It was obvious he would eventually be needed back in the Oslo office and I was quite sure he would be sent to London now and then to work – and that he and I would meet up eventually. In fact, we kept in touch for a long time, one way or another. He crafted me a beautifully mounted pendant as a wedding present and sent me a photograph of each of his two sons with their Mum the very days they were born, a couple of years apart.

It was the same in choir practices. The questions kept cropping up about what would happen to the choir. It was at this emotionally difficult time I was to discover just one more diversion to enjoy. Out of the blue, Rektor Anderson caught me in the corridor one day. He stopped me and asked if I had time for a conversation.

'Have you got a minute? There's something I want to ask you – a favour, if you like?' He smiled. 'Could you come with me to my study? Right now, if you have time?'

Chapter Twenty-Seven

Swan Songs

I followed Rektor Anderson to his study. It was sizeable compared to our tiny staff room next door. He also had a better view of the fjord, across the grass flats with all sorts of aquatic birds busy nesting or chatting to each other in front of it, with a clear view beyond to the launch site established in the early 20th century to mark the starting point of Northern polar expeditions. The mast erected there commemorates Roald Amundsen's expedition to the North Pole in 1926. Anderson grinned sheepishly when I commented on his privileged outlook as he invited me to sit in one of his several comfy chairs. I had only been inside his study twice before, but never all the way in, nor invited to sit. I looked round, intrigued.

The Rektor and I rarely spoke apart from casual greetings, although he always smiled if we happened to pass each other in the corridor, when he might ask me how things were going – always in such a way that assumed the answer would be 'fine'. He generally kept on walking as he spoke. Occasionally, he even called me by my first name. But I had come to presume that he preferred to be more formal and would usually appreciate the briefest of encounters. I also believed he did not want to interfere with what I was doing, since he knew Øystein was my overall boss. Mostly, however, I thought he just wanted to avoid any conversation about anything important, terrified in case he had to have a serious conversation in English.

But now, as he welcomed me into his office, he had even opened the door for me and let me go in first, which was the English manner I rarely met either in the South or the North of Norway. I had come to understand how Norwegians believed manners were much deeper and more important inter-relational expressions of behaviour than just an occasional visible or practical gesture. Whenever I had any conversation about English manners or 'etiquette' - the French word that always mystified Norwegians - Norwegian friends spoke about how important it was to treat people with dignity and respect, whether men or women. Opening doors or pushing chairs into or pulling them away from tables or letting certain people 'go first' was not that much of a priority to a people who believed that everyone mattered and should always be treated courteously and with decency. They simply could not see the point of these gestures, specifically towards women. They were just that: gestures. In themselves they certainly could not see how that alone showed that people treated each other with equal respect and dignity.

'What IS the point,' Alf had asked once in a lesson 'of opening doors for women if you also presume it's their job to scrub the floors and wash the nappies while you go to your office, where your secretary - female, of course - brings you a cup of coffee and meets your practical needs all day long without reservation or hesitation?'

It was a good question. I had learnt early on that no-one at any level of seniority in the Norwegian work force would dream of expecting their coffee to be brought to them. Even in the remote North, belief in gender equality was both practised and advocated. Norwegians gathered from what they read or films they watched that work-place expectations, especially in the UK and America, were much more used to women supplying every male need than any Norwegian counterpart would tolerate – even 60 years ago.

So, I noted the Rektor's courtesy and was careful to say 'thank you' with a smile, to his face.

Once we were comfortably seated, Rektor Anderson said, 'I won't keep you long. I have a favour to ask you, that's all. I'll come straight to the point. Do you could think it's at all possible that you could take your choir to sing at a music event in Berlevåg in early June? It would mean going along the fjord to a festival organised there every two or three years, by local councils in this part of Finnmark. It's a way of encouraging young people to get together to mingle and make music.'

His phone rang at that point, but he ignored it. 'If you felt able to do this, the school office would sort out the arrangements – getting to and fro, booking the tickets on the *Hurtigruten* and dealing with the fares and other expenses. So, you wouldn't have to do any of that. It would all be taken care of and any personal expenses would be re-funded of course. The only thing is, if you agree to do this, you'd have to be responsible for the safety and well-being of the students. As well, of course, as the music,' he added with a grin.

He paused at this point, probably trying to take in my initial reaction to what he was saying. But not for long. He continued, 'Someone told me that Bjørn Hansen is a member of the choir. Is that right?' I smiled and nodded. Anderson continued, 'So you would have one other colleague with you - if he's able and willing to go, that is. The two of you would be in charge, which would make it easier for you to manage, wouldn't it? I haven't asked him of course. He's not on my staff. But if he couldn't join you, someone else would be assigned. So, you wouldn't be entirely on your own.'

I was relieved to hear that. I couldn't think there would be any difficulties on such a trip, but it was good to know I wouldn't be solely responsible, nevertheless.

Anderson continued, 'I very much hope you'll say yes. I think the whole community, the school and the town, would appreciate it if they could be represented in this way. It might be fun for all the choir members too, mightn't it?'

I was impressed by Anderson's approach. It was a big ask of a Norwegian teacher at that time and he had no idea how I would respond. I could easily have declined on the grounds that I was not sure whether my *Friundervisning* bosses would appreciate a precedent such as this being set. I was sure enough of the organisation's aims and objectives to know that taking a large number of Gymnas students on an overnight trip was really pushing the boundaries. I also knew that Norwegian teachers at that time were not used to having contact or working with students out of school hours. It was not a regular part of the culture. There were no clubs and societies so asking people to do things in addition to what was contractually required felt odd, even sometimes difficult. In general, employees were not asked or pressurised to do things out of hours if that meant giving up any personal time.

'You're right about Bjørn Hansen.' I tried to sound positive. 'He IS in the choir. He has the most beautiful tenor voice, incidentally. Anyway, he's always helped with bits of necessary administration. I've never actually asked him to do anything. He just does whatever's necessary. Actually, everyone helps out, especially the older students. It's never been difficult to get things organised. So, I'm sure he'll be more than willing to help if he's given permission to leave his classes. But can you tell me more about this event?' I asked.

'The festival is in a few weeks' time, just before the school year ends. I'll confirm the actual date in due course. But there is plenty of time to get the choir ready, isn't there? I must confess I don't really know anything about choirs. But I do know you can definitely choose what you'd like to sing. I think the organisers expect up to four items each, although I need to check that. What d'you think? What's your initial reaction?'

'Personally, I think it would be great. But it's not up to me. I'll have to ask the choir members what they think and whether they'd be willing to do it. However, I don't imagine for one minute they'll say no. They're so enthusiastic, I'm sure they'd be up for almost anything!' I laughed, and so did Anderson. 'Anyway, I'll ask them at our next practice the day after tomorrow. I'll see what they say and get back to you. Is that all right?'

'That's absolutely fine. Thank you so much. And meanwhile, I'll check the exact dates and find out anything else I can to help you plan. I'll get back to you too. Let me show you out.'

Once again, he opened the door for me. This time, he also offered his hand to shake and smiled as he did so. 'Thank you!' he said as I passed through it. 'We've never done anything like this before – taken part in a festival somewhere else, I mean,' he said, grinning broadly. I took his hand, and shook it heartily, smiling back as I did so.

Almost everyone in the choir was waiting when I arrived at the next practice. One or two were busy writing – probably keeping up with homework.

'Hello, everyone!' I took off my coat. It was beautifully warm as always inside, even at this evening hour when hardly anyone was on the premises apart from a few teachers marking books. Whatever the temperature was outside, however far below freezing, inside one could prance around in a bikini and feel as warm as toast. Not for the first time, I rejoiced that I was warm enough to get the evening started without us all having to do star jumps. Although it was May, the evenings were cool. The wind could still bite.

'Sorry if I'm late everyone – or maybe you're all early?'

'You're not late, Miss Russell,' Per Johann announced. 'A few of us have been doing homework together so we came on to the practice together too. We thought we might as well carry on doing what we had to do waiting here, as well as anywhere else. Others joined us en route. It's become, what you might call a kind of "work party".'

Per Johann pronounced the last two words in inverted commas, believing he had made a witty joke. He waited to see how his punch line had gone down, his two forefingers still held up in parenthesis around the two words.

I smiled at him and flipped a smacking down hand gesture as if to signal what a bright and amusing young man I thought he was. 'Well! You're obviously on form tonight.' I said. 'Have you heard that expression in one of your James Bond films, Per Johann?' I asked.

'Possibly,' he said. 'I don't actually know where I picked it up. But I CAN say it as I did, can't I? It IS the right expression, isn't it?'

'Indeed, it is. But I don't suppose knowing that will have done much to help you with your homework, which I hope you've finished, by the way?' I paused. 'But seriously, it's impressive that you can make an actual joke in a language that's not your own. Well done!' I did not wait for him to respond. I wanted to move on. 'Anyway, before we get to sing, I've something I want to ask you all.'

The room had already gone quiet. No one ever wanted to miss out on any badinage of Per Johann's – especially if it had anything to do with Miss Russell. More importantly though, now everyone wanted to hear what it was I wanted to ask.

There was complete silence. I explained what we/they were being asked to do and what kind of commitment it might mean in terms of rehearsals and travelling. I also explained it was not compulsory. Only those who really wanted to be included should commit themselves. And they would all have to have their parents' permission. But I could see from the lit-up faces that there was real enthusiasm to seize such an opportunity. The mood began to change. Now that there was the prospect of yet another event, I could sense a general lifting of spirits. The trip might well bring the year to an exciting and enjoyable climax.

'I'll need to know by this time next week how many of you are able to come. But for starters, could you put your hand up if you'd LIKE to go – just so that I can get an idea of what we might choose to sing, please?'

Every hand went up at once.

'That's wonderful. But please discuss it at home to make sure you have your parents' approval. I expect I'll have much more information for you all next week. We also need to come to a decision about what to sing, so if you've any thoughts about that, could you let me know.'

A buzz of chatter hummed for a minute or two while I began to organise my music and prepared to start the practise. Breathing exercises would kick us off, followed by scales sung with fun embellishments. When I was ready, I called everyone to order. We were was just about to start when Grethe interrupted.

'Have **you** any thoughts about what we might sing, Miss Russell?'.

'Ah! Well!? Maybe! But I really don't want to talk about that now. I'd rather wait to hear YOUR suggestions first. I really do want us to sing what YOU want to sing.'

It became clear through the following week that everyone wanted to go. So, the next thing was to decide on our programme, get the music ready and then get the singers up to a certain standard and ready to perform. After all, the festival was only four weeks away.

In the practices that followed, there was much joy around at the prospect of an actual choir trip, with all the fun and new experiences it would bring. That there was something to look forward to instead of dreading the end of term with all the sadness of endings, would be a bonus. I felt grateful for that. For some, just the prospect of travelling on the *Hurtigruten* was exciting. Many choir members had never travelled on it before. Or if they had, only for small trips. So, the excitement grew at the prospect of such a fun endeavour to round off the academic year.

The great day came at last. It was a typical northern, early June day: not cold, but definitely cool, especially in the early morning. Since it was during the period of Midnight Sun there were a number of tourists on board the *Hurtigruten*, doing the coastal tour from the South round the North Cape and back again to experience 24 hours of daylight inside the Arctic Circle. These were the early days of a developing tourist industry. Compared to today's cruise liners, the *Hurtigruten* was basic. Trips in June were expensive. Even so, they were beginning to gather growing numbers of adventurous travellers, especially from the United States.

We waited on the quayside and saw our boat approach the harbour. We watched as it rounded its entrance and slowly made its way to dock where we all stood. I could not help thinking how different it felt now from that early morning 10 months previously when there had been no-one in sight, and I stood alone, in trepidation, wondering if I had made a terrible mistake. It could not have felt more different this same early morning. I felt accepted, not just by all these amazing youngsters, but also by the whole town. I knew I was part of the lives of everyone waiting with me to get on board. I belonged. This time my anxiety was not about whether I had made a mistake coming here at all: rather, it was of impending loss. I could not help asking myself how I was going to cope when it came to the point when I actually had to leave?

There was a party of elderly Americans on our ship - from the deep South, I thought, judging by their accents. Although it was early in the morning, there were already voyagers on deck watching us board, including several women who wore smart travelling clothes. Most of them wore heeled shoes – even on deck –

and lots of jewellery: bright necklaces and sparkly brooches. They were obviously intrigued by the lively Vadsø party.

'These young people are really enjoying themselves, aren't they?' said a lady who had been watching us nearby. She spoke in a drawling, somewhat flat-tened-sounding English. 'You're in charge of them, aren't you? They seem so excited. It's almost as if they've never actually been on an outing together before. Is it some kind of school trip you're on?'

'Yes, it is. And yes, I am. And you're right, many of them haven't.'

I had replied in my perfect BBC Received Pronunciation English which I and my colleagues had been told to use whenever possible. Being able to speak like that was one of the reasons why we had been recruited in the first place. I really made the most of it now and I decided to put it on a bit and sound as much like the Queen as I could.

I continued, almost without pause. 'It's not easy to get about in this part of the world. The geography and the climate do not lend themselves to going out on a trip just for the sheer pleasure of it.' I paused, relishing the look of total astonishment on the woman's face. I presumed it was because of the way I spoke. It spurred me on. 'Although it's true that what we do get to see when we travel around is magnificent. The scenery is always wonderful, whatever the weather and however rough the sea turns out to be, don't you think? I expect you're finding it all very different from the sort of terrain you're used to in America, especially in the South!'

The lady's mouth fell wide open. She appeared completely stunned, and for a moment, so taken aback she was unable to speak. Before she had time even to think of what to say next, I added, 'I hope you're all enjoying your trip too?'

Finally, she found her voice, although she remained, seemingly, utterly flummoxed. 'Aw, gee honey!' she said in her slow, Southern drawl, 'Your English is almost perfect! They really train you people good, don't they?'

'Thank you!' was all I said by way of reply. I smiled feebly.

I was aware that a few girls standing close by had heard and understood every word the American woman and I had exchanged.

'Miss Russell, you **have** to tell her,' they urged. 'You have to tell her that your English IS perfect. Tell her, tell her! You can't let her think that her American is superior to your English!

I laughed. 'I don't think so. I don't want to tell her. I'd rather she thought I was a well-educated Norwegian. I'm not sure she'd understand what on earth I was doing here if I told her I was actually from England. I'm afraid she'd find that quite difficult to absorb.'

The American lady continued to watch us, listening and smiling ever so benevolently, that I could not help feeling patronised. I wondered if those on a Midnight Sun cruise from foreign parts had expected us all to be rough, illiterate peasants rather than civilised, educated and lively students. Our party of school teens after all was no different from any other teenage school trip anywhere in the world.

***

The venue for the festival was a school for students from a wide area in Finnmark, for whom daily access, especially in winter, was totally impossible. It was one of those rarest of institutions – a Norwegian boarding school. Thus, it had all the scope and facilities necessary for visitors: dormitories, kitchens, dining rooms and sitting rooms, in addition to ordinary classrooms and meeting areas. It was a sophisticated complex with a well-equipped sports hall as well as a school hall for meetings, concerts or film shows - a sizeable space with fine acoustics. I knew at once that the choir would be able to sing well there. Singing in a great space with wonderful acoustics always inspired them. It was a fabulous venue for the choir's end-of-year performance.

I was delighted that several Sami students made up some of the boarders. They were from families who still followed their reindeers' annual pilgrimage across the *vidda* with all their families, goods, and chattels. They would not be able to go to any local school as they moved across the *vidda* with their reindeer. Apparently, they liked boarding anyway: it allowed them to blend in with their Norwegian colleagues. Because this was a special event, the Sami students wore their national costumes - bright blue and red woollens and furs with their distinctive coloured caps and fur flaps to keep their ears warm. They stored their tools, equipment and needs in the front of their jackets – the *paesh* - which always made it look as if they had extended tummies. The rest of their worldly goods would traditionally be pulled along behind them on flat-bottomed sledges called *pulks* - an early version of a suitcase on wheels.

One of the Sami students, Andreas, introduced himself to me in flawless English. 'How do you do?' he asked extending his hand. 'This is how I should greet you, isn't it?' He flushed slightly but continued undeterred. 'We heard you were coming. I mean **you** personally, an English person. So, I've been looking forward to speaking English with you. Can you understand what I'm saying, by the way?'

'Indeed, I can!' I assured him. 'I'd be absolutely thrilled if my Norwegian pronunciation and intonation were even half as good as your English. And I'm delighted to meet you too. You look wonderful in your costume, by the way. It's great that you're wearing it today. The colours are splendid!'

Although I am only roughly five feet four myself, I was actually at least an inch or so taller than Andreas. The Sami people tend to be shorter than their Norwegian, Viking brothers and sisters, but his height in no way diminished his general air of competence.

'What year are you in?' I asked.

'I've one more after this one. I'm taking my *Artium* next year and then I really want to go to university.'

The *Artium* exams were roughly equivalent to English A Levels, and I understood Andreas was on the brink of changing his way of life completely, which would mean moving from one culture to another, as well as moving away from 'home'.

'So, you'll move away from Finnmark, from your family and your roots too. That won't be easy, will it? Do you know what you want to study?'

'Yes. I want to be a doctor. So, I'll need to get very high marks indeed if I'm to get into a good school AND study medicine, coming from MY background.' He smiled. 'But then, I can only do my best.'

'Well! I wish you all the very best in all your endeavours. If your science is half as good as your English, you should be all right.'

Andreas laughed. His faced creased into smiles and his eyes lit up. He was indeed a most delightful person. I thought he would have the most excellent of bedside manners. 'Thank you!' he said.

I remembered what I'd been told about how the Nazis saw the Sami people – that they had no civilisation, were uncultured and ignorant peasants without even decent houses to live in. How wrong they were! Their beautifully warm and well equipped *lavvus* – or Sami family tents – met all their daily needs as they followed their reindeer across the *vidda*. The central fire-place also kept the prolific Finnmark *vidda* mosquitoes away. Smoke from their central - *stroke*

- oven was persuaded to disappear through an expertly crafted smoke hole which allowed it to escape efficiently, leaving the inside of the *lavvu* smoke free. So reliable and comfortable were they, that *lavvus* were a God-send to many in 1944/5, when the Germans burned absolutely everything they could in Finnmark as they retreated south. The Sami people also set up a *lavvu* in front of the Storting in the late 1970s during the Alta Controversy. Far from being some kind of outback, rural temporary camp site, it became an international focal point during the protest. Always beautifully warm and dry, *lavvu* provide real comfort in any low temperature.

I also remembered that many Norwegians believed until recently that the Sami people were backward. I doubted whether any of them had come across an Andreas or any other serious Sami students I had met since I arrived in Vadsø. I was delighted to be able to sit next to him at one or two meals, so I was able to ask him endless questions about Sami life and culture. He told me more about what it meant to Sami folk, having to learn Norwegian by law since the 1850s, and then later compulsory for them to go to school. Members of his own family were keen not to lose too many elements of Sami culture, even as it became increasingly difficult to maintain the way of life they had known for centuries. They also valued access to decent education. Sadly, increasing numbers of Sami were enticed to live in developing towns and cities where there were jobs and money and other inducements to what many of his fellow Sami thought was an easier, more reliable way of life.

***

After we arrived, we were offered the standard fare of welcoming coffee and *smørbrød*. When everyone was suitably fed and watered those in charge of the festival event prepared to get it started. There was no strict timing. The programme would start when it started, take the time it needed and finish when everyone had sung, and there was no more music to be shared. No one had to make a hazardous journey home after all. Then, there would be *middag* - or dinner - for everyone in the dining-room followed by bed around midnight, or later, I guessed. Not that it made that much difference at this time of the year since it was light all the time, and many people found it difficult to stick to a definite sleep schedule anyway. They napped when they could. It was the complete opposite of the dark period from mid-November to late January, when people could not help falling asleep at the oddest times, and often struggled to stay awake in the middle of the day.

There were only three choirs participating, but two of them had two slots on the programme. Vadsø's singers were programmed to sing in the middle of the proceedings. We had prepared four items including two negro spirituals, We Shall Overcome and Swing Low Sweet Chariot. The former had been especially requested by a number of choir members in view of recent conversations many of us had had about Rhodesia – known today as Zimbabwe. The madrigal group had prepared three of their favourites to sing also. The sound they made was excellent, and their performance went down a storm. Most people did not know about this particular sixteenth century English music and had never even heard of it.

To round off our participation, the choir had prepared Handel's Joy to the World and the well-known Funiculi, Funicula which was always such fun to sing and went with a swing. There was riotous applause and whistles at the end. I wondered whether the audience wanted to show appreciation for our willingness to have come come all that way, or our actual performance. Eventually, since the applause did not stop, I invited the choir to sing, We Shall Overcome once again, and asked everyone else to join in. It nearly brought the house down.

It was a special trip and an appropriate climax to the choir's year. When we all sat down for our final meal there was over an hour of community singing, joke telling and speechifying. It felt like a special passing out ceremony. Formal photographs were taken of all the musicians who had taken part. A newspaper article praised the occasion and had good things to say about the Vadsø choir. I was much moved by everything. It was a great tribute to all the singers and a memorable rounding off to the year. The thought of leaving still hurt. But the year felt appropriately and finally phrased in conclusion to this particular expedition. I, for one, will never forget it.

Chapter Twenty-Eight

Wild Picnics

In addition to days of celebration May was also dominated by the spring thaw, because of the unique, soft quality and warmth of the sunlight. The dregs of ice and snow changed from pristine white to clear, running water. Cleaner, earthy browns, a range of brilliant, lush greens and distinctive greys and browns revealed themselves in a landscape that was constantly changing. The town seemed different too. People appeared re-energised. Roads and tracks became visible once again. The few private cars there were emerged from hibernation as snow ploughs disappeared.

Most spectacular, however, were the days of Midnight Sun, from May 17th to July 28th. Continuous daylight for several days either side of those dates meant that the many weeks of light helped people to put the long, dark days of winter behind them. The sun was omnipresent and enormous. The skyscape continually took my breath away - a daily preoccupation. Although it may have looked like summer-time, with this massive red or yellow ball moving from side to side across the horizon like a balloon, there were days when it could still be really cold, even days when it snowed. But although the flakes were thick, they did not settle for long.

Milder temperatures also led to tons of melted snow across the *Finnmarkvidda* hurtling towards and merging with newly made rivers of enormous torrents careering towards the open sea. I had never before experienced such a powerful sight or heard such a deafening sound.

The process of millions of tons of snow melting into cascades of fast-flowing water was dramatic to witness. The popular thing to do at weekends for this crucial period of three or four weeks was to find a viewing spot by one of Vadsø's nearby rivers to watch the thaw in exactly the same way as it is possible in English summers to watch the sun disappear behind the late evening horizon. The water nearest Vadsø flowed through what is known today as *Varangerh-alvøya's* National Park.

One of the first trips the Flysts undertook as soon as the roads were free of snow and ice, was their annual picnic to a favourite spot they had found close to what, if I remember rightly, was either the Ridelva or the Storelva. It was so long ago now that I'm no longer entirely sure which it was.

This year, the family invited me to join them. The prospect of a picnic in the Arctic seemed ridiculously impossible to me. But I was soon to be amazed by its reality.

As we parked, and before we had even got out of the car, the roar of the gathering flow of water was deafening. It was impossible to hear anyone speak, even if they were standing right next to you. I was surprised how anxious I felt. If the noise was as loud as this when we were at least a couple of hundred yards away from the water what on earth would it be like close to it? Was it actually safe to be here? What if the banks of the river were overcome by the power of the flow? I calmed my thoughts by presuming that Jon and Bente would not even think of taking their children anywhere that was not safe. I kept telling myself this, and hoped the butterflies in my stomach would eventually settle down!

'We've come to this same spot for the last three years,' Bente told me in the car en route. 'You'll see why when we get there,' she added mysteriously. 'It won't be easy to have any kind of conversation once we've parked, but if we look at each other when speaking, I'm sure we'll be able to communicate easily enough. Actually, I'll be surprised if you'll want to say much since it will be such an overwhelming surprise to see the river as well as experiencing how loud the water is.'

I was not disappointed. Every step we took from the car towards the river bank considerably increased the decibels. I had never experienced a phenomenon like it when we finally found a place to stand and watch, somewhere close to Skallelv, I believe. I stood utterly amazed as together with Jon and Bente and their children, I saw the tons of rushing water hurtling from left to right in front of us as it roared on to the sea. It is an experience I have never forgotten. I was stunned - both by what I saw as well as the incredible noise we could all hear - like an endless roll of overhead thunder surrounding us.

'It's quite a sight, isn't it?' Jon said. 'An experience really: impossible to describe,' he continued more slowly. All five of us stood still in respectful, silent awe for several minutes before he spoke again. 'We can never believe it ourselves when we first see it. It's the same every year, wondering if the experience will be the same as we remember from last year. We come here, to this exact spot, about this time – and we never fail to be totally amazed by just how much water there is, and just how loud a noise it makes as it accumulates and swirls along. Even though we know it will be a mighty sight when we get here, nevertheless, it takes us all by surprise every single year, isn't that right Bente? Children?' All three nodded in agreement.

'We discovered this spot the very first year we were here, quite by chance, following the noise once we'd found a place to park. But before we could see how far it might be possible to go for a walk and explore what had been hidden for months under snow, we were drawn by the roaring noise. We found we could stand without being too dangerously near the water, where we could be crushed to death against the rocks in just a few seconds! Fortunately, the noise alone makes the children cautious and stops them from getting too close.'

'I've never seen or heard anything like it.' I said. It seemed a feeble statement. In no way could it communicate what I was experiencing!

'It's a sight and experience I'll never forget,' Bente reiterated. Then, she laughed. 'And I say that each year.'

'You'd think the top of the world would be a neglected and savage place,' she went on, 'but it's somehow dignified and orderly in spite of its power. And I expect it's a lot calmer beneath the cascading surface, close to the bed of the river. It must be, surely, since we know how many exquisite and sizeable salmon are caught from this **very** river every year. When we first heard about that too, it was difficult to believe. But seeing this incredible torrent makes the truth even more impressive. I mean that it's possible that healthy life can be sustained under all this power. You'd think it would kill off anything trying to thrive inside or underneath it.'

Bente had to shout at the top of her voice so that I could hear. I was speechless and could only nod in reply. I just kept on saying, 'It's amazing' under my breath. I kept thinking how awesome nature is and how fragile and puny I felt in comparison.

The five of us stood silent for several minutes before we made a move to settle ourselves to the serious business of enjoying our picnic. Jon and Bente did not have to worry about the children falling in the water or getting caught in it accidentally. It was obvious that both youngsters had a healthy respect for the strength of what they could see and hear, and they naturally kept their distance from the river.

The picnic spot made an ideal base for everyone in a sheltered cluster of rocks well away from the river itself. There, we could at least hear each other speak without having to shout above the thunderous noise. We were also spared a constant soaking from the water spray. We could sit, sheltered and comfortable in a cosy grass dip, surrounded by five stones arranged in such a way as to form a natural windbreak.

When I first saw this spot, 30 yards or so from the riverbank, I wondered if someone had actually placed the rocks where they were, close enough to the river, from what felt like front row seats. The rocks were arranged in a rough circle. We could comfortably lean against them and hear each other speak without having to shout. Bente assured me the rocks were a natural formation as she spread out several thermal blankets, for all of us to sit on.

I still remember our picnic to this day. Some years later, when our own children were small, we would sometimes, on a Saturday, drive out into Derbyshire – close to where we lived – to spend time in a small, ancient stone circle on the moors that acted as a glorified playpen. We would take books, newspapers, food and drink, bats and balls and other toys. Everyone was supremely happy for four or five hours at a time. Of course, the stone circle was bigger than Bente's snugly arranged five rocks. But memories of our Arctic picnic came flooding back every time we visited the Derbyshire circles – enjoying similar experiences, albeit some 1600 miles from Finnmark, and at a place in the Peak District that was nothing like as dramatic as the banks of our Finnmark river.

I could not help wondering what the journey of one small drop of water would actually be like: what would it experience as it hurtled along, thrusting towards its destiny, finally flowing out into the ocean? For thousands of years, rich and plentiful in and to all sorts of life, the river had charted almost exactly the same course. Fifty-five years ago, I presumed it would go on doing so for many centuries to come, continuing to give life to some of the world's biggest fish that support a vital part of that Arctic region's economy. But that was before climate change.

Today, there is much less snow melting off the *vidda*, the Finnmark rivers are nothing like as deep as they used to be, and their flow is less dense and hectic. However, the Arctic Circle is still rich in all forms of wild-life, and the Barents Regional Council - founded in 1993 with representatives from Denmark, Finland, Iceland, Norway, Russia, Sweden, and the EU, together with observers across the world with a remit to make sure that sustainable development is maintained in the Arctic Region - pays attention to such precious realities as respecting and maintaining the Arctic's natural, living riches. Many creatures such as Reindeer, Wolves, Foxes, Arctic Hares, Elks, Musk Ox, and even a few

Brown Bears, as well as sea animals such as Polar Bears, Seals and a plethora of other forms of sea creatures and varieties of birds rarely seen anywhere else, which might otherwise be in danger of extinction, are kept safe and protected from that. It sees it as an important aspect of its general remit to maintain and prosper the whole area's many unique resources.

I went on several picnics with the Flysts, experienced much and learned a lot about the changes to its environment that came with Spring. It helped me understand something of what I had been told about people topping up their annual finances from salmon fishing in the spring and summer. I could see how that was possible, simply because of the sheer scale of the harvest. Other things began to make sense too. I came to see how impossible it was, as I had heard people say, to even contemplate driving south to visit friends and families before the snow had completely melted and run off the roads at the end of the school year in midsummer.

All roads south – such as they were - from Finnmark were closed for at least nine months of the year: from September to the following May. If they were not actually under snow or ice-bound, they mostly consisted of mud and slush instead of tarmac: more like sophisticated tracks than arterial roads. But it was possible to drive south from Finnmark and back again for at least two or three months in the summer. Many people did so, leaving Finnmark as soon as the school term ended, to spend summer en famille visiting relatives or gathering at a family cabin by the sea. Return journeys were made well before the autumn snows began to fall, when the roads became icy and dangerous once again. Today, however, there are first class main roads in all directions in Finnmark. It is even possible to take a bus trip the whole length of the country, from Oslo to Kirkenes. It takes about 25 hours. Such a trip would have been unthinkable, 55 years ago.

Currently, several main rivers and their tributaries are still a key part of Finnmark's life. They not only supply food locally and commercially, they are also vital contributors to the social and economic glue of Finnmark's life and culture. Additionally, their riches provide a vital source of income to many Sami families. To date, the water is still crystal clear and pure, and the fish are plentiful. Finnmark still hosts some of the world's keenest and most professional fishermen. I still recall how wonderful it was to be able to breathe the clean, sharp air too. But none of us know what will happen going forward if the climate continues to warm these special places in Finnmark. Or what might happen to its environment if, or rather when, the determination to explore and harvest the vast amount of underground wealth known to exist in that county on top of the world is given permission to do so.

***

Many families enjoyed similar *Finnmarkvidda* expeditions towards the end of May and through the whole of June, to enjoy the chance to get out and about and seek rare and cherished, so called, 'Finnmark fruit', or 'Arctic Gold'. May was too early in the year for *multer* – or 'cloudberries' in English - to be ripe for picking. But it was not too early to look for places where the fruit was in early growth, promising to be ripe for harvesting in several weeks' time. *Multer* were, and are, not easy to find, and once located, important unwritten protocols known by local people had to be followed by unspoken rules of etiquette acknowledging the finder's right to harvest the berries later on when ripe. It was considered extremely anti-social to harvest a crop found originally by someone else, even though none of the berries belonged to anyone specifically. There was no law against it, but a form of social isolation, inevitably followed if anyone disrespected the unspoken code of *multer*-picking.

It was vital the berries were ripe. Picking them when unripe was regarded as worse than impolite. It was positively anti-social, even illegal in some places – at least it was in my days in the Arctic. Picking unripe *multer* was viewed as an act of vandalism, not least because *multer* were of such limited supply and difficult to find. In July and August – knowing and following the proper picking time and the correct picking protocol was thought to be as important as knowing which side of the road to drive on! It will have changed substantially nowadays, not least because it has become popular to freeze *multer* to serve as a special treat at Christmas, so market forces are at play and the whole *multer* protocol has changed, except in the remotest parts of Finnmark.

Harvesting all kinds of nature's bounty remains a popular pastime for many. My southern friends have always been particularly keen to pick wild mushrooms. Carefully sought out, they flourish in parts of the mountains within walking distance of winter cabins. A day's hike could include picking a plentiful supply of edible fungi, rich in B vitamins and selenium, enjoying some of the day's crop for supper.

The ways *multer* are picked may have changed over the years, but the special way to eat them has not. The best, way requires pressing the tongue against the fleshy part of the fruit to enjoy the mild, sweet flavour. It can taste sour, almost bitter, if the pips get in the way. Served with cream, however, and as a desert to follow a first course of reindeer meat, it is a meal that certainly used to be regarded as a luxurious delicacy in Finnmark. Both reindeer and *multer* have unusual flavours to experience, savour and enjoy. *Multer* remain the most expensive of all berries in Norway. No wonder they are still referred to as 'Arctic Gold'.

Chapter Twenty-Nine

Iceland

Whilst writing about May, I remembered another unique and special experience. During my year in the South, I was fortunate enough to be included in the visit of the choir I had joined, to Iceland. I'm not sure I've ever known what this was to celebrate, but I believe it had something to do with honouring Iceland's 20 years of independence from Denmark, the outcome of the referendum they held to become self-governing in 1944. Whatever the reason, we were invited to sing at two concerts over an extended weekend. The first event was to be broadcast from the National Icelandic Broadcasting Studio in Reykjavik. After a couple of days in the capital, we flew to the northern town of Akureyri for our second concert. We were asked to wear national costume – both male and female *bunads* – presumably as a mark of national solidarity. I did not own one, nor indeed was I entitled to wear one. But a kind choir member, who could not go to Iceland herself, lent me her Trondelag *bunad* which featured red, green and blue Rococo style roses, woven into a colourful, vibrant pattern against its black woollen cloth background, especially around the hem where it was clearly visible.

In Reykjavik, Iceland's capital, we sang the Norwegian composer David Monrad Johansen's Nordic piece, *Voluspaa,* in Old Norse. The work tells a story from an old Norse Saga, or, more accurately, Edda. The Edda is a collection of Icelandic poetic literature that forms the main source of Nordic mythology. It celebrates pre-Christian beliefs at a time when Icelanders were on the brink of embracing Christianity. A prose Edda was collected and written down some time in the first two decades of the 13th century by the Icelandic historian and scholar, Snorri Sturluson, whose writings include ancient Norse myths with stories of Creation and Norse deities. *Voluspaa* heralds the birth of a beautiful new world arising from the ashes of death.

J.R.R.Tolkein was familiar with some of the text of *Voluspaa's* Eddas and occasionally, like Johansen's lyrics, references them in his Lord of the Rings trilogy. He even used names for some of his dwarves from the *Dvergatal,* which tells stories of the first man and woman. It also relates stories of the World Tree and describes some of what were thought to be hidden secrets of knowledge.

Written towards the end of the first century about the creation and the destruction of the world, *Voluspaa* makes three Norse gods *Odin, Hoenir* and *Loki,* creators of man. The work may have been partly inspired by a particularly contemporary and dramatic extensive volcanic eruption in Iceland, the like of which we still witness today. The story of the last battle might also reference mankind's vulnerability at the same time as the old gods are being replaced by forces too strong for them to keep in check. In any event, *Voluspaa* acknowledges a declining pagan faith even as it anticipates the coming of the Mighty Ruler, which many scholars think is a definite early reference to Christianity and which Snorri actually references as he reconciles the decline of paganism to emerging Christian beliefs.

Although it must have been translated for us from Old Norse into Norwegian, I fear I have long since forgotten both its detailed content and its specific meaning. All the sleuthing I have done since has not enlightened me, save to say that I discovered the work has attracted even greater acclaim in recent years, and become known as Johansen's best work. However, I believe the piece definitely commemorates great deeds of heroes and heroines, similar to those in Snorri's sagas, including some of the larger-than-life heroes of ancient myths and legends. These would include some subsequently accomplished by real life heroes like Olaf Tryggvason, an early Norwegian King who worked to bring Christianity to a disunited, pagan Norway. He laid the foundations for that to be achieved after his death in 1000 by Olaf Haraldsson – King of Norway in the early eleventh century, now known as St. Olaf - who was killed at the Battle of Stikklestad in 1030.

Snorri also wrote about deeds from heroic tales that parallel many Greek myths, or the kind of deeds Wagner includes in his Ring Cycle. This world of Ancient Wisdom and hobbit-like pursuit of heroic quests is also contained in Scandinavia's rich collection of Nordic mythology. It celebrates pre–Christian, heroic deeds in Norway, Iceland, Greenland and the Faroe Islands with much of the folk lore that precedes and surrounds them.

The only part of Iceland that lies within the Arctic Circle is the tiny island of Grimsey, a boat trip away north from Akureyri. We could not see the midnight sun itself at all while we were there. Nevertheless, the radiance of the sun's rays, even from below the horizon, meant that daylight prevailed round the clock for the whole of our stay in Akureyri. There was no dusk or dawn or even twilight. We did not visit Grimsey, but mentioning it now reminds me of the small island of Herm in the Channel Islands, comparable in terms of size, and beauty. There are many memorable experiences that have come to mind since I recalled my exceptional trip to Iceland. I have unearthed photographs I had forgotten I had even taken which have brought back memories captured in colour of that special trip.

In our two or three days in Reykjavik, we also had time to enjoy its open-air swimming pool, close to the centre of the city, heated by natural, underground volcanic geysers. This geothermal water heats most of Reykjavik, and roughly 90 per cent of Iceland's homes. The supply of this natural energy means that even in Iceland's cold climate, heating is cheap. All homes and buildings are naturally warmed and the city's streets are always free from snow and ice. Although we were there in May, the air was cold so far north, and it was strange to be able to swim in the heart of a capital city, in an open-air pool, watching busy people with their briefcases, or shopping bags, pushchairs and bicycles pass by all around. Road traffic also moved around us. People were warmly dressed in buttoned-up coats with woolly hats while we swam alongside, warm as toast.

We also sampled, or rather chewed, an abundance of dried fish - stock or cod mainly – cooked and served to us in a variety of dishes. (I have to admit it tasted pretty unappealing then, but today there are many recipes to be found online whose basis is dried fish. My Norwegian friend and I had a meal of dried fish on the boat from Bodø to the Lofoten Islands a few years ago which reminded us of the more-leathery style of cooking! Cooked properly, however, it can be absolutely delicious.) Wooden racks of drying stock and cod were hung everywhere. From a distance, they looked like endless pairs of socks interspersed with underwear hung out to dry, cheek by jowl on dozens of washing lines. In Iceland, the fish – a domestic equivalent to keeping chickens - had to be caught, cleaned and processed before being pegged on to lines to dry.

We were fortunate to have been able to visit Iceland when we did. The increasing numbers of visitors there since the mid-1960s has meant that protective fencing has had to be installed round ancient sites and places of special interest to keep them safe from direct access. At the time of our visit, we were all allowed to clamber freely wherever we liked.

And for the whole of our trip, we were regarded as important guests. So, before we left Reykjavik, we were treated to a private visit to *Thingvellir*, which lies some 40 miles outside the capital. This singular, small earth mound with its few, large and scattered natural stones, was unfenced in those days, so we had direct access to it. *Thingvellir* is where the *Allthing* had met – Iceland's original great assembly or site where civic decisions were made - since the early 10th century. The *Allthing* is generally accepted to be the world's oldest Parliament which first met on the mound at *Thingvellir* in 930 AD – probably before the content of *Voluspaa* was even much known. There, laws were discussed, disputes settled, and policy was agreed. It was at *Thingvellir* in 1000 that Christianity was accepted by democratic decision. Gatherings were regular until its last session in 1798, whence the Assembly moved elsewhere and then, later still, was housed inside its own special building in Reykjavik, where it has remained since 1881.

During our visit to *Thingvellir*, we were summoned by our choir master to come together to sing the Norwegian national anthem. As we sat on the Icelandic Parliament mound, we could not help but sing our hearts out. It felt moving and powerful. I knew I was privileged to be there: I was neither Icelandic nor Norwegian.

Today, thousands of tourists visit Iceland each year and make an important contribution to the island's economy. Indeed, following the banking collapse of 2008, which had the severest possible consequences for newly expanding Icelandic banks, the government has done a great deal to develop and encourage a profitable tourist industry. Now, along with many other ancient sites in the world, including Stonehenge, *Thingvellir* is fenced off to protect it from damage and deterioration that might obtain from too much trampling. Nowadays, no one can sit on this precious site and sing.

I have retained and developed my interest in Iceland not least because my younger Norwegian goddaughter's two children have an Icelandic father. Unsurprisingly perhaps, folk often joke about the undeniable truth that most Icelanders must be related to each other, however remotely, since the entire population amounts to fewer than 360,000 people. On the island of Iceland itself, most people choose to be known by their first name only. Indeed, in a recent conversation I had with a diplomat at the Icelandic Embassy in London, she insisted I should just use her first name. 'It's what we do! It's our custom always just to use first names,' she said. But because they live in Norway, my goddaughter's children have to use their surnames too, which are different from each other as Jonsdottir is his daughter and Jonsson is his son.

Approximately just 6,000 Icelanders lived in the Northern fishing town of Akureyri some 60 years ago - where we were to stage our second concert. We flew to the small fishing town over Iceland's rugged, uniquely barren, but beautiful landscape, apart from small parcels of cultivated land with the plethora of sheep and horses that lived in open countryside. I had no experience or knowledge of Finnmark until a few months after this trip to Iceland, but the many similarities

I have since discovered that exist between Iceland and Finnmark, interest me. This is especially so nowadays, because the Oslo government is trying to fathom ways to encourage and facilitate Finnmark's greater inclusion in the affairs of the rest of Norway. The 40,000 plus square miles of the island of Iceland are comparable to the 48,600 square miles of Finnmark. In that smaller space however, Iceland gives home to a population of just over 350,000 people, whereas only 75,000 plus people live in the larger area of Finnmark. Iceland is a volcanic island in the middle of the ocean. Much of its land is rock and larva, whereas Finnmark's terrain is currently hundreds of square miles of rich, mossy tundra, with the hidden prospect of vast amounts of untapped wealth from minerals below ground, as yet both uncultivated, and - much more significant - unmined. I cannot help wondering how long it will be before Finnmark's mineral wealth will be harvested, whatever the resistance – not least from the Sami people and their protection rights guaranteed in the 1970 Treaty after the Alta struggle - has to be overcome to get it to the surface. Then Finnmark's new prosperity will surely rival Iceland's wealth, derived from the liquid gold of its underground geysers that enable the production of extraordinarily cheap electricity.

My visit to Iceland with the Norwegian choir birthed in me an interest in the country whose fortunes I have since followed in the press. I was amazed at its growing wealth, even in 1965, considering how few people make up the population. In the decades following, its prosperity steadily increased. By the turn of the Millennium its three major banks – Kaupthing, Landsbanki and Glitnir – had managed to accumulate huge amounts of capital by massive borrowing from the international credit that was so readily available in the run up to the crash of 2007/8. This was only possible because since 2001, Icelandic banks had been de-regulated and therefore, were seriously exposed when the crash came, and extremely hard hit. The crash created a debt for Iceland that was seven times as large as its total GDP. That could not possibly be sustained or repaid. The huge wealth that had been accumulating through its banking system was wiped out at a stroke and left Iceland's central bank in no position to lend any money for any reason to anyone for quite some time. Shareholders, investors and creditors all lost heavily. Up to 500,000 non-Icelandic investors lost everything they had.

For three years, Iceland had to submit itself to an IMF bail-out. Iceland's banks were put into receivership and thousands lost huge amounts of money, while its currency depreciated rapidly. In relation to its size, the banking collapse in Iceland was the largest ever experienced in any country in economic history. Significant unrest and financial depression followed with a debt of some ISK9,550tn. Various public sectors in Europe, including institutions in the UK, had borrowed from Icelandic banks believing their rate-payers would be advantaged by the good deals at low rates of interest that were on offer. Unfortunately, the Market Capital of the Icelandic Stock Exchange fell by 90 per cent. Kent County Council, having invested in Icelandic Banks, lost £50m; Transport for London, lost £40m – to name but two examples. Some 14 Icelandic bankers were given prison sentences for their financial mismanagement. However, since 2011, Iceland's growth and prosperity has been more than totally restored, as has her capital growth. Chemical industries, fishing and tourism flourish. Even the USA has aluminium smelting plants in Iceland because electricity is so cheap there.

Remembering the flight to Akureyri also calls to mind the dramatic travel disruptions of 2010, when Eyjafjallajökull, one of Iceland's volcanos, threw out relatively small amounts of larva which disrupted air travel for several days. No one could predict how much more would be coughed out, or the extent to which hot ash spewed upwards into the air would cause serious problems of visibility for aircraft. It was an expensive disruption – although a minor hiccup compared with the current Covid toll - across western and northern Europe. Indeed, for six days air travel for almost the entire world came to a complete halt in April. Future Icelandic volcanic eruptions are unpredictable but have not prevented Iceland's continual and growing prosperity.

Having righted herself after the banking crisis, Iceland now continues to move her economy forward especially in fishing. But the overwhelming current prosperity that has pulled her out of economic decline is due to the sale of extremely cheap electricity. Iceland is the only country in the world that can claim to harvest 100 per cent of its energy and heat from renewable sources. Scientists also say that as yet, Iceland has not tapped even as much as 25 per cent of its underground renewables.

Iceland is now much closer to the wealthier sophistication of the rest of Scandinavia than is Finnmark. The dormant wealth of Finnmark, however, cannot be overestimated. But, even without the competitive delivery of cheap electricity, Iceland's underground riches will also be substantial. It also has untapped resources, and together with its well-developed fishing industry and its energetic pursuit of tourism, it will be able to make the best of even more riches yet to come.

***

Our choir was only in Iceland for five days. I remember little about the northern town of Akureyri, except that we received as much warm hospitality and positive response to our singing as we had done in Reykjavik. But while I was away for that short period of just five days, virtually every flowering plant and shrub in the town where I lived in the South of Norway seemed to have burst into blossom. I could hardly believe my eyes when I got home and looked out from my sitting-room window. The sight made the song from the musical Oklahoma, about spring bursting out all over, seem understated. The view was one of total transformation from the uniform greens and browns I had left, to a landscape of multi-coloured beauty that greeted my return. It felt even more extraordinary to get back from a few days of stark and barren wilderness, to be met in Norway by a dramatic, sudden burst of colourful, bountiful spring.

The memory of such a dramatic contrast, lives with me still. May in Norway before the impact of climate change was hugely different from anything I had experienced before. The scale of contrast was echoed in Finnmark, not only the following year, but also in May 2019 when I returned after 55 years. It was chilly in Vadsø, but as we drove across the Finnmarkvidda on our return and meandered round the glorious Northern *fjords* on the *Hurtigruten*, the glories of spring were everywhere: the colours and quality unsurpassed. The range and shades of different greens was extraordinary. To date, life in Arctic Finnmark remains gloriously natural and as yet, unspoilt. But I fear this state of affairs will not hold for much longer once the natural riches of Finnmark begin to be forensically explored and the yearning to recover them to help boost the nation's coffers becomes overwhelming.

Chapter Thirty

Compline

It was on one of the special Arctic picnic trips with the Flysts that reality struck me - forcefully. My departure from Vadsø was now only weeks away. The *russ* students had left school altogether two days following May 17th. After clearing up, they had flown to a beach in Denmark, the customary destination back then for a week of fun for Norwegian *russ* students. All my other classes were still hard at work for a few more weeks, looking forward to Midsummer's Day – when the school year would end. Indeed, all Norwegians looked forward to that particular day when families would decamp, possibly to their own or a relative's cabin by the sea, build bonfires to celebrate the summer solstice, party, picnic and swim. The outdoor life of the summer holidays began everywhere in earnest.

In the South, my friends and I had often sat by the water where their garden met the *fjord*. We sang at several outdoor picnics around Midsummer. 'Annie Laurie' was our favourite choice. We would sing in two parts, and those passing in boats en route to late evening summer jollies on nearby islands waved to us now and again as they sailed past, sometimes with upturned thumbs of approval. Occasionally, we even received applause. The acoustics out by the water were fantastic on long, summer days: sound seemed to carry for miles.

Even in the North, it was usually warm enough at Midsummer to party outside. In the Northern Hemisphere, the mid-June summer solstice occurs when the sun reaches its highest and northernmost point in the sky. That is the official time to mark the start of summer. But since it occurs in the Midnight Sun period, neither the light itself nor the length of daylight is noteworthy. So, in Vadsø, June 20th - Midsummer's Day – was not particularly different from any other day during the Midnight Sun period. It would not have been significant at all were it not that it also marked the end of the school year. Soon, I would have no more classes to prepare for, or students to teach; no more choir practices to organise, and no more adults or students with whom to speak English over pots of tea. There would be no more picnics, or *Hurtigruten* trips, or evening 'at home' tea parties. I felt real physical pain from such thoughts.

On one of our picnics, Jon and Bente were discussing their holiday plans. Bente, Anna and Anders always went to Trondelag to see all four grandparents as soon as school broke up. The family moved between both sets of parents' farms for the whole of the seven-week summer break. On the other hand, Jon Flyst only had four weeks of leave, so could not drive south until a couple of weeks after his family. His journey took him three days on roads that were passable, although not entirely reliable - if there had been a lot of rain, for example. But they were fine as a rule from July to September. Today all routes throughout the whole country, including Finnmark, are superb, with first class highways, excellent bridges and tunnels where necessary, and sophisticated venues for rests, refreshment and sleep, especially the latter since distances between places are so far. Nowadays, driving north to south can be almost as quick as other forms of transport - factoring in time allowed to get to and from airports and from airports to actual destinations.

'We'd love you to meet our families and friends - and show you where we hail from,' Bente said. 'We always go home for the summer and we'll move back there once we finally leave Vadsø. We'd love you to know where we'll be then. You WILL come for a few days and stay with us there, won't you? We'd love to show you round Trondheim too. It's the oldest and most special part of the country and Trondelag is a beautiful farming area and rich in Norwegian history - as I'm sure you know. So, please, do come.'

'I'd love to,' I said. 'How kind of you to invite me. I'd love to visit Trondelag and Trondheim. I know it used to be an important Viking trading area and that Trondheim Cathedral is the most Northerly Medieval building in the world. That IS right, isn't it?'

'Indeed, it is.' Bente was obviously pleased that I knew something about her home town. 'The Cathedral was built on top of St. Olav's burial place. He was killed at the Battle of Stiklestad in 1030 – now a small village some 60 miles North of Trondheim on the E6. He brought Christianity to Norway and moved us from the Viking to the Medieval period. Even though Olav Harraldsson was killed by King Knut, his death turned him into a martyr that produced a devoted following all over northern Europe and started a steady procession of northern pilgrimages to Trondheim, or Nidaros as it used to be called – and actually still is on important, formal occasions. Pope Alexander III made him a saint in 1164. After the Reformation, he continued to be honoured by Lutheran Protestants. So, although Stikklestad was only a small battle, its impact on our national identity remains huge.'

'I think I knew some of that.' I said. 'But since I haven't yet managed to explore that part of your country, it will be wonderful to do so! I'm in no hurry to get to my southern friends. They know to expect me when they see me - as long as I manage to get to them eventually.'

'That's great!' Bente seemed genuinely pleased. 'I usually leave with the children as soon as school finishes. If you don't mind waiting for Jon, you could drive south together. That way, you'd see a lot more of the country, and you would be company for him. I know he'd welcome that. It's such a long drive to undertake alone.'

'I'd enjoy that enormously,' I said as I began to realise how special it would be to be driven through such a remote part of the world - like having my own taxi. To start with, I knew it would mean I could see the heart of Sami country - Karasjok and Kautekeino - because our route would be confined to the only main road straight through at least one of those towns. 'I don't know much about the country between here and Trondheim either and have always wanted to explore it.' I felt fortunate indeed.

Bente seemed delighted. I was too - not least because it took pressure off organising an immediate, speedy departure at the end of term. I could leave my packing until the school year had finished, even though my tenancy with the Flysts in the formal sense was due to end at Midsummer. It would make leaving an altogether more gradual process and much less stressful than it would have been if I'd had to say my farewells alongside packing up.

As the days passed and the process began, I realised just how hard saying my final farewells actually was. Plus, it seemed there were so many people from whom I had to take my leave. It was as if each class insisted on a full, ceremonial closure. I tried to keep my spirits buoyant. I handed out an English address with promises to keep in touch, with offers of hospitality if and when anyone made a trip to England, as well as warnings that I may have moved after just a few months if work demanded.

Apart from those I taught, I wanted to say proper farewells to the adult friends I had made – my colleagues, the ladies in my adult groups, parents I had come to know personally. Some invited me for tea wanting to chat one on one. A few got together with others to make up small parties. I wanted to say a proper goodbye to so many who I'd got to know, befriend and love. Even so, I was not at all prepared for it to be the demanding experience it was. The endless round of final adieus was difficult and emotionally taxing. And I had not reckoned on being given so many gifts either. It was almost too overwhelming to cope with.

But I wanted to say goodbye as graciously as possible. At the big Gymnas where I taught in the South, there had been a splendid farewell event to celebrate the end of the year for everyone. All students, staff and parents were invited, not least to bid farewell to the *russ*. But there could be no such ceremonial formality in Vadsø since the Gymnas there had such a huge catchment area for one thing, and, in comparison to the South, a tiny school population with a much, much smaller school hall than the one in the South.

I needed to pack some of my belongings into crates and get them to the harbour for shipping to England. This needed thought and planning. My own travel arrangements could be made later. But since I would be spending time in Trondheim and then in the South, I needed to think carefully what I would need to have with me, and what I could pack to ship straight to England.

Our travel dates were finalised when Jon told me exactly when we could leave. Once that was agreed, he produced a map to show me the route and where we were to stay overnight. He had made this trip several times already, so had it all carefully worked out. We would be leaving Vadsø travelling West with the Verangerfjord on our left, as far as the Tana River. We would need to cross that at some point and then turn south through a bit more of Finnmark before driving through some of Finland and Sweden, parallel to Norway's narrowest parts which had roads that were perilous to car tyres and slow to drive along. Eventually, we would cross back into Norway somewhere north of Trondheim. Jon was already on first name terms with his hosts in Karasjok and Northern Sweden. It was marvellous to have that whole trip mapped out for me. I had no organising responsibilities at all.

Once they knew I would be leaving by car with Jon, literally everyone said to me 'You're going to have to cross the Tana river, then. That will be a really special experience for you. Just you wait and see!' They kept on saying similar things every time the topic came up about exactly how it would be. A certain look of amusement always accompanied their comment – together with a wry smile. It was all rather mystifying.

Whenever I tried to press for further explanation I was met with hoots of laughter. 'You'll see!' was all anyone said. I wondered if they were simply teasing me. I had come to understand how different Norwegian humour was from English: Norwegians often laughed heartily at things that just made me smile.

Saying goodbye to Mette was hard. Her eyes were misty when she opened her door to show me out after an evening of drinking endless cups of coffee and never-ending chat.

'I AM sorry you're leaving. I shall miss you. I've loved working together, being involved in all the English teaching. It's been great fun – inspiring too.

'Have you heard anything from *Friundervisning* about next year?' I asked, not for the first time.

'Not yet. They've said they'll be in touch before the end of the month though. I really hope I can go on with it next year. We'll definitely be here then. We have another whole year's break before we go back to the South, and my husband returns to sea. But we'll just have to see what they decide in Oslo.'

We chatted and laughed over the coffee and *smørbrød*, exchanged addresses and promised to keep in touch. Mette knew I would be around for a week or two yet, and we might cross paths still. But we both understood that this was to be the formal round up of our work together and our proper final farewells to each other.

As I walked home, I pondered whether or not I should write to my *Friundervisning* boss myself and ask about a successor. Since I had been the first *Friundervisning* appointment to Vadsø, I was surprised they had not asked me anything at all about the following year's appointee. I wondered whether funding was an issue. It was expensive to send Denis, Colin – our colleague in Harstad – and myself, so far north. We had to be paid more. All public workers were given additional allowances so far north, and had their travel costs paid, which *Friundervisningen* also had to honour. Or maybe politics was a concern? Remembering the greeting I had in the first few weeks of my year, maybe official channels knew that attitudes to receiving English teachers might be different in the Arctic Circle? It felt odd that I had not been told anything. But then, it was also no longer my concern. Eventually, I decided I just needed to think carefully about what I should say in my final, formal report.

It took a couple of weeks to say goodbye to everyone and to cope with the sadness of leaving. But, eventually, the day came when it was time to go. Jon had packed the car the night before, so all he had to do was make sure all the taps were turned off inside, and all the windows properly fastened against any freak storms. Then, he performed his final task which was, for the one and only time each year – to lock his front door.

I thought I had said all my absolutely final farewells to everyone I had planned and wanted to and had exchanged my last parting hugs and shed my last tears. But outside Jon's house a small farewell party had assembled to wave us off. Seeing them standing there took me by surprise. It seemed such an unusual sight and it brought tears to my eyes – as the car began to move and hands were waved energetically and goodbyes were said over and over, accompanied by blown kisses and shouts of 'au revoir'.

Jon backed his car into the road and turned his steering wheel southwards.

***

Many Southern Norwegians living temporarily in the North knew the importance of the Tana River. It provided the only crossing from Vadsø to the South. The ferry point on the river was vital to anyone who needed to leave Finnmark. They could not go further south without using it. A desultory series of rough tracks and poorly maintained so-called roads were virtually impossible to navigate at that time of year.

Inevitably, the roads in Finland and Sweden were less beaten up by the effects of extreme weather and were better maintained than those of Arctic Norway. Since they carried more traffic, they were kept clear of the more severely damaging hazards of snow and ice. Obviously, there were also many more tax payers to pay for road maintenance than in the Arctic Circle. In any case, the climate was less severe even just a few hundred miles further south, so the roads were guaranteed to be less churned up by the severe frosts and heavy snowfalls that occurred on a regular basis in Finnmark.

All those driving south told of similar experiences. At first, when the Norwegian roads had joined the main routes into Finland, there would be little, if any, traffic. What little transport there was would not be able to drive at great speed: in other words, the roads would be safe. The pace of life would seem similar. Sami settlements dominated the area where Norway met Finland at its Northern point, as well as in the parts of Finland through which it was necessary to drive. That particular part of the world was, and still is, an area often referred to as Lappland. The point on the Tana river where northern travellers would need to cross to continue south was sited where many Sami people lived.

The manually operated car and passenger ferry was operated on a daily basis by the Sami themselves. It was they who made sure there would be someone there to facilitate the process every day at a certain time. There was no official timetable. It was the Arctic Circle after all. But everyone knew there would be a ferry available every day to cross the river at about 2pm or soon after. Anyone who knew that Jon and I were taking this route had been only too keen to tell me the same thing – that this would be a special experience that I would always remember and had tried not to laugh. The closer we got to the crossing, the more filled with anticipation and curiosity I became.

Meanwhile, I found that taking in all the splendid, rugged scenery we drove through helped soothe my inner churnings about leaving. I did not want to spoil the journey by missing the opportunity to absorb the amazing grandeur all around us because I felt overcome by sad thoughts. So, I tried hard to pay attention as we drove. There were virtually no other cars. I could only ever remember one going the other way on the first day. It was as if we had the whole Northern World to ourselves, in all its extraordinary, majestic dignity. I knew I would never see the like again. We chatted intermittently, exchanging random comments about this and that, but mostly we were both absorbed by the wonders of the journey.

We passed continually between huge, rocky cliffs, beautiful and brutal. There were any number of waterfalls, some temporary, with drip drops of melting snow from the surrounding *vidda*. Others were natural and constant, powering their way into distant lakes.

After a couple of hours, we approached the ferry crossing point. We knew we had made good time. A Sami ferryman never appeared before 2pm. Once on the other side, we would have to drive for a further couple of hours through Finland to reach our destination for that night. Briefly, we would be back in Norway once again at a well-known, thriving town, renowned as the centre of Sami culture and history.

It was almost exactly 1.30pm when we arrived at the Utsjok crossing point. Jon was relieved to be in good time. We got out of the car to stretch our legs. It felt good to move about after sitting for so long. We wandered around breathing in the good, clean air for 20 minutes or so. We both kept our eyes open to see if anyone else was going to join us on the ferry. We were also eager to catch sight of the ferryman, expecting him to appear at any minute.

I noticed some of the wild plants growing there that I had not seen before. I picked a few, planning to press them once I had managed to discover what they actually were. Flowers were rare in that part of the world so they had drawn my attention. Time passed. Two o'clock came and went. Three o'clock passed – and then, four. Jon was getting agitated. He was clearly worried.

'Are you worried that someone might not be coming today?' I asked. 'This IS the right place, isn't it?' Surely, this was not what so many people warned me would be mildly amusing? Surely, they had not meant that we would get to the crossing point only to find that no one would come at all?

'It is. And, I suppose I'm not really worried. Anyway, as you see, the ferry is tied up obviously waiting to go from here to the other side. It's not even as if we're waiting for it to come from over there to over here. It's just that I've never had to wait quite so long before.'

Jon was looking anxiously around as he spoke. 'I'm just beginning to worry whether or not anyone is going to come at all today. Sometimes, the people who live round here can be quite casual about timing. But they generally do what they say they'll do – even if it IS at a different time. And' he added, 'there may of course be people over the other side who want to come over here. They can't do that until the ferry gets to them.'

I felt helpless. I also wondered what he meant by 'anyone living around here'. I could not see any sign of life in any direction and I also began to wonder what we could do if no one turned up at all. Would there be anywhere close by to stay the night if necessary? But then Jon said, trying to sound more confident to convince himself perhaps, 'Someone will come eventually, I'm sure.'

I felt glad I was not in charge of our travel arrangements. I knew it would not be easy for Jon to change our plans. In any case, there was no phone nearby even if we had decided we wanted to. There was not even a telephone in the tiny hut that served as an assembly point-cum-waiting room. At least it was somewhere dry to sit. I understood how important it was to reach our first destination that night. If we did not, the whole of Jon's schedule would be kiboshed. There was nowhere else we could spend the night. The only other alternative would have been to sleep in the car. 'Perish the thought!' I said to myself, knowing it would not be at all comfortable at the same time as I recognised that this was not a part of the world where anyone actually lived, never mind whether or not it was safe and civilised enough for us to find any hotels or guest houses.

In my year in the North, I had learned to shed many of my intense anxieties about time and speed. But even though I had learned to be less rigorous about such things yielding to the inevitable constraints of climate and lack of sophisticated facilities, nevertheless, I thought to be so very late was all a bit too casual. It was irresponsible just not to turn up when you were supposed to at such an important place, where people depended on you and who would be helpless if you were not there to do your job. Surely it would be understood that such extreme behaviour would have consequences? Being late was one thing, but to be SO late as to make people feel concerned and helpless - surely the most casual of timekeepers would understand that that was difficult to take?

Just before 5pm, Jon thought he spotted movement on the horizon.

'Is that someone in the distance walking towards us?' he asked. 'Can you see? Or am I imagining things?'

'Where?' I put my hand to my brow and focused on the direction where he was pointing. 'You're right! Yes! I see. I think it IS a human being. D'you think it could be our ferryman?'

'I hope so. I really, really hope so.' Jon sounded more desperate than optimistic. I was already worried about how tired he must be feeling by now, knowing there was still a fair distance to drive once we'd made it to the other side. I could relax once we were across the river, but Jon could not.

As the figure approached, the unmistakable shape and ambling gait of a Sami man - known for, and proud of, their shorter stature than the average Viking - came into closer view. When he was only yards away, he waved a greeting.

'Hello there! Are you wanting to cross?'

Jon did his best not to sound exasperated. He was, as ever, polite and to my great admiration, completely self-controlled. 'Yes! We are!' he said. 'We've been waiting for over three hours.'

Jon, like me, was expecting an apology or at least an explanation. But the ferryman seemed unabashed. He was smiling broadly as he approached. A curious response, I thought. I could see how irritated Jon looked. He must have felt exasperated. Could the ferryman not see and appreciate that?

'We still have another three hours' drive before we get to our destination for the night.' Jon continued. Now, I thought he sounded really cross. Usually, he was the most equable and amiable of men. 'This is really too bad. We expected you to be here ages ago. As I said, we've been waiting more than three hours.'

I had never heard him speak so sharply. The ferryman continued to grin from ear to ear. Completely unmoved by Jon's exasperation he made no apology at all, not even an explanation. He was not rude or unpleasant. He just continued to smile broadly. And once he was actually standing beside us, he simply stood, extended his arms wide in a gesture of genuine surprise and total incredulity, and sounding mildly exasperated, he simply said,

'Well! Goodness me. If you were in such a terrible hurry, why on EARTH didn't you come yesterday?'

Jon and I stood and stared at each other, open mouthed - speechless.

***

This exchange of words seemed to me to be a fitting epilogue to my adventures in the Arctic Circle. The next few weeks spent ever further south allowed me to re-enter a world I had left behind for a year, slowly and enjoyably. Weeks later, and on reflection, I saw how my time in and around Trondheim had successfully facilitated my smooth transition from one world to another. The people were the same – large hearted, generous spirited, energetic and vigorous – but perhaps because the climate and environment was kinder and less austere, life further south was less challenging. The environment also felt softer; the prevailing human spirit seemed altogether more placid, quieter and relaxed. The greenery of the landscape, the rich golden expanses of abundant, ripening crops everywhere punctuated by so many trees made the whole ambiance more welcoming – reassuring even. It took me by surprise that I needed to adjust to what was definitely a different rhythm; to adapt to gentler expectations and accept what felt like an atmosphere that was overall more serene and predictable.

For quite some time, I missed the natural exuberance of my students. I realised how much freer they seemed than their southern counterparts with whom I was now back in contact. They also seemed more willing to risk and explore attitudes and ideas: more prepared to test and dare. It was difficult to put my finger on specific examples, although the fact that the school had been the responsibility of a youthful Gymnas Rektor was definitely one. That would have been the choice of the local authority in Vadsø with which the National Ministry of Education would just have had to agree. Also, after my difficult start, the more than willingness of people to engage with difference and accept someone from a different background was notable. Yet wherever I went and who ever I met while I was with the Flysts people were astonished to hear I had just been in Vadsø for a year. It seemed they needed to check that I was both sane and well-adjusted before they went overboard to praise what they thought was genuine and unusual courage.

Ann, Margaret and I took the bus along the exact same route that Jon and I had driven from Vadsø to the Tana River on our way from Vadsø to Honningsvåg. There was a tiny ferry crossing for local use close to where Jon and I had boarded. A large, strong bridge had replaced it for at least the last 50 years of constant use allowing heavy lorries and vans to drive through the northerly parts of Sweden, Finland and Norway. However, an even bigger, stronger and much more impressive bridge was in the throes of final construction two years ago. It may be in full use by now – if not delayed by Covid constraints. Clearly, the volume of traffic and the size of vehicles has increased ever further – even to include pantechnicons that could easily accommodate the very ferry itself that Jon and I took in 1966.

Chapter 31

A Couple of Highlights

Our Three Arctic Musketeers' trip in 2019 came to a climax with a notable visit to a service in a church that has come to be called a Cathedral, even though it is in fact a local, parish church. Located in Tromsø, a city generally called 'the Gateway to the Arctic' it is sited some 400 kilometres inside the Arctic Circle. In the last 50 years, Tromsø has become a well-established cultural centre, with a university built in 1968 that offers teaching in a range of subjects and advanced research opportunities especially Auroral Light, Space Science and Sami Culture. Tromsø is also often referred to as the 'Paris of the North', hosting as it does The Arctic Symphony Orchestra founded in 2009, which shares a central teaching and rehearsal base with Bodø.

Tromsø has been a significant trading centre since the 13th century, although never as well-developed as Trondheim. Its population of some 67,000 is considerably fewer than the 170,000 in Trondheim. Like so many Norwegian towns and cities, Tromsø is partly on mainland with a dramatic bridge, connecting it to the adjacent island of Tromsøysund. Getting about is facilitated by a plethora of underground tunnels in its centre.

I had been wanting to visit what has become known there as the Arctic Cathedral ever since it was consecrated in November 1965 by Bishop Monrad Norderval, a few months before I finally left Norway in 1966. But that was before Jon and Bente had asked me to travel home via Trondheim to stay with their families, and I decided not to double back up north after my visit there. I had often wondered about including it on one of my regular visits to Norway, but it had never been the right time, or possible – until 2019. After our days in Vadsø, leaving Honningsvåg at 5 45am on the *Hurtigruten*, we sailed for the whole day until midnight when we arrived back in Tromsø in time to attend the confirmation service the next day, to which Sigmund and May Line had welcomed us when we had stayed overnight with them in Tromsø on our way from Oslo to Vadsø.

The confirmation service is an important rite of passage for Norwegian adolescents. The majority of these services are performed in local churches, although there are increasing numbers of secular ceremonies delivered in civic buildings too. The dignity and respect for this occasion is as great and as memorable whether spiritual or secular, honoured as it is by a *bunad* dress code. The future for all youngsters concerned is marked by the receipt of substantial gifts of money and expensive presents which help towards future costs of further education and training.

The Arctic Cathedral, or *Ishavskatedralen,* is the parish church of Tromsøysund, the large island connected to Tromsø's centre on the mainland, connected by its famous white bridge. The Arctic Cathedral stands proudly in the midst of the Tromsdalen Valley. Its tall triangular frontage and striking interior houses a congregation of some 600 worshippers. Attending a service there turned out to be a highlight of our trip, providing a fitting climax the day before we flew home.

The name Arctic Cathedral has been acquired out of admiration and affection. It is not a Cathedral. The actual, smaller and older, Protestant Cathedral in Tromsø is located at the other side of the city, notable for the fact that it remains the only Norwegian Cathedral made of wood. Built in 1861, it is probably the most northerly Protestant Cathedral in the world. These days, it serves more as a church administrative centre rather than a place for regular worship. It was not open on the Sunday when we visited Tromsø. Whereas the Parish Church of Tromsøysund, or Arctic Cathedral, is in regular and continual use. It's A-shaped frontage is easy to see from many locations - the *fjord*, main roads or from the air.

Margaret, Ann and I were thrilled by our day's voyage on the *Hurtigruten* from Honningsvåg to Tromsø. All day we had been enveloped by stunning landscapes and scenery sailing through a plethora of *fjords*, along coast lines of busy harbours as well as small and scattered settlements. Historical wharves and storehouses were pointed out to us by the captain. Quaint villages had been left unaltered from the days when tall sailing ships delivered vital cargo to isolated places along the coast. We were told over the tannoy at some point that the retreating Germans had actually refused to burn some of these quaint harbours, in spite of instructions to do so, because the soldiers assigned to the task felt they were too historically special. That made the three of us feel even more thrilled to be able to catch sight of them. People came out to wave, whistle and hoot as we passed some settlements, and the *Hurtigruten* acknowledged their greetings with ritual blasts on its horn.

Dead on time almost to the minute, we sailed into Tromsø under its famous bridge and into the harbour. Although it was close to midnight, the sun was high in a cloudless sky. We caught sight of the so-called Cathedral as we glided into dock.

True to his word, given as he had left us at Tromsø's airport a week earlier, as recorded in Chapter 14, Sigmund called me the next morning to let us know he would pick us up at 10am to take us to the Confirmation service at the Cathedral. We were the first congregants to arrive, so we had plenty of time to orientate ourselves and absorb our surroundings.

Sigmund told us much about the building and interesting details about how the church was run. Margaret said how much it reminded her of Coventry Cathedral, designed by Sir Basil Spence and re-built from scratch on the same site after it had been bombed by the Luftwaffe in 1940. I knew the Arctic Cathedral had been designed and built by the Norwegian architect, Jan Inge Hovik. But Sigmund explained there were problems with the original windows behind the altar. When the sun streamed straight through them, it made it difficult for the congregation to see the pastor clearly. So, it was decided to replace the original windows with stained glass. There had been no difficulty in raising the money for the project and I understood that raising money for any church needs was never a problem. The new window portrays Christ's Second Coming and has suggestions and overtones reminiscent of the tapestry of Christ Seated on His Throne in Coventry Cathedral.

There are beautiful glass facades of the cross, in rays of light and other symbols at the main entrance. Inside, the wooden furniture is powerfully simple and straightforward. I knew the magnificent organ installed in the gallery behind us had been acquired in 2005 with its 2,940 pipes and bellows made from reindeer hide. Once again, there had been no difficulty in raising the necessary money for any of these expensive and innovative additions. I could not help thinking how ironic it was that however easy it had been to get people to give to pay for the organ, it was nevertheless almost impossible to get anyone in the congregation to actually sing in the service to the hymns it accompanied!

We were introduced to people who served as stewards and sidesmen, including a young Englishman with certain liturgical responsibilities who had emigrated to Norway from North London, from the same suburb where I had lived from the age of five until I left for my two years in Norway: small world!

Gradually, the church began to fill up as families and friends arrived. A spectacular array of colourful *bunad* designs and accompanying silver and gold adornments assembled in the next three quarters of an hour. There were also many smart suits and formal dresses – all to respect and honour the special nature of the occasion. By the time the service began, the church was full.

My feelings about the service are similar to those I experienced as we had flown into Vadsø airport in our little turboprop airplane seven days previously – joy and elation, and a whole range of emotions I could not even name. But I remember most of all the sheer beauty of the church itself, the wonderful smell of wood, and the gracious way we were treated as visitors. It thrilled me that the organist came from Germany, and that the female quintet had chosen to sing 'Mary Did You Know?', written by a Southern Baptist in the USA. It also thrilled me that Anthony, to whom we had been introduced, had chosen to leave North London to live in Arctic Norway, and that we, unknown visitors from the UK, were treated like visiting royalty. I also remember feeling embarrassed that we were under-dressed for such a special event, and I felt sad that few people in the congregation sang. Everyone sat to sing the hymns that were displayed at the front, so that did not help open enough physical air corridors in their lungs to make joyful sound in songs of grateful praise.

I remember one other detail. In the week between our overnight stay with Sigmund and May Line and our return visit to Tromsø for this service, we had spent our three days in Vadsø. One of the many surprises that struck me in addition to the plethora of coffee shops and eateries, the well-equipped garage and the new clothes shops down the main street, was the existence of one large and well-stocked antique shop. Quite by chance, or as I choose to believe, by Divine Serendipity, wandering round the shop I had come upon three small cream-coloured pottery angels. They simply ASKED to be purchased as our parting gift and were well-received when we presented them to May Line and Sigmund when we said our good-byes after the service as we were dropped at our hotel.

There could not have been a more fitting climax to our Arctic Musketeer trip. We left Tromsø early the next morning and were back in England later that same day. It had been quite simply a glorious trip with a wonderfully fitting and memorable infusion of appropriate worship to round it off.

***

I had made two good friends in the choir during my first year in southern Norway. My great friend with whom I have been close all my life, and another young lady the same age as myself, who worked in the town's only bank. Sadly, she died last year, and even more sadly, once I was back in England, and subsequently established my own family, we lost touch and never recovered it. Our friendship was based on getting out and about, going places and doing things which my life-long friend was not free to do since she welcomed her first child into the world during my year in the South. My bank friend and I went out dancing some nights, which was fun. We sat together as fellow sopranos at all choir events. We went to Iceland together. Prior to that, I spent Christmas in Norway with her family.

Undoubtedly the most memorable thing we did together, however, was to spend a weekend in Rjukan. Rjukan is currently a well-known skiing centre, and even though I am not Norwegian, I fear I mind that it is now somewhat spoilt by the plethora of ski cabins that have been built there in the past 50 years.

Rjukan's other great claim to fame, however, is that it has hosted a Hydro-Electric plant for many years, and thus Hollywood's 'The Heroes of Telemark' was filmed in that very town in 1965. This tells the true story of the fight during World War II to prevent the Germans from being able to make heavy water in order to be the first to build an atom bomb. It has all the glitz and glamour of Hollywood stars in the lead roles too – Kirk Douglas and Richard Harris.

Norwegian film-makers have recently made a docu-drama of the story in addition to a production they made some years ago which includes details from the original saboteurs themselves. The story is an important one because, if Germany had been able to manufacture the atom bomb before anyone else, that would most definitely have changed the face of history. Efforts from both Norwegian and British saboteurs concluded with the sinking of the ferry carrying trucks full of the heavy water as it crossed the *fjord* to the train waiting to carry the cargo to Berlin.

My friend and I decided we would like to spend a weekend in Rjukan at the same time as the film was being made. So off we went to witness the action and the drama as well as bask in the beauty of Rjukan's environment. The town itself is sited in North Trondelag, just south of the *Hardangervidda* and close to the *Gausta* Mountain. It stretches along the *Vestfjord* valley. At that time, it was a lovely, understated, mountain skiing retreat. It was also a typical Norwegian mountain village – or small town – with a close-knit community, a church, one hotel, a school, and good roads to neighbouring towns and villages.

My friend and I had booked ourselves in to the only hotel. It was a shock to arrive and find the town full of folk – mainly men – in German uniforms, wandering freely among everyone else who lived there with no animosity or tension or fear. I confess that just seeing actors dressed in German uniforms made it feel scary It took us several minutes to get our bearings, and also our courage - to walk up to the hotel from the ferry that had brought us across the lake from the train.

It was an even greater shock to enter the hotel and find it filled with German uniforms, worn by actors, clearly. They were lolling around, drinking beer, laughing and chatting - everyone in good spirits. There was a lot of friendly banter aimed especially at my friend who a typical, Norwegian blond bombshell, was quite capable of giving as good as she got. As we checked in, we learned that the town was abuzz with chat about the fact that the film crew had left some arc lights on in the church when they'd finished filming a day or so previously. It had caused some damage to the structure, and although the film crew insisted that they would put things to rights and they did, they were currently seriously unpopular.

The other highlight I remember was that there was only one place to eat in the town – the hotel dining-room. My friend and I found ourselves eating supper only a couple of tables away from the starring actors. My friend kept telling me not to stare!

'Leave them in peace,' she kept saying. 'They are entitled to eat their meal without being gawped at.'

'It's part of their job, isn't it?' I said. 'Being the centre of attention, I mean.'

'Well! even if it is, surely they're allowed to enjoy their food.'

'I think I'm going to ask for their autographs,' I said looking for a suitable notebook and pen in my handbag.

'You can't do that! You wouldn't dare...'

But I was already on my feet. I walked across to the table where Kirk Douglas and Richard Harris immediately put down their cutlery on their dinner plates, pushed back their chairs and stood up.

'Ma'am?' one of them said. I don't remember which.

'Forgive me for interrupting your meal,' I said. 'But please may I have your autographs?'

They both said 'yes, of course.' They asked me what I was doing in Rjukan. Did I live there? No, I explained, that I taught English in Telemark and felt really fortunate to be doing so: it was so beautiful and the people so welcoming and friendly. I hoped they had found that too, and that they were enjoying being in Norway. A few more pleasantries were exchanged before I apologised for interrupting their meal, hoping their food had not gone cold, wished them a good evening and returned to my table where my friend was agog to hear what had been said between us.

I learned two special facts last year. In the TV docu-drama made by Norwegians, we learned of a concert organised to divert German guards to its venue so that there would be fewer of them at the lake or on the ferry making the saboteurs' task easier. One of the musicians who helped organise the concert in Rjukan to divert attention was probably the choir master in whose choir I sang in the South and who took some of us to Iceland. Secondly, one of his three sons is currently the GP of one of my god-daughters who lives in Oslo.

I still have the two special autographs. At the time of writing, Kirk Douglas has only recently died, at the age of 104.

Afterword

Utøya

It was not many months after one of my regular trips to Norway that, some 24 kilometres North West of Oslo, on the island of Utøya, the dreadful events of July 22nd, 2011 occurred. I have never been to Utøya myself, but I know its location, and that it was a special place used by the AUF – the youth wing of the Democratic Socialist Party. Young people would go there to socialise, have fun and talk seriously about the future of their country and its place in the world. The DSP has changed its political roots over the years. Jens Stoltenberg - now NATO's General Secretary - was 'head boy' during his particular AUF year.

However, Norwegian politics has also changed much in the last 20 years, so it is difficult to say where the political allegiance of its young people might fit in today's world. My grandchildren tell me that citizen camps exist in the UK, but I do not know what their specific focus might be, so I do not know if they bear comparison. Utøya is singular because it is an island devoted to host enthusiastic youngsters for such causes. Together with everyone else in the world, I was appalled to learn what happened on that fateful day.

The film, '22 July' directed by Paul Greengrass of Bourne Supremacy fame, was released on Netflix a few years ago. It is a beautifully crafted and thoughtful film with Norwegian actors deliberately speaking in English to emphasise the world-wide significance of what happened that day. Greengrass decided to produce the film only after he had consulted Jens Stoltenberg, Norway's Prime Minister at the time and also had approval and consent from those who had been attacked and injured, as well as the relatives of all those who were seriously maimed or murdered. His film tells the story in accurate detail.

The incident took place at a time when many countries in the West had genuine and justified concerns about Islamic extremist terrorism. After all, it was only 10 years since the twin towers had been levelled in New York. Certainly, not everyone in Norway was at ease with immigrants from the Middle East receiving refuge in their midst.

270

The film focusses on the story of a seriously injured survivor, Viljar Hansen from Spitzbergen. He was shot more than once and had to have bullet fragments removed from his brain. To this day small pieces of shot remain there which are too dangerous to remove - and could shift at any moment, which would lead to his instant death. The deep grief that he, his family and many of his friends experienced is all-pervasive and shocking and runs as a theme through the film. His parents are anxious about the bullet fragments still in his head, naturally, but are also thankful he is alive. His brother feels constantly depressed, guilty that he is not suffering too.

The film also shows how Viljar learned to cope physically and emotionally with the various operations he has had to endure and the inevitable demands of learning to walk and move his limbs again. It also explores how he was able to find the courage and strength to give evidence at the trial, making it clear that he was still coping and would have to go on managing his injuries for the rest of his life, as well as showing the depth of real, sobering grief that just one family experienced.

Through Viljar's story, the film explores the perpetrator's motives without expressing any sympathy for him. In the same way, the Norwegian press and government, while not giving Andreas Breivik the oxygen of publicity, were willing to explore the reasons behind his actions. The surrounding details of that shocking day help emphasise the whole country's determination to pursue justice and healing for the attacked, not headlines for the perpetrator.

It feels important to me to mention this film and the event it describes, not just because of how singularly shocking it was, but also because I feel it shows so much of what I personally experienced it meant to be Norwegian when I lived there. Many beliefs and attitudes expressed in the film show remarkable resilience from victims who have chosen to go on living their lives as far as possible to the full. Islamic terrorists have caused havoc and pain in many places in the West, not least in New York and on the London Underground. But trying to wipe out a large cohort of a particular group of young people starting out on life was a piece of singularly calculated evil.

Thinking about how the nation responded to those ghastly events might be a particularly fitting focus on which to draw the thoughts of this book to a close. Not just because Breivik's murdering spree was beyond description but because the response of the Norwegian people bears testimony to their innate resilience and pacific reasonableness. There is sorrow and anger – of course. But the response to the perpetrator is not vindictive or punitive but conducted with all the dignity and justice of due legal process, advocated by many Western democracies. Pain was widespread but dignified. Sorrow was universal, shared with the world in the compassion of deep grief.

Breivik claimed his act was one of war against the influx of Islam in Europe. He was desperate to explain his personal, hideous slaughter was justifiable action to protect the way of Norwegian life. The reluctant, but professional conduct of his assigned lawyer through the entire proceedings, together with the dignity and poise of those who, in spite of their personal physical and psychological damage, gave evidence at his trial, is a memorable example of legal due process however ghastly the crime, as well as a fine example of the superiority of grace.

Viljar, the 'hero' of the film, decided he **must** give evidence at Breivik's trial, in spite of his injuries and the obvious emotional trauma of having to face the man who tried to kill him. He lists his injuries in court. Among them, he is blind in one eye.

'But' he says, with a wry smile, 'that's a relief in a way, 'cos I don't have to look at Breivik.'

Viljar later concludes, after answering endless questions and having made it clear how absolutely awful the whole experience was and remains, with his simple, defiant statement: 'I still have family and friends and memories and dreams. I have hope and love.'

Breivik has been sentenced to indefinite solitary confinement. The film concludes with him being shown into his isolated cell.

The King and the Prime Minister made several important speeches immediately after the dreadful events on Utøya: both struggled with their emotions every time they spoke. King Harald shed tears at the service in Oslo Cathedral and had to swallow hard, acknowledging his own experience of what it means to be part of a family as a husband, father and grandfather. Jens Stoltenberg also swallowed hard and held back tears when he gave an address at the Cathedral Service.

Ten years on from that ghastly event, several plucky and dignified survivors still go into Norwegian High Schools on a regular basis to talk about their own experiences of Utøya, the current dangers of both Islamic extremism and the potential reaction to it from both hard right and hard left.

'How could this happen', one journalist asked, when recently reviewing the film and referring to the events of that fateful day, 'in Norway?' His particular astonishment evident because he describes Norway as 'surely one of the best countries to live in in the world?'

One plucky, young survivor of the attack told an American CNN interviewer in her exquisitely fluent English, 'If one man can display so much hate, consider how much love we can show together.'

Amen to that!

Glossary

Allthing: Iceland's Parliament, the oldest parliament in the world, was founded in 930. After many changes over hundreds of years it moved to a building in Reykjavik in 1844. Elections of 63 members are held every 4 years.

Bløtkakker: Creamy sponge sandwich cakes.

Brennevin: Distilled spirits.

Bunad: National Costume, both for men and women.

Domkirke: Cathedral.

Finnmarkvidde: Finnmark's mountainous plateau – its large stretches of uninhabited landscape and tundra.

Frekk: Cheeky, audacious, presumptuous, disrespectful, brazen, impudent, conceited.

Friundervisning: Founded in Oslo in 1864, FU is Norway's oldest organisation for study. NSF, or Norske Studenters Friundervisning, founded nationally and officially in 1948, offers adult education in vocational subjects, languages, culture and leisure. Originally designed to allow mature Norwegians to engage with the academic environment and extend their knowledge and experience, it has morphed into more sophisticated and wider curricula in recent years. Its name was changed in 1965 to Folkeuniversitet – The People's University - Its aim is to promote learning and cultural experience for adults inside their communities, in collaboration with relevant local organisations and facilities, including the work-place.

Fylke: County

Gakti: Traditional Sami clothing. Bold in colour – mostly blue – worn when herding reindeer, and on ceremonial occasions. Adornments indicate marital status and place of birth. Today, gakti are made of wool and adorned in silk: in previous times, they were made from reindeer skins.

Gymnas: High School, Sixth Form College, Grammar School.

Hjemmebrent: Home brewed, illicit wine or spirits – Hooch or Moonshine.

Hurtigruten: Literally, coastal express. Realistically, the reliable coastal steamers – currently, also cruise ships – that travel along the coast from Bergen to Kirkenes, stopping at 34 ports every day, travelling in both directions. The Hurtigruten fleet consists of 11 ships at sea every day.

Hygge: Cosiness, comfort from both warm fires and warm fellowship: being snug, safe and comfortable: often, a special, memorable experience.

Ishavskatedralen: Tromsdalen's Parish Church in Tromsø, affectionately and generally called the Arctic Cathedral - because of aspects of its architecture.

Jante and Janteloven: See Chapter 15

Jentekor: Girls' choir or singing group.

Kofte: Traditional Sami costume for women.

Kommune: The Local Authority.

Lavvu: Tents used by Sami people in North Norway. Less vertical than a tepee, designed to be warm and secure against all kinds of extreme Arctic weather. Easy to erect when following migrating reindeer herds.

Laerer: Teacher, School Master or Mistress

Magerøya: A Large Island in the extreme North of Norway on which the most northerly point of Norwegian land is located.

Multer: Cloudberries, ground level growing fruit native to Arctic tundra, which used to be a rare and expensive treat. Now more easily available, and often eaten at Christmas instead of just at Midsummer.

Nidaros: The Medieval name for Trondheim when it was the capital city under Norway's first Christian Kings.

Nikkers: Male, knee breeches: Skiing and National Costume.

Nordlaendinger: Original, genuine, born and bred Northerners.

Peis: An open fireplace.

Pensum: The whole syllabus of a school or of an individual subject.

Pulk: A human type of reindeer sleigh

Pålegg: Sandwich fillings of meat, cheese, fish, salad, vegetables and fruit, 'laid on top' and not sandwiched between slices of bread.

Paesh: The plump front expansion of Sami jackets acting as carrier bags or small suitcases to carry tools and equipment essential for reindeer husbandry.

Quisling: A traitor collaborating with enemy forces. So- called after the Norwegian puppet Prime Minister who collaborated with the Nazis and was executed by firing squad after the war.

Reisende: Literally, a traveller. But a 'reisende lektor' is a peripatetic teacher at high/secondary school graduation level.

Rektor: Headmaster, Headmistress, Principal or Vice-Chancellor.

Russ: Equivalent to what used to be called 'Sixth Formers.'

Smog: Intense air pollution that is much denser than thick fog.

Smørbrød: Open Sandwiches: see 'Pålegg'.

Sparksøtting: A sledge.

Sprawklairer: An invented name for a language teacher.

Stue: The Living, Sitting Room or Snug.

Snorri Sturluson: The Icelandic poet and historian who was senior adviser of the Allthing from 1224 to1230.

Syttende Mai: May 17th – Norway's National Day that celebrates the establishing of Norwegian independence as a sovereign country and the foundation of a national constitution in 1814. It's a day of national celebration and serious partying.

Saerdeles: This literally means 'extremely,' or 'exceptionally.' As 'S', it used to be the highest mark given for a piece of work in an earlier exam system, the attainment of which was a crucial passport to Higher Education.

Thingvellir: The mound outside Reykjavik where the Allthing met regularly until 1798.

Valhalla: According to Snorri Sturluson, Valhalla was believed to be the destination of all slain, Viking warriors.

Vidda: Vast area of tundra: bleak, windswept plains.

Vinmonopolet: From 1923 almost until the Millennium, importing wines and spirits was a government monopoly. Choice and availability of alcohol was tightly controlled, because of the dangers of drinking in a cold climate and the influence of the Christian Democrats in Parliament. The government 'off-licence' used to be the only place to buy alcohol, at enormous expense and only between 9am and 5 pm on week-days: never on Sundays. Recently, restrictions have softened. Supermarkets sell some wines. There is more choice in restaurants, although at great expense. All forms of alcohol are heavily taxed, so many make their own alcoholic drinks, which is not strictly legal. *Hjembrent* - home brewed alcoholic drink – may be devastatingly potent.

Voluspaa: A prophecy from an Old Norse seeress that led to the Poetic Edda about the creation of the world. A key primary source to inform understanding of Norse Mythology.